Organization and Innovation

THE IRWIN-DORSEY SERIES IN BEHAVIORAL SCIENCE

EDITOR   JOHN F. MEE   *Indiana University*

ARGYRIS *Interpersonal Competence and Organizational Effectiveness*

ARGYRIS *Organization and Innovation*

CARZO & YANOUZAS *Formal Organization: A Systems Approach*

CUMMINGS & SCOTT *Readings in Organizational Behavior and Human Performance*

GUEST *Organizational Change: The Effect of Successful Leadership*

KELLY *Organizational Behaviour*

KUHN *The Study of Society: A Unified Approach*

LAWRENCE & SEILER, WITH BAILEY, KATZ, ORTH, CLARK, BARNES, & TURNER *Organizational Behavior and Administration: Cases, Concepts, and Research Findings* rev. ed.

LYNTON & PAREEK *Training for Development*

MASLOW *Eupsychian Management: A Journal*

MASSARIK & RATOOSH *Mathematical Explorations in Behavioral Science*

O'CONNELL *Managing Organizational Innovation*

ORTH, BAILEY, & WOLEK *Administering Research and Development: The Behavior of Scientists and Engineers in Organizations*

PORTER & LAWLER *Managerial Attitudes and Performance*

PRICE *Organizational Effectiveness: An Inventory of Propositions*

RUBENSTEIN & HABERSTROH (eds.) *Some Theories of Organization* rev. ed.

SCOTT *The Management of Conflict*

SEILER *Systems Analysis in Organizational Behavior*

WHYTE *Organizational Behavior: Theory and Application*

WHYTE & HAMILTON *Action Research for Management*

Organization and Innovation

By CHRIS ARGYRIS
**PROFESSOR OF INDUSTRIAL ADMINISTRATION
YALE UNIVERSITY**

Innovative organizations

1965 · HOMEWOOD, ILLINOIS

RICHARD D. IRWIN, INC., AND THE DORSEY PRESS

First Printing, June, 1965
Second Printing, August, 1966
Third Printing, December, 1968
Fourth Printing, January, 1970
Fifth Printing, March, 1971

PRINTED IN THE UNITED STATES OF AMERICA
Library of Congress Catalog Card No. 65–22411

To

Roger Barker

who helped me to realize that in order for research
and teaching to be meaningful and need fulfilling
they require risk taking, trust in one's own experience and probably most important, self-acceptance.

PREFACE

It is my belief that there is a role for research that can be of help to individuals and to organizations and which can also help illuminate (even in a small way) some aspects of individual and organizational theory. For too long, the social sciences have been plagued with the dichotomy of basic versus applied research and one could do one or the other but not both.

The difficulties with this dichotomy has been illustrated recently in the field of engineering. In my own school, engineering and the physical sciences began as an integrated activity (Sheffield Scientific School). Unfortunately, for both engineering and the sciences, they were separated. Now they are being merged again. The sciences now acknowledge the important role of engineering that draws from and adds to basic theory. Engineers, in turn, have realized that their activity can become sterile without the close contact with the established disciplines. Thus we have engineering schools changing or adding to their organizational charter *applied science*. They have learned, as Gordon states, that when a creative engineer designs for the future he must often work as a scientist. The scientists, in turn, realize that to achieve some of their great advances, they have to work as engineers.[1]

Gordon differentiates three broad categories of engineering. First are those engineers who have talent for detecting deficiencies in the capabilities of existing engineering systems, and whose impulse is to conceive from abstractions or from a broad body of science wholly new superior systems. Such engineers can relate quite abstract and seemingly unrelated concepts. They are composers rather than arrangers. "Their work is predominantly intellectual, and it depends on a profound knowledge of science. They may work as scientists, but their knack of seeing the useful . . . characterizes them as engineers."[2]

In a second group are those engineers who can devise and build

---

[1] Gordon S. Brown, "New Horizons in Engineering Education" *Daedalus*, Vol. 91, No. 2, Proceedings of American Association of Arts and Sciences, Spring, 1962, pp. 341-361.

[2] *Ibid.* p. 346.

engineering systems by an orderly, creative arrangement of already existing knowledge. They are arrangers and inventors rather than composers. Finally, there is the group of persons expert in assembling, operating, and maintaining the existing systems from drawings, descriptions, or experience.[3]

Behavioral science applied activities may also be ordered along the same continuum. For example, the gamut may run from the creative "action research" characteristic of Kurt Lewin just before his death, to the development of new measuring instruments "derived" from theory; to those instruments that are reliable and valid but contribute little to theory; to the development of norms for tests, and finally to the competent administration of various kinds of tests in schools and clinics.

I should like to view this research as being related to the first two of those research endeavors where there is a desire to draw from and add to theory and a purpose to be of some value to the society. I hope that the research will result in some new light being shed on such basic issues as the nature of (1) interpersonal competence, (2) organizational innovativeness, and (3) theory of individual and organizational change.

I also hope that the set of categories developed to observe and quantify aspects of interpersonal and organizational competence may provide a useful observational device for other kinds of individual, small group, and organizational behavior.

If one holds the values above regarding research, then one is inclined to conduct studies in natural settings. Usually such field research begins with a descriptive phase where one studies what one sees without introducing value judgments (other than those inherent in the research process). In the second phase, where changes are attempted, values come into play. In all the change attempts, the attempts is to enhance individual-organizational competence.

The mixture of descriptive and normative, quantitative and qualitative may tend to provide an uneven texture to the research. Part of the unevenness, I suspect, will be eliminated as the theory and methods become more sophisticated and as the "research permission" granted by the host institution becomes more liberal.

---

[3] *Ibid.* p. 347.

However, a certain degree of unevenness will probably exist because of the nature of the task chosen. I have tried to do my best to differentiate the testing of hypotheses from the illustration of them and these two from the more applied action orientation stage.

Another characteristic of field research aimed at being capable of making changes in the "real world" is derived from the multi-dimensionality of the real world. This naturally leads to research that includes more and more complicated chunks of reality. This is one reason why action research that aspires to make some contributions to theory tends to become wholistic or systems research.

The desire to explore the interrelationships among the many levels of a system makes it difficult to allocate time and resources to explore, in detail the interrelationships within each level. Yet, it is the latter kind of activity that scientists who are working in the established disciplines perform. Some, understandably, may wish that I had gone into more depth in certain of the levels discussed. I can only plead my own limitations as well as the consideration that others should be encouraged to conduct studies in "width."

The Organization of the Book

In Chapter I, I present a new set of categories that can be used to observe individual and group behavior and to quantify variables related to interpersonal competence and problem solving effectiveness. In addition to exploring several methodological issues, I attempt to define hypotheses and predictions that are explored in the remainder of the book.

Chapters II, III, and IV each contain a report of a study in an organizational setting. Chapter V describes an attempt to change certain values and behavior of the Board of Directors (an internal one) of an organization as well as to measure the impact of these changes.

In Chapter VI, I extrapolate from the data and the relevant literature a model of the probable relationship among interpersonal competence, internal organization, environment and innovation.

Appendix A contains a more detailed description of the categories used in the theoretical scheme. Appendix B provides further interobserver reliability studies.

In Appendix C, I include a study of the use of the system of categories to quantify individual and group interpersonal competence. This study appeared in *Applied Behavioral Science* and I acknowledge my appreciation for permission to reprint it.

Acknowledgements

Clayton Alderfer and Fritz Steele helped me from the early stages of the manuscript. They were the first two observers to be trained. Both performed exceedingly well; both made important modifications and suggestions.

Lee Bolman and Roman Weil came in during the later stages for a shorter period of time. However, they were very helpful in clarifying substantive as well as stylistic issues. Mrs. Joan Swanson was responsible for the typing of the manuscript. Martin Evans made many helpful comments on the manuscript.

This work was done under the generous grant of the National Institute of Mental Health. I am especially indebted to Dr. Raymond F. Gould. I am also indebted to the many executives, scientists, and engineers who gave of themselves in order that the research could be conducted.

NEW HAVEN, CONNECTICUT   CHRIS ARGYRIS
June, 1965

TABLE OF CONTENTS

CHAPTER 1

Research Objectives and Methods

THE FIRST objective of this book is to present the preliminary findings of studies made of how varying degrees of interpersonal competence among top managers influences their, and the organization's, innovativeness, willingness to take risks, and problem-solving effectiveness—as *perceived* by the participants. It is only because I found ways to discover them that I limit myself to *perceptions*. I have been unsuccessful in finding relatively objective measures of innovation, extent of risk taking, and problem-solving effectiveness.

Since these factors are presumably crucial in research and development organizations, I thought it would be interesting to study them in such supposedly innovative organizations. The first two studies upon which our findings are based, therefore, were conducted in research and development organizations. The third study was conducted in a management consulting firm.

The second objective of this book is to present a new system of categories which can be used to observe variables related to interpersonal competence and with which useful predictions can be made and tested.

Innovative Organizations

It is becoming increasingly clear that modern organizations may not survive unless they are able to innovate.[1] It is equally clear that

---

[1] Richard Nelson, "The Economics of Invention: A Survey of the Literature," Rand Corp. Research Memo RM–2146–1, revised January 15, 1959; ASTIA, No. AD 209021.

the costs of innovation are growing rapidly while the useful life span for any new idea is decreasing. Caught in this squeeze, organizations must not only innovate, they must also transform their ideas into salable products quickly or they will lack the funds to support continued innovation.

In the past decade there has been a stream of studies on innovation and creativity. Among these, two recent major reviews—by D. W. Taylor[2] and by C. W. Taylor and F. Barron[3]—conclude that there are five approaches usually taken to the study of innovation. They are the study of (1) products, (2) processes, (3) tasks, (4) persons, and (5) environmental variables (or the study of some combination of these).

These same reviews conclude that the least understood of these factors is the environment in which innovation is supposed to flourish. Taylor, and Taylor and Barron agree that:

> We are perhaps more in the dark about the environmental conditions which facilitate creativity than we are about any other aspect of the problem. Beyond obvious conditions such as the need for ample time in which to work freely on problems of one's own choice, little is known. Research, then, on the *general environmental conditions*—cultural, professional, and institutional—conducive to first-rate scientific research needs major encouragement. We are aware of no area in the social sciences where research is simultaneously so vitally needed and so sadly neglected.[4]

Having decided to study supposedly innovative organizations, I had next to determine where I should focus my limited resources. Elsewhere, I have suggested that the lower one goes down in the hierarchy in organizations, the greater the probability that behavior is controlled by systems of technology, organizational structure, and managerial controls.[5] The higher up in the organizational hierarchy one goes, and the less programmed or routine the activity, the less influence these factors tend to have over behavior and the more will interpersonal relationships tend to become the crucial variables.

---

[2] See Donald W. Taylor, "Thinking and Creativity," *Annals of the New York Academy of Sciences*, Vol. 91, Article 1, (December 23, 1960) pp. 108–27.

[3] Calvin W. Taylor and Frank Barron, *Scientific Creativity: Its Recognition and Development* (New York: John Wiley & Sons, Inc., 1963).

[4] *Ibid.*, p. 373.

[5] Chris Argyris, *Integrating the Individual and the Organization* (New York: John Wiley & Sons, Inc., 1964).

Research organizations may also be viewed as systems which have the power, information, and rewards and penalties centered at the upper levels. The use of these factors by top research management would seem, therefore, to be critical. We would anticipate that the way these factors tend to be used would be strongly influenced by the relationships the upper-level executives and their subordinates have with one another. This is one of the predictions to be explored in these studies.

In focusing upon top management, I am not suggesting that the other levels do not have an impact upon organizational innovativeness and problem-solving effectiveness. I begin with the top management because I believe that the top men have the broadest influence in the organization. Indeed, I would argue that changes in interpersonal relationships, values, and norms must *begin* at the top if they are to be effective. I realize that there are some who believe that such changes can be profitably begun at the lower levels. Unfortunately, little data exist to prove either contention. I have participated in attempts to change interpersonal relations at the lower levels of management only to find that very few of the new insights were used until, and unless, the top men emotionally felt them, as well as used them, especially under stress. I have also experienced several instances where the top management, by a seemingly innocent policy memo, undid months of progress at the lower levels.

Changes in the interpersonal environment are not accepted lightly by subordinates. Few subordinates will alter their behavior until they have clear evidence that they will be rewarded for doing so. Otherwise, as one second-level supervisor kept telling the writer, "Stay loose, Doc, stay loose; that's my advice."

On the Resultants of Interpersonal Competence

Recently, White has defined competence to mean "capacity, fitness, or ability."[6] The extent to which individuals produce the intended effect is the measure of competence.[7] The phrase "intended effect" requires further discussion. If White means that an individual tends to be competent when he achieves whatever effect

---

[6] Robert W. White, "Motivation Reconsidered: The Concept of Competence," *Psychological Review*, Vol. LXVI (1959), pp. 297–333. Robert W. White, "Sense of Interpersonal Competence," in Robert W. White (ed.), *The Study of Lives* (New York: Atherton Press, 1963), pp. 72–93.

[7] *Ibid.*, p. 73.

he intends, then I would not agree that this is sufficient. I prefer to define interpersonal competence as the individual's ability to produce intended effects in such a way that he can continue to do so.

It is possible for an individual to accomplish his intended effect, and to resolve his problem, but in so haphazard a manner that this leads to only temporary results. Problems that are not truly solved cannot imply as much competence on the part of the problem solver as problems that are solved in such a way that they remain solved. (I am, of course, speaking of those problems whose solution the individual can control.)

But even this condition is not sufficient. Problems may be "solved" so permanently, that people do not speak to each other again. The problem-solving process then is dead, or seriously impaired. More frequent is the case where the problem is solved, but enough hostility and mistrust have been generated that the individuals will tend to be less effective when they meet again to solve new problems.

I should like, therefore, to focus upon three resultants or "outputs" of interpersonal competence. The higher the interpersonal competence of the individual, the greater is:

1. The awareness of relevant problems (relevant problems are those that have effects).
2. The ability to solve problems in such a way that they remain solved.
3. The probability that the problem-solving process involved has *not* been harmed or negatively influenced.

It follows from the above that the lower the interpersonal competence, the less the probability that the individuals involved (1) will be aware of the relevant problems,[8] (2) will solve them effectively, and (3) will not harm the problem-solving process. If individuals with relatively low interpersonal competence *are aware of relevant problems, they should not be able to solve them;* or if they *are able to solve them, they should do so at a cost to the problem-solving processes involved.*

If it can be shown that individuals with relatively low interpersonal competence are able to be aware of relevant problems, or to

---

[8] Relevant problems are those that can be shown to have effects on the issues involved.

solve them permanently, or to do so without harming the problem-solving processes, then this theoretical framework is in difficulty.

I hope that it is clear that by selecting interpersonal competence I am not attempting to depreciate intellective, technical competence. The opposite is true. I am interested in seeing how interpersonal competence facilitates or inhibits intellective, technical competence.

The System of Categories

Beginning with the outputs or end products of interpersonal competence, it is possible to reason backwards, trying to make

TABLE 1–1

	Individual		Interpersonal		Norms		Performance Difficulty	Outputs
				(Plus)				
	experiment	i f	help others to experiment	i f	trust	i f		
	open	i f	help others to be open	i f	concern	i f	↑	Increased competence
	owning	i f	help others to own	i f	individuality	i f		
Zero								
	not owning	i f	not help others to own	i f	conformity	i f		
	not open	i f	not help others to be open	i f	antagonism	i f	↓ Defensiveness	Decreased competence
	reject experimenting	i f	not help others experiment	i f	mistrust	i f		
				(Minus)				

explicit what sorts of necessary (but not necessarily sufficient) behavior would be required to lead the resultants listed above to be as high as possible.

The results are presented in Table 1–1. The reader will note a *zero line*. The variables above the line are hypothesized to facilitate—while the factors below the line are hypothesized to inhibit—interpersonal competence. The position of each factor is not arbitrary. Generally speaking, the further away from the zero line (for the positive or plus factors) the more difficult the behavior should be to perform. The further away from the zero line (for the negative or minus factors) the greater the defensiveness involved in the behavior.

There must be exceptions to these generalizations, and empirical research is needed to spell them out. For example, I believe that different *patterns* of the categories will be more effective under different conditions. Under conditions of personal threat, owning and openness may be more facilitative than risk-taking. Under conditions of a crisis, conformity may be more facilitative than individuality. Antagonism may arouse an indifferent person to become more involved, while trust could be threatening to an individual who had grown up in a climate of mistrust.

Before I define the categories two assumptions ought to be made explicit.

Assumption I: Behavior Is Not Neutral. All behavior that can be classified within the categories is considered to be relevant. It can either add to, or detract from, interpersonal competence. Any behavior that cannot be classified according to the categories is hypothesized to be irrelevant. Such an hypothesis, while typical of research endeavors, is dangerous. It is typical since schemes of categories are frequently used as guideposts to what is relevant. It is dangerous in that the categories can be incorrect and data necessary to bring this to light might tend to be excluded. Constant search for flaws, but especially continued research to test the categories, are the two ways researchers have to decrease the probability of such difficulties. Thus, an extended program of research has been planned to see how well the scheme can help us understand interpersonal competence (and thus be able to predict and control behavior associated with it).

Assumption II: Ideas (i) and Feelings (f). All behavior is classified, for research purposes, as being primarily at the ideational (intellectual) or feeling (emotional) levels. This bifurcation is arbitrary and goes against the current thinking that these two aspects of behavior are highly interrelated. The reason for it is to help in making more explicit the relationships between the ideational or intellectual and the feeling or emotional levels. As more knowledge is accumulated and the relationships are made explicit, the necessity for the arbitrary bifurcation is expected to decrease.

For our purpose it is assumed that all feelings include an ideational component, but ideas do not include a feeling component (or, if they do, it will tend to be so suppressed that it will not tend to be observable). If it is, it becomes categorized as a feeling.

Behavior on the idea level will be connoted by (*i*) and on the feeling level by (*f*).

The Definition of the Categories

Level I: Individual

1. *Owning up to (i or f)*

The first category refers to the behavior of the individual being aware of and accepting responsibility for the behavior that he manifests. The individual is able to identify his behavior, communicate it, and accept ownership of it.

2. *Not owning up to (i or f)*

Being unable or unwilling to be aware of, identify, and own up to one's behavior.

3. *Openness (i or f)*

Behavior that enlarges the individual's scope, or pushes back his boundaries of awareness and responsibility. The individual permits and encourages the reception of new information.

4. *Not open (i or f)*

The behavior that constricts the individual's boundaries of awareness and responsibility. The individual discourages the reception of new information.

5. *Experimenting (i or f)*

That behavior which represents some risk for the individual. The purpose of the risk taking is to generate new information on the i or f level. The individual may be observed manipulating his internal or external environment in order to create new information. The risk is evaluated in terms of the probability that such explorations could upset the individual's self-acceptance.

6. *Rejecting experimenting (i or f)*

The behavior that prevents the system from taking risks.

The next six categories are the same as those above except that they focus on the behavior that helps or does not help others to do the behaviors described above.

7. *Helping others to own up (i or f)*
8. *Not helping others to own up (i or f)*
9. *Helping others to be open (i or f)*
10. *Not helping others to be open (i or f)*
11. *Helping others to experiment (i or f)*
12. *Not helping others to experiment (i or f)*

Level II : Norms

Sociological and anthropological theories suggest that the cultural aspects of behavior must be understood if a more complete picture of human behavior is to be developed. We believe that this is the case in the study of competence. The second or *norms* level is therefore designated to include aspects of the cultural factors.

Norms may be hypothesized to develop "out of" those inter-actions among the participants that have proven useful (to the participants) in maintaining the steady state of the system. They are, as the sociologists and anthropologists would call them, func-tional for the system. Norms may be defined as "coercive mecha-nisms" created by the individuals to sanction behavior to maintain the steady state of the system. They act to enhance or to inhibit competence. Norms arise in a group like streets may arise in a community. Individuals desire to create some order in their trans-portation, so they create streets for cars. Once the streets are created, they act to coerce people to drive on them. Norms, there-fore, are commonly perceived and sanctioned patterns of behavior that act to influence those individuals' behavior who desire to remain, or are coerced to become part of, the system (be it a relationship between two people, a group, or an organization).

The norms included are:

13. *Individuality (i or f)*

The first norm includes that behavior that acts to induce the individuals to express their ideas or feelings. The norm acts to influence the members to protect and develop the uniqueness of the individual in a group or organization.

14. *Conformity (i or f)*

That behavior that acts to inhibit individuals from expressing their ideas or feelings. The norm acts to influence the members to help suppress the uniqueness of the individual in a group or organization.

15. *Concern (i or f)*

The behavior that acts to induce people to be concerned about others' ideas and feelings. The norm acts to influence the members to help protect and develop the uniqueness of others' ideas and feelings in a group or organization.

16. *Antagonism (i or f)*

That behavior that acts to induce people to reduce their concern about their and others' ideas and feelings. The norm acts to influence the members to disintegrate the concerns for others' ideas and feelings. (Indifference would be considered as antagonism.)

17. *Trust (i or f)*

That behavior that induces members to take risks, to experi-ment. The norm acts to influence the members to take risks, on the ideas and feelings levels.

18. *Mistrust (i or f)*

That behavior that restricts and inhibits members from taking risks and experimenting. The norm acts to influence the members to disintegrate risk taking and experimenting.

Trust is a highly complex variable which we hope to make more clear as we proceed. At this point let us hypothesize that trust tends to arise in a relationship when A senses that B is concerned enough about B and A to permit A to take a risk with his self-esteem without B punishing A for taking a risk, or minimizing A's risk, or helping A to see the risk in such a way that it tends to decrease A's sense of self-esteem.

Imbalance Behavior

Early in the exploratory studies we came upon behavior that had to be scored both as plus and minus. For example, individual A would say to B, "I believe in people having their say, but in this case, x is true. You're wrong and you'd better change your mind if you wish to succeed here." This bit of behavior would be scored *own i* (A is owning up to his beliefs) and *conform i* (and inducing B to conform to them). If B is to believe the plus-minus character of the behavior it would communicate to him contradictory messages. On the one hand it implies that A believes in individuality, yet he creates conditions of conformity for B.

Following "imbalance theories" this behavior was labeled *imbalance* (creating) behavior.[9] Brown concludes that ". . . human nature abhors imbalance. . . . A situation of imbalance is one that calls for mutually incompatible actions. . . . Imbalance in the mind threatens to paralyze actions."[10] This is our assumption about the impact of imbalance behavior upon competence striving. Plus-minus behavior creates imbalance because it communicates contradictory messages to the receiver.

Although space prohibits going into detail, I should like to point out that imbalance scores may be valid indicators of the changeability of an individual or group. I believe that the unfreezing process will tend to be more difficult when the individual (for example) has high imbalance scores. The logic, in *summary* form is as follows: If

---

[9] We are thinking of the work of Fritz Heider, Osgood and Tannenbaum, Festinger, Abelson and Rosenberg. Our reading is presently limited to the work of Fritz Heider and the excellent summary and critical article by Roger Brown, "Models of Attitude Change," in R. Brown, *et al.* (eds.), *New Directions in Psychology* (New York: Holt, Rinehart & Winston, 1962), pp. 1–85.

[10] *Ibid.*, pp. 77–78.

man abhors experiencing imbalance behavior, then manifesting it may be caused by defenses in the sender. The defenses may be personality or situationally related. Moreover, if man abhors behaving in an imbalanced manner, then those who do must have a set of defenses that inhibit them from being aware of their behavior. In short, the imbalance behavior may indicate that an individual has, at least, two sets of related defenses: one that "causes" the imbalance behavior and one that inhibits the sender from realizing that his behavior communicates contradictory messages.

Examples of imbalance scores are:

own i or *f* with any combination of *conform i* or *f, antagonism i* or *f* or *mistrust i* or *f*.

open i or *f* with any combination of *conform i* or *f* (etc).

experiment i or *f* with any combination of *conform i* or *f* (etc.).

help others own i or *f* with any combination of *conform i* or *f* (etc.).

help others open i or *f* with any combination of *antagonism i* or *f* (etc.).

help others experiment i or *f* with any combination of *mistrust i* or *f* (etc.)

not own i or *f* with any combination of *individuality i* or *f, concern i* or *f, trust i* or *f*.

not open i or *f* with any combination of *concern i* or *f* (etc.).

not experiment i or *f* with any combination of *trust i* or *f* (etc.).

The Pyramidal Values

The system of categories above would be more useful if they could be used to generate a priori hypotheses about what would be found in studying the relationship of interpersonal competence to the three criteria described above.

One way to accomplish this was to follow the lead of anthropologists like Kluckholn who showed that much of the human behavior of the Navajos could be understood if one knew the basic values that they held. More recently administrative theorists like Herbert Simon[11] and psychologists such as Donald W. Taylor[12] have developed theoretical frameworks using values as key concepts in understanding behavior. Values, all these behavioral

---

[11] Herbert A. Simon, *Models of Man: Social and Rational* (New York: John Wiley & Sons, 1957).

[12] Donald W. Taylor, "Toward an Information Processing Theory of Motivation," in Marshall R. Jones (ed.), *Nebraska Symposium on Motivation* (Lincoln: University of Nebraska Press, 1960), pp. 51–79.

scientists agree, are internalized cultural commands which tend to coerce or canalize (to use Gardner Murphy's[13] term) behavior in a particular direction.

Using this view of values, I asked if there are any values about interpersonal competence that are endemic to organizations. Is there anything about organizations that naturally leads to the development of certain values about effective human relationships? If so, perhaps they could be used as a basis for developing hypotheses.

Elsewhere I have suggested that pyramidal organizations imply a strategy of effective human relationships.[14] This rational strategy emphasizes (1) the centrality of organizational objectives, (2) the suppression of relevant feelings and the emphasis upon intellective, cognitive thinking, and (3) the use of power and control to obtain the compliance of the participants.

Such a strategy of organizing human effort tends to imply three basic values about effective human relationships. They are:

1. The important human relationships are those that are involved in accomplishing the objective of the formal organization.
2. Effectiveness in human relationships increases as the participants are rational and decreases as they become emotional.
3. Human beings can have their energies canalized in the organization's interest if they are directed, controlled, and appropriately rewarded or penalized.

Since the initial formulation of these values, they have been found to be implicit not only to administration but also to teaching and religious activity as well as to the research process. Either these values are basic cultural ones or human beings, wherever they interact to achieve objectives, tend to organize using pyramidal-type values.

Some A Priori Hypotheses

If we conceive of the categories defined above as a system of variables and the criterion variables as outputs, then the pyramidal values may be viewed as the inputs. These inputs may be said to influence the system of variables and the outputs in the following manner.

---

[13] Gardner Murphy, *Human Potentialities* (New York: Basic Books, Inc., 1958).
[14] Chris Argyris, *Interpersonal Competence and Organizational Effectiveness* (Homewood, Ill.: Irwin-Dorsey Press, 1962).

In any given administrative group where people are striving to solve problems or make decisions:

1. From the first value, I would hypothesize that task-oriented behavior will be emphasized and rewarded.
2. From the second value, I hypothesize that idea (i) behavior will tend to be much more frequent than feeling (f) behavior.
3. To the extent that people are rewarded for (primarily) contributing ideas to the achievement of the objective and are controlled through scarce rewards and competition, I hypothesize a high incidence of people attempting to "sell" their point of view in order to maximize the possible rewards and minimize the possible penalties.

Consequences:

People will focus primarily upon "selling" their ideas. Contributions made by others would not be heard as intended.

Frustration will be high, but not dealt with because feelings are not admissable.

Struggle will be frequent for "air time" to get across one's view and/or to defend an already made position.

The probability that members do not listen to others will increase. Listening will be primarily in terms of those views one can agree with or one can safely compete against.

Predictions from the Above to the Categories

Prediction 1. In terms of the categories, *own i* should be most frequent with *concern i* and *conform i* next. *Concern i* should rank second (in frequency of occurrence) where competition and "win-lose" situations are not frequent. Where these conditions are pronounced, then *conform i* should be the second most frequent behavior (because "selling" would be scored as contributing to conformity).

To the extent that people are controlled through scarce rewards and to the extent they are competing with each other on a win-lose basis, one should observe attempts by individuals to strengthen their position and simultaneously weaken the position of their adversaries.

Consequences:

People should tend to ask questions primarily to obtain information that helps them to ascertain the weak and strong points of the others' positions. This should help increase their probability of winning.

Prediction 2. Since questions are scored as *open i*, these scores should be the next most frequent behavior observed (to *own i, concern i, conform i*).

Prediction 3. If the motive for questions is as we described it above, then the "real" strategy of using questions eventually to harm others should become evident when, in any given situation, the individual has asked all the questions that he wants to ask. I would predict, therefore, that a series of *open i* scores should tend to be followed by such scores as:

own i–conform i *not helping others to own i–conform i* *own i–antagonism i*	Because he is finally telling the individual where he is wrong.

Prediction 4. Another prediction would be that even if this sequence did not occur the minus scores just listed should be at least as frequent as the *open i* scores.

Consequences:

Feelings should exist that in this group
   a) People are attempting to show each other up.
   b) Openness and concern cannot be trusted.
   c) Frustration is part of life.
Feelings will not be communicated because of the value against emotionality.

Prediction 5. *Feeling* scores should be very *low; idea* scores should be very *high.*

Consequences:

People will tend to play it safe and be cautious rather than to take risks related to emotionally laden topics.

Members will tend to be prepared to defend their view rather than to explore it openly.

Prediction 6. *Experimenting scores* and *trust scores* should be very low; *helping others to own, to be open,* and *to take risks* should be very low; *not helping others to own, to be open,* and *to take risks* should also be low because to manifest such behavior openly is to violate the value of loyalty to the system.

Consequences:

As interpersonal feelings of frustration, mistrust, and hostility pile up, they will not tend to be expressed openly because of the value against emotionality.

One safe way for people to "blow up" is to create crises where emotionality is permitted (crises are usually created by people with power because they violate the value against emotionality).[15] Another relatively safe way for the tension to be released is through the expression of imbalance behavior.

Prediction 7. Imbalance scores should exist when feelings tend to be expressed. Their frequency should be at least as high as the *open i* scores.

If these predictions hold, then I may predict further that members of organizations in problem-solving groups (of any kind) will tend:

1. *Not* to be aware of all the problems that are relevant to their problems. Interpersonal issues and issues that potentially threaten members' organizational positions will tend to inhibit their awareness.
2. To use problem-solving processes that lead to relatively ineffective and temporary solutions of difficult problems.
3. To use problem-solving processes that lead to a further deterioration of problem solving as well as interpersonal competence.

To put this more boldly, to the extent people hold pyramidal values, there will tend to be a general predisposition toward low interpersonal competence which, in turn, can become so low that their level of effectiveness in solving any type of problem that involves interpersonal issues will tend to be lower than the participants believe is the case.

The Potency of the Categories

I stated above that the categories were positioned in such a way that those which were further away from the zero line were also the most difficult to perform (see Table 1–1). If the consequences of the pyramidal values just stated are valid, then the degree of difficulty of some of these categories will tend to be altered. Some behavior will now tend to be more important and more difficult to perform than other behavior. For example, idea (*i*) behavior will tend to be much easier to manifest than *f* behavior. Thus the hypothesized weighting given to *own, open* and *experimenting* may hold as long as this is limited to *i* behavior. On the feeling (*f*) level, *owning,* and *openness* are going to be more difficult than *experimenting i* (but not more difficult than *experimenting f*).

---
[15] *Ibid*

Also, *helping others* should be difficult but not as much as the expression of feelings.

On the norm level, again, *i* behavior will be more easy to manifest than *f* behavior. Furthermore *concern i* will be easier and more frequent than *individuality i* (which also represents a switch from the original chart). Finally, on the *f* level *individuality* and *concern* will be more difficult than *trust i* but not more difficult than *trust f*.

These considerations have led to the development of the potency schedule shown in Table 1–2.

TABLE 1–2

POTENCY OF CATEGORIES

Individual	Weight	Interpersonal	Weight	Norms	Weight
own i. . . .	1	helping others to own i. . . .	5	individuality i. . .	2
f. . . .	9	f. . . .	9	f. . .	8
open i. . . .	2	open i. . . .	6	concern i. . .	1
f. . . .	10	f. . . .	10	f. . .	10
experiment i. . . .	4	experiment i. . . .	7	trust i. . .	4
f. . . .	16	f. . . .	16	f. . .	16
not own i. . . . − 8		not helping others to own i. . . . −3		conform i. . . − 2	
f. . . . −14		f. . . . −5		f. . . − 8	
not open i. . . . − 9		open i. . . . −3		antagonism i. . . − 4	
f. . . . −15		f. . . . −6		f. . . −12	
not experiment i. . . . −14		experiment i. . . . −4		mistrust i. . . − 6	
f. . . . −16		f. . . . −7		f. . . −16	

The Research Methods Used

I have used three different research methods in each of these studies:

Questionnaire. A short sentence completion questionnaire was developed to infer if people held the pyramidal values about effective human relationships. In one study a more complicated version was developed (by Lee Bolman) in order to create, if possible, a way to measure the *degree* to which the individuals held the pyramidal values. Both questionnaires, although showing promise, are extremely primitive, and much further research is necessary.

Semistructured Interviews. Each subject was interviewed at least once with a standard set of questions. The process of interviewing that I used is described in detail elsewhere and I will not repeat it here.[16]

---

[16] Chris Argyris, *Understanding Organizational Behavior* (Homewood, Ill: Dorsey Press, 1960).

Observations. The third research method is the use of the new system of categories. I hope that it represents a small contribution to the observation of human behavior. Over one hundred meetings were observed. The meetings were mostly concerned with problem solving, they ranged in size from 2- to 50-man meetings, and from meetings that lasted a few minutes to those that went on for several days.[17] Since the development of a reliable and valid observational scheme was a central objective of this study, I should like to discuss the way the scheme was used in more detail.

The Way the Categories Are Used to Observe Behavior

The observer's frame of reference in scoring the behavior may be described by these two questions:

1. What is A's behavior doing to the system? How is A functioning? Is he owning his ideas, experimenting, not helping others, etc.? "Answer these questions from your (the observer's) view." Thus A could be, in the eyes of the observer, "not helping others" in his behavior toward B. It could be that B actually experiences the same behavior as helpful. This discrepancy will not be corrected unless the observer is able to show other data to support his view.
2. What impact would this behavior have on the creation of group norms? The observer also focuses on the impact of the individual's behavior upon the norms of the group. In making this decision he has some help from accumulated empirical experience. There are certain norms that tend to be correlated with specific types of behavior.

For example:

Helping others to own frequently leads to a norm of *concern* because helping others is showing concern for others.

Experimenting with one's feelings and ideas frequently leads to *trust* because experimentation includes taking risks and this is the major criterion of trust.

Openness *could* lead to *concern* if he is open to understanding others; to individuality if he is focusing on his self.

Not helping others to own leads to *conformity* because it attempts to require them to behave as the actor desires.

Other guideposts that have been developed to help in scoring behavior are:

---

[17] In Appendix C, I suggest how the same system can be used to study T groups.

1. Any interruption is always scored as a *not helping others*—(*i* or *f*) followed by the scoring of the content of what the interruptor said.
2. If two or more people interrupt the behavior it is scored as the *group not helping others*—(*i* or *f*).
3. Whenever in doubt the observer is told to select the category with the least potency so that the scores tend to be on the conservative side.
4. Any helping score is scored in terms of the category of the statement of the person being helped.
5. All questions receive an open score on level I.
6. Every statement that includes the phrase "I feel" is scored as an *f* score except when because of previous observation it is clear the individual is an intellectualizer who says "I feel" for "I think."

In the majority of the studies, tape recordings were made of all sessions. The observers scored behavior from the tapes. The procedure given to them were as follows:

1. Turn on the tape recorder and let it run for a specified period of time (which varied with each project).
2. Begin with the first full contribution. Score that statement as the first unit. Do not add another unit unless that person's behavior is no longer represented by the category just noted or if a new person speaks. In short, a unit is scored any time a different person speaks or any time an individual's contribution changes from behavior representing one category to another.
3. Continue the scoring for a specified amount of time in accordance to the following sampling procedures (which were varied with the research programs).

Interobserver Reliability Studies[18]

Three individuals (the writer and two graduate students) participated in the initial interobserver reliability studies.[19] Eleven studies in T groups, problem-solving groups, executive decision-making groups, and case study groups were used. The total number of units scored was 4,958. In these initial studies, in order to maximize learning, each observer scored several units separately, and then

---

[18] Other interobserver reliability studies are presented when relevant to the discussion.

[19] There are many issues that cannot be discussed because of space. For details (including an item analysis) see Appendix B. The graduate students were Fritz Steele and Clayton Alderfer. The writer acknowledges their help given to, and patience with, the writer as well as their skill in observing groups.

comparisons were made. Disagreements were noted first, and then a discussion was held until agreement was reached (in five cases no agreement was possible). Under this procedure the minimum percentage agreement among any two observers *before* any discussion took place was 86 percent. With this procedure, all one can state is that when two observers score behavior, and they have periodic opportunity to discuss their independently arrived at scores, there is relatively high interobserver reliability.

Several studies were also conducted to ascertain the interobserver reliability when all the behavior is scored by each observer and comparisons are made without periodic comparisons (thereby canceling the opportunity for mutual learning). The results were as follows: The first study of 200 units was conducted with one observer who had not scored tapes for nearly a year. He spent about ten minutes in practicing scoring a tape and then began. The percentage agreement was 70 percent. There was an 18 percent disagreement on units. In 12 percent of the cases the observers had missed units. A second study was then conducted of 218 units. The percentage agreement rose to 80 percent. There was a 14 percent disagreement on units. Each observer missed some units. The total for these was 6 percent.

No studies were made of the degree of agreement in the definition of a unit because the overwhelming majority of the units (about 90 percent) were of the type that were identified simply by a different individual speaking. However, such studies are necessary if the full utility of the framework is to be ascertained.

The Procedure for Analyzing and Scoring Individual and Group Behavior

In discussing the procedure for analysis and scoring behavior, I will use the T group setting as an example because it is the most difficult to score. It includes all the operations used to study problem-solving groups and more.

After each meeting, a sample of the verbal behavior was taken from the tape recording of the session. The sample was taken to mirror, in the observer's eyes, the behavior characteristics of the session. With few exceptions the sample size remained constant for each session. It was usually about 200 units on both the individual and the norms level. (Step I [see page 22] shows an example of part of a data sheet.)

From the data sheets, summary sheets were developed for each individual and the group. All categories, with appropriate idea or feeling designation, were listed, and the frequency of behavior in each category was tabulated. Having determined the frequency of behavior in a particular category, one then multiplied it by the appropriate weight for the category. Thus each category received a weighted score. These scores were then totaled for each of four larger categories: Individual or Interpersonal Positive, Individual or Interpersonal Negative, Norms Positive, and Norms Negative. (Step II shows an example of the procedure, based on the data taken from the data sheet of Step I.)

The thinking behind this method of developing scores was that contribution to, or inhibition of, effectiveness was a function of the amount of type of exposure manifested by group members. It also seemed useful, to give the scores more intuitive meaning, to let ± 1.0 be a limit. Consequently, each of the four weighted scores were divided by the highest possible (or lowest possible) scores to develop an *index* of competence. In each case the highest weight was 16 and each base point was developed by multiplying 16 times the total number of units of behavior. (Step III shows how this is done.)

As we shall see, indices developed in this manner seemed to reflect adequately most problem-solving meetings, as well as trainer and observer qualitative notions about member effectiveness in T groups in cases in which amount and quality of exposure were low, amount and quality of exposure were high, and when exposure was high and quality low. But when exposure was low and quality was high, the scores seemed to suggest more competence than seemed empirically justifiable. Consequently, it seemed necessary to adjust such scores.

In addition to the empirical reason, there is a theoretical reason for developing an "adjusted" score, which I can best describe by reminding the reader that two criteria of competence are the awareness of problems and the relatively permanent solution of these without influencing negatively the problem-solving process. Elsewhere I suggest that the higher the self-esteem, the higher the possibility that the above would occur.[20] Self-esteem develops when human beings experience psychological success. Finally, psychological success is defined as achieving realistic goals that involved a risk to the individual's self-esteem if he failed or succeeded.

Returning to the individual who does not tend to say much in a group, he is probably minimizing his opportunity for challenge and risk. A silent person may enhance his scope of awareness but, from our view, he should find it difficult to *behave* these new awarenesses. If he cannot behave them, then the others in the world around him (group members, staff, observers, etc.) will not tend to perceive him as increasing his competence.

It may be argued that the silent observers can learn in such a way that without exposure and risk taking, they can behave competently. This hypothesis, as well as ours, is subject to empirical test. One test would be to take the person who does not expose himself frequently but who, when he does, seems to behave competently, and place him in a test situation. For example, a two-man situation could be developed where he is supposed to help another individual to solve some interpersonal problem. It would be our hypothesis that disinterested but competent observers as well as the individual being "helped" will tend to evaluate the subject's behavior as *not* helping. Another test would be to ask our subject to describe, in writing or verbally, a situation where he believes that he (the subject) has helped someone to increase his awareness and to solve his interpersonal problems more competently without decreasing the "client's" self-esteem. It would be predicted that a content analysis of these incidents by competent but disinterested observers will tend to lead them to conclude that he did not accomplish his objective as he (the subject) thinks he did.

On the other hand, there is the case where the individual is silent in a group because he is highly competent but the rest of the members are not. If this individual maintained his silence, he too would receive a low competence score. However, upon interview we would find out why he behaved infrequently. Subjecting him to the tests above should confirm his competence.

If the individual does not expose himself, he has reduced his potential for learning, but he still could learn from watching the

[20] Chris Argyris, *Interpersonal Competence and Organizational Effectiveness,* *op. cit.*

exposure of others. How much an individual could learn depends, in part, on the behavior of others. (In part, it also depends on his ability to see what others do.) To take these views into consideration for developing quantitative scores, it was decided to weight their scores by the proportion that a particular behavioral unit appeared in the total group sample for that session. Competence, it was felt, was reflected by the individual behaving in increasingly more positive ways. Competence scores were somewhat arbitrarily chosen to be all plus scores on the individual and the norm levels. Incompetence scores were represented by the minus scores. Then the proportion of competence and noncompetence scores in the session could be determined. Each low exposer's scores would then be multiplied by the appropriate ratio, and his indices would be changed.[21]

The group scores were developed by summing all the scores in each behavioral category. (Group units, such as group not helping own, would be included.) The same indices, appropriate for individuals, were developed for the group.

The last step in completing the scoring consisted of developing imbalance scores between levels and between ideas and feelings. This was done by forming a table that allowed one to read individual and group totals simultaneously. (Step VII shows the imbalance taken from the initial data sheet.)

One final comment. Presently our scoring procedure assumes that every time an individual talks, he could have taken a risk. This assumption is clearly optimistic about people's capacities, and it results in relatively low scores. Further, it is not in line with psychological theory. Risk behavior is highly potent and energy consuming. We would hypothesize that an individual can have only a finite number of emotional and/or intellectual peaks. There will be a need for rest. Also, risks provide the individual and the group with rich opportunities for exploration. Consequently, some

---

[21] A different procedure was used in scoring the T group. While it does not make sense psychologically to exclude the trainer's scores, there does seem to be an operational reason for doing this. Trainers, one would hope, tend to boost the group scores, but this is not always so. It may turn out that some trainers tend to be less competent than some members. Such a separation of trainer scores from the group would reverse this. But there is also a need to adopt some operational criterion for a group being no longer dependent on its trainers for growth. Such a criterion might be that dependence ceases when the group score without trainer(s) matches the group score with trainers.

STEP 1: THE DATA SHEETS

(As Data Are Taken from the Tapes)

Name	Individual or Interpersonal	Ideas	Feelings	Norms of Unity	Ideas	Feelings
Joe	own	x		concern	x	
Group	n.h. own	x		conf.	x	
Mike	own	x		concern	x	
Joe	open	x		concern	x	
Mike	own	x		concern	x	
Mike	open	x		concern	x	
Bill	exp.		x	trust		x
Mike	h. exp.		x	trust		x
Bill	open		x	concern		x
Mike	own	x		concern		x
Bill	own	x		concern		x
Joe	n.h. own		x	conf.		x
Bill	h. own		x	concern		x
Joe	own		x	conf.		x
Mike	h. own		x	concern		x
Group	n.h. own	x		conf.	x	
Joe	n.h. own	x		conf.	x	
Bill	own	x		ind.	x	
Mike	own	x		concern		x
Bill	own	x		concern	x	
Joe	open	x		concern	x	
Joe	own	x		conf.	x	
Mike	h. own	x		concern	x	
Bill	own	x		conf.	x	
Bill	own	x		concern	x	
Bill	own	x		antag.	x	
Joe	n.h. own	x		conf.	x	

STEP II: THE SUMMARY SHEETS

			Frequency	Total	Score
Joe $N_i = 8$	own	i	//	2	2
		f	/	1	9
	open	i	//	2	4
		f			
Individual sample size for a session	exp.	i			
		f			
	h. own	i			
		f			
	h. open	i			
		f			
	h. exp.	i			
		f			
Total Individual or Interpersonal Positive				5	+15

Step II (Continued)			*Frequency*	*Total*	*Score*
n. own	i				
	f				
n. open	i				
	f				
n. exp.	i				
	f				
n.h. own	i		//	2	−6
	f		/	1	−5
n.h. open	i				
	f				
n.h. exp.	i				
	f				
Total Individual or Interpersonal Negative				3	−11
ind.	i				
	f				
concern	i		///	3	3
	f				
trust	i				
	f				
Total Positive Norms				3	+3
Joe					
$N_i = 8$	conf.	i	///	3	−6
		f	//	2	−16
	antag.	i			
		f			
	mistrust	i			
		f			
Total Negative Norms				5	−22
Bill	own	i	//// /	6	6
$N_i = 9$		f			
	open	i			
		f	/	1	10
	exp.	i			
		f	/	1	16
	h. own	i			
		f	/	1	9
	h. open	i			
		f			
	h. exp.	i			
		f			
Total Individual or Interpersonal Positive				9	+41

Step II (Continued)			*Frequency*	*Total*	*Score*
n. own	i				
	f				
n. open	i				
	f				
n. exp.	i				
	f				
n.h. own	i				
	f				
n.h. open	i				
	f				
n.h. exp.	i				
	f				
Total Individual or Interpersonal Negative				0	0
Bill $N_i = 9$	ind.	i	/	1	2
		f			
	concern	i	//	2	2
		f	///	3	30
	trust	i			
		f	/	1	16
Total Positive Norms				7	+50
	conf.	i	/	1	−2
		f			
	antag.	i	/	1	−4
		f			
	mistrust	i			
		f			
Total Negative Norms				2	−6
Mike $N_i = 8$	own	i	////	4	4
		f			
	open	i	/	1	2
		f			
	exp.	i			
		f			
	h. own	i		1	5
		f	/	1	9
	n. open	i			
		f			
	h. exp.	i			
		f	/	1	16
Total Individual or Interpersonal Positive				8	+36

Step II (Continued)			Frequency	Total	Score
Mike $N_i = 8$	n. own	i			
		f			
	n. open	i			
		f			
	n. exp.	i			
		f			
	n.h. own	i			
		f			
	n.h. open	i			
		f			
	n.h. exp.	i			
		f			
Total Individual or Interpersonal Negative				0	0
	ind.	i			
		f			
	concern	i	////	4	4
		f	///	3	30
	trust	i			
		f	/	1	16
Total Positive Norms				8	+50
	conf.	i			
		f			
	antag.	i			
		f			
	mistrust	i			
		f			
Total Negative Norms				0	0

STEP III: COMPUTING THE SCORES $(N_{ie} * = \dfrac{19}{3} = 6;$

(Therefore No Adjustment Is Needed) †

Base point $= 16 \times N_i$

Therefore: Joe's base point $= 16 \times 8 = 128$
Bill's base point $= 16 \times 9 = 144$
Mike's base point $= 16 \times 8 = 128$

	Individual or Interpersonal		Norms	
	Positive	Negative	Positive	Negative
Joe	15/128 = .117	−11/128 = −.086	3/128 = .023	−22/128 = −.172
Bill	41/144 = .284	0 = 0	50/144 = .347	−6/144 = −.042
Mike	36/128 = .281	0 = 0	50/128 = .390	0 = 0

* N_{ie} = group sample size for a session less the trainer's interventions over the number of members present at a session.

† These scores are used primarily in the studies reported in Appendix C.

Step IV: Correcting for a Low Number of Individual Interactions in a Sample
(Although this particular sample did not require correcting for a low number of
interactions, an additional hypothetical case is added to show how it is done.)

Definitions:

N_{G-T} = group sample size for a session less the trainer's interventions.
N_i = individual sample size for a session.
M = no. of members present at a session.
N_{ic} = $\dfrac{N_{G-T}}{M}$ = cutoff point for individual sample size.

For all N_i's and N_{ic}'s the following weighting scheme should be employed:
Growth score = all plus feeling scores and all helping scores.
Nongrowth score = all the other scores.
The weighting scheme should be applied only to positive scores.
To apply the weighting scheme, compute p_i, p_g, q_i, and q_g.

p_i = proportion of group growth scores in a session on the individual level.
$1 - p_i = q_i$ = proportion of norm nongrowth scores in a session on the individual level.
p_g = same as p_i except on group level.
$1 - p_g = q_g$ = same as q_i except on group level.

Recompute all individual scores where $N_i < N_{ic}$ by weighting all growth scores by p_i and p_g and all nongrowth scores by q_i and q_g.

Example:

Session #7 $N_{G-T} = 150$, $M = 15$
Norm
Scores $p_i = .10$ $p_g = .20$
          $q_i = .90$ $p_g = .80$

$N_{ic} = 10$
$N_i = 4$

John		Frequency	Score	Weight	New Score
own	i	2	2	0.90	1.80
	f	1	9	0.10	.90
	i				
exp.	f	1	16	0.10	1.60
			27		4.30
	i	1	2	0.80	1.60
ind.	f	2	16	0.20	3.20
	i				
trust	f	1	16	0.20	3.20
			34		8.00

Old Index
  Individual or Interpersonal Level 27/64 = 0.422
  Norms of Unity Level   34/64 = 0.531

New Index
  4.3/64 = 0.0671
  8/64 = 0.125

Step V: Tabulating Group Scores (For the Example,
Let Us Assume that Mike is the Trainer.
Therefore, $N_G = 27$; $N_{G\text{-}T} = 19$)

		N_G		$N_{G\text{-}T}$	
		Frequency	*Score*	*Frequency*	*Score*
own	i	12	12	8	8
	f	1	9	1	9
open	i	3	6	2	4
	f	1	10	1	10
exp.	i				
	f	1	16	1	16
h. own	i	1	5	0	0
	f	2	18	1	9
h. open	i				
	f				
h. exp.	i				
	f	1	16	0	0
Total Individual and Interpersonal Positive		22	92	14	56
n. own	i				
	f				
n. open	i				
	f				
n. exp.	i				
	f				
n.h. own	i	2	−6	2	−6
	f	1	−5	1	−5
n.h. open	i				
	f				
n.h. exp.	i				
	f				
g.n.h. own	i	2	−6	2	−6
	f				
g.n.h. open	i				
	f				
g.n.h. exp.	i				
	f				
Total Individual and Interpersonal Negative		5	−17	5	−17
ind.	i	1	2	1	2
	f				
concern	i	9	9	5	5
	f	6	60	3	30
trust	i				
	f	2	32	1	16
Total Positive Norms		18	103	10	53

Step V (Continued)

		N_G Frequency	N_G Score	$N_{G\text{-}T}$ Frequency	$N_{G\text{-}T}$ Score
conf.	i	6	−12	6	−12
	f	2	−16	2	−16
antag.	i	1	− 4	1	− 4
	f				
mistrust	i				
	f				
Total Negative Norms		9	−32	9	−32

Step VI: Computing Group Scores
(Base Point of $N_G = 27 \times 16 = 432$; Base Point of $N_{G\text{-}T} = 19 \times 16 = 304$)

	Individual or Interpersonal Positive	Individual or Interpersonal Negative	Norms Positive	Norms Negative
Group including trainer	92/432 = .215	−17/432 = −.039	103/432 = .238	−32/432 = −.074
Group without trainer	56/304 = .184	−17/304 = −.056	53/304 = .174	−32/304 = −.105

Step VII: Tabulating Imbalance Scores

	Individual or Interpersonal— Group Imbalance own i conf. i	own i antag. i	Idea—Feeling Imbalance own f conform i	concern f own i	Totals
Joe	1			•	2
Bill	1	1		/	3
Mike				//	2
Group Totals	2			///	7

behavior will be appropriately directed toward openness and concern. So far we have been unable to resolve this problem. We have not paused too long, however, because it is our belief that if a better procedure is arrived at, it will not change the relative but simply the absolute scores.

CHAPTER 2

Organization A

THE FIRST of the three studies upon which the findings in this book are based took place in a physical science industrial laboratory. It contained about 150 employees, of whom 100 were professional and semiprofessional. At the top of the hierarchy was a director of research. Next were two associate directors and an administrative director. The two associate directors had section and group supervisors reporting to them. Below them were about 40 engineers and nearly 50 technicians.

I interviewed all the top management (4); almost all of the supervisory staff (12 out of 13); almost all the engineers (36 out of 38); and about 50 percent of the technicians (26 out of 50). I also observed ten meetings where ten different superiors were in charge.

THE VALUES OF THE TOP MANAGEMENT, SUPERVISORS, ENGINEERS, AND TECHNICIANS

The first step was to infer the values that the subjects held about effective human relationships. A questionnaire was used, entitled the Managerial Behavior Questionnaire, which was developed initially by Fritz Steele and later by Lee Bolman. The questionnaire presented the respondent with a series of eight situations which might be encountered in organizational life, and asked the respondent how he would deal with the situation, why he would have dealt with it that way, and how sure he felt of his answers.

A content analysis system was developed, again by Bolman, which attempted to diagnose the extent to which the members held the "pyramidal values." By pyramidal values I mean (1) exclusive emphasis upon getting the job done, (2) the suppression of emotions and the highlighting of rationality, and (3) the assumption that the most effective commitment and motivation of the participants is obtained through direction, control, and appropriate rewards and penalties.

The answer to a single question was taken as a scoring unit and was checked for the presence or absence of each of the three pyramidal values and each of the three "newer" values. By newer values I mean (1) the emphasis upon maintenance of the system (in addition to achieving its objectives), (2) the expression of emotions (in addition to rational thoughts) when they are relevant, and (3) the use of psychological success, confirmation, and feelings of essentiality as motivators for human effort.[1] The presence of a pyramidal value was given a minus score, weighted by the degree of sureness which the respondent felt in his answer (in a scale ranging from 1–7). Thus if two of the pyramidal values were present, and the respondent indicated a degree of sureness of 6, he would receive a score of −12 for that question. The newer values were given positive scores and weighted in the same way. On the questionnaire as a whole, the possible range of scores is from −168 to +168, although these extreme scores would be extremely difficult to obtain. A minus score indicates that the respondent was oriented toward the pyramidal values; a plus score indicates the opposite.

Among 26 engineers who filled out the questionnaire, the mean score was −74.46, with a standard deviation of 21.91. This is a strongly pyramidal score and indicates that the respondents place a very high value on avoiding personal relationships, suppressing emotions, and using hierarchical control. A group of 18 technicians obtained a mean score of −70.94, with a standard deviation of 25.97. The supervisors (n = 15) obtained a mean score of −60.4, with a standard deviation of 25.42. This difference between the supervisors' scores and those of the engineers approaches statistical

---

[1] Chris Argyris, *Interpersonal Competence and Organizational Effectiveness* (Homewood, Ill.: Irwin-Dorsey Press, 1962).

significance.[2] Using t-test, $p < .10$, the engineers were more oriented toward the pyramidal values than their superiors.

An example of the way the replies were scored might be of help to the reader. The subject was asked how, if he were chairman of a meeting, he would handle an individual who became emotional. A typical example of a response of a subject who adhered to the value of a rationality and de-emphasis of emotionality was: "Since outburst is of an emotional nature, I would assume a high degree of irrationality, irrespective of whether the cause lies in something which was said at the meeting or not. Accordingly, if the meeting is near conclusion, I would adjourn, or call a recess temporarily, respectively." Another response was, "Ask him to quiet down or leave the room."

The development of the questionnaire used was in the formative stages. Much more research needs to be done to develop it further—as well as to ascertain its reliability and validity. The latter will be inferred by comparing it with data obtained in the interviews and from the observations. The results, to date, are encouraging. Adequate reliability studies are not available at this time, partially because the instrument is still in a transitional form. However, in a check of ten randomly selected questionnaires, the percentage agreement of Mr. Bolman and another rater (scoring independently) was 76 percent. The rank-order correlations were .81 (Spearman's R) and .60 (Kendall's T).[3]

CONCLUSIONS FROM THE OBSERVATIONS OF SUPERVISORS' LEADERSHIP BEHAVIOR

During the course of the study I observed ten problem-solving meetings (see Table 2-1). Each was formally administered by a different supervisor, although some meetings contained more than one supervisor as participants. Most of the meetings dealt with

---

[2] The overall mean for all three groups combined was 69.81 with a standard deviation of 26.8 (the latter indicating that the variation among groups is greater than the variation within groups). The range in the group as a whole was from −119 to +23.

[3] Those interested in the theory and method involved in the questionnaire should see Lee Bolman and Department of Industrial Administration, "Managerial Behavior Questionnaire" (New Haven: Yale University, 1964) (mimeographed).

TABLE 2–1

FREQUENCY OF CATEGORIES MANIFESTED IN PROBLEM-SOLVING MEETINGS

	1* (n = 201)		2 (n = 198)		3 (n = 250)		4 (n = 143)		5 (n = 168)		6 (n = 168)		7 (n = 200)		8 (n = 100)		9 (n = 131)		10 (n = 107)	
	n	%	n	%	n	%	n	%	n	%	n	%	n	%	n	%	n	%	n	%
own i	156	78	146	74	205	82	105	74	133	79	135	80	144	72	78	78	102	78	86	80
own f			1	.005																
concern i	52	26	122	62	123	49	89	62	79	47	64	38	89	44	47	47	56	43	58	54
concern f	87	43	54	27	88	35	38	26	60	36	72	43	92	46	38	38	62	47	32	30
conform i	31	15	46	23	39	16	34	24	24	14	25	15	37	18	20	20	25	19	14	13
conform f			4	02																
open i	30	15	18	09	22	09	12	08	12	07	29	17	18	09	13	13	8	06	8	09
open f																				
individuality i	32	16	5	02	17	07	4	03	17	10	6	04	1	.005	2	02	5	04	9	08
individuality f																				
antagonistic i	14	07			3	01	3	02	6	04	8	05	19	10	2	02	4	03	5	05
antagonistic f																				
n.h.o. own i																				
n.h.o. own f																				
h. own i					3	01			5	03							2	02	2	02
h. own f																				
own i–conform i	79	39	42	21	65	26	33	23	56	33	61	36	54	27	54	54	47	36	22	21
own i–antag i	30	15	19	10	14	06	2	01	15	09	4	02	5	03	3	03	5	04	4	03
open i–conform i	1	.005			3	01					1	.006	3	02			2	02		
open i–antag i	1	.005	4	02							1	.006								

* Individual and Group scores are considered as separate universes. All individual scores should approximate 100% and the same for all group scores. Thus n = 201 means 201 units on the individual level and 201 units on the group level.

technical problems, such as the defining of research objectives, the evaluation of ongoing research projects, the review of budgets, the development of a new product, and the need for greater communication among research personnel.

From a research point of view, it is interesting to note that the scores obtained in all meetings—except 1, 6, 7, and 9—are in accordance with our expectations of how people would behave if they held the pyramidal values.

Thus *own i* was most frequent, with *concern i, conform i, open i, individuality i,* and *antagonism i* following in that order. Also feeling (*f*) scores were extremely low, as were the scores for trust, mistrust, and helping and not helping others. Turning to the apparent exceptions, sessions 1 and 6 were administered by two supervisors who were described by their subordinates during the interviews as "highly competitive," who "love a good fight," who'd "just as soon tell you off," and who "respect subordinates who fight." These data permit us to infer that these two supervisors were predisposed toward being competitive or counterdependent. This is one of the conditions under which *conformity i* is predicted to exceed *concern i.* Sessions 7 and 9 were concerned primarily with intergroup problems. The high conformity scores within the groups were caused by supervisors defending their own sections in a win-lose situation.

The frequency of the imbalance scores was also as predicted. *Own i–conform i* is most frequent, with *own i–antagonism i, open i–conform i,* and *open i–antagonism i* following in that order.

According to the theoretical scheme used in this analysis, we would conclude that in the supervisory group:

1. There was a high degree of owning up to ideas, of expressing opinions. However, it was not shown in the table that the amount varied among members. In all cases the superiors tended to speak much more than did the subordinates (more about this later).
2. The most frequently supported norm was *concern* for ideas. The second most important norm was *conformity* to ideas. The third most important norm, whose frequency was less than half of *conformity i,* was *individuality i.*
3. Openness to ideas from others was high when:
   a) a subordinate wanted to learn the view of the superior.

b) a superior wished to "show up" a subordinate. The superior asked questions in order to show the subordinate the incorrectness of his thinking.
4. *Antagonism i* was relatively low in all the sessions except the first. All but one unit of these were made by a supervisor who, according to the reports in the interviews, is the most competitive individual in the laboratory.
5. *Not helping others* was slightly more frequent than *helping others* because of the interruptions that tended to occur among participants during the meetings.
6. Behavior that was hardly ever observed:
   a) the expression of positive or negative feelings.
   b) risk taking.
   c) trust.
   d) mistrust.
   e) overtly refusing to give one's point of view or overtly refusing to listen to someone else's point of view.

Some Predictions Made from the Findings Above

The pattern above is expected from individuals who hold the pyramidal values regarding effective human relationships. According to the theoretical viewpoint, this pattern tends to lead to low interpersonal competence. When low interpersonal competence occurs, there should be, according to this viewpoint: (*a*) little awareness of important interpersonal problems; (*b*) few interpersonal problems that are solved effectively; and (*c*) a constant deterioration of the effectiveness of the problem-solving process.

These predictions should hold true for all interpersonal problems *and* for those technical and administrative problems that have strong emotional and interpersonal components.

In order to explore these hypotheses, I interviewed the subjects to explore the superior-subordinate and the peer relationships. If it is true that the supervisors' interpersonal competence is low, then I predicted that interpersonal difficulties should be reported between the two and that the superiors should not be highly aware of them. All the interviews were tape-recorded and transcribed in full. The analysis was made from the typewritten protocols.

Superior-Subordinate Relationships. Although 50 percent of the supervisors admitted they probably did something that inhibited their subordinates, 67 percent believed that their relationships with the subordinates were basically sound. If they did upset the subordinates, it was when they passed down pressure from above them (58 percent).

The subordinates' view was quite different. Sixty-one percent of the engineers and 62 percent of the technicians saw their supervisors as not being interpersonally competent.

Some typical comments were:

1. I wish my boss would be more open and straightforward with me. Every now and then he would come and say "How's that report coming" and remind me to get together with him. Well this reminding business is for the birds. I think if he wants me to get together with him, he should say so. One of the problems with my boss is he doesn't know how to talk to you without making you feel as though you must be nothing short of stupid.

2. He's about the worst man I have ever worked for.

RESEARCHER: Could you elaborate a little more?

He is extremely rigid in his supervision, and he tries to be mean to you, to humiliate you in every possible way that he can. He's a coward and a bully and he bows down to those higher up and he blasts those people below. He won't stick up for his men. He's very bad on raises and he squeezes a company dollar as if it were coming from his own pocket. He takes the attitude that the most important thing in life is to get respect as a boss, rather than to get respect as a supervisor, a competent supervisor. He eternally demands respect, but he doesn't know how to earn it.

3. My supervisor has a tendency to embarrass an individual right in front of a group of people, especially when it comes to a particular job. There may be two or three engineers around and he will pinpoint one particular person. He has a tendency to embarrass him right in front of the whole group instead of calling him down in his office and talking it out.

4. At times I think my supervisor is arrogant. Too militaristic, I would say. I butted heads with him once and he left me flat. I am very, very leery of him, I don't know whether I should trust him or not. I am afraid that if I do give him my confidence he will stab me in the back, so I am very hesitant about this, but openly I have no aggressive attitudes toward him. I don't make him feel that there is any withdrawal on my part towards him. But I am still cautious.

Not all supervisors were perceived in this negative manner. For example:

1. One thing around here we do have are very capable managers with a lot of experience. They seem to be well-educated fellows

and I think most of them are respected for their technical competence.

Comments such as "impatient," "dominating," "insensitive," "makes me feel lower," "a tendency to embarrass" lend support to the possibility that the subordinates' negative reactions were caused more by the superior's relatively low interpersonal competence than by the formal power position he held. The fact that 34 percent of the technicians and 39 percent of the engineers reported their supervisors were "fine" also supports (but does not prove) that differential power between superior and subordinate was not the major cause.

Another indication of the interpersonal difficulties existing between superiors and subordinates was that "poor relationship with my supervisor" was the dissatisfying experience most frequently recalled by the technicians and engineers (46 percent and 36 percent, respectively) during the interviews. For example:

1. There are some dissatisfying experiences. For instance, I can think of a few weeks ago my immediate supervisor, in my opinion, made a complete fool of himself, which he does rather often, and he shows how little he knows about the subject.

RESEARCHER: How does he do this?

Instead of admitting he doesn't know, which I admit in a lot of areas, he'll go on and on. His best excuse is not being able to explain that particular question. Whereas, in the meantime, he's made three or four completely erroneous and rather foolish statements in trying to explain it. Mind you, this doesn't frustrate me as much as it frustrates a couple of fellows I work for. I just feel very sorry for him.

Another indication of a major difficulty was found in the replies to the question "Do you know how your superior feels about your work?" Sixty-two percent of the technicians and 61 percent of the engineers replied "Only indirectly" and 35 percent and 22 percent (respectively) stated "No." This finding was especially significant since the organization required all supervisors to formally evaluate each subordinate.

If the superiors utilized the same behavioral pattern in the evaluation sessions as they did in their meetings (and 83 percent said that they did), then the results should not be surprising. How can one have an effective personal evaluation session where the expression of feelings, risks, and trust were not sanctioned, where helping behavior was practically zero, and where the concern for ideas and conformity were the two most potent norms? If a subordinate disagreed with a supervisor's view he immediately would have to discuss interpersonal and emotional issues and yet this could not be encouraged. No wonder French[4] recommends, and Rowe[5] agrees, that these types of evaluation sessions be radically revised or eliminated.

Some typical views were:

1. I'm never sure. I will say that I'm caught up with, on the one hand, thinking that he's extremely fair, and, on the other hand, thinking that he's extremely unfair. Well, this is too conflicting of course. I think it's a little difficult to know exactly what he's thinking. But I keep getting the feeling that he's not fair.

RESEARCHER: What has he done that makes you think he might be unfair?

Well, I get little criticism of my work, considering that I'm doing a capable job. Then comes money time and he doesn't seem to have any for me. For instance, you hit me at a real crucial point. The time has gone by when I'm supposed to have received a raise, and I haven't heard. Right now I'm toying with the idea of going up and asking him "Why didn't I get a raise?"

2. Sometimes we have discussions, but so far I have found out that one of the things I don't like too much is that the superior sort of softens whatever he has to say. I don't particularly care for that. If I'm not doing the right job, I like to be told because I want to do it right. If what he feels is right is not what I feel is right, and I have a conviction along this line and I can substantiate it, then I'll argue with him about it.

Another example of interpersonal difficulties may be found in the area of reports and report writing. May I remind the reader that I am not suggesting that I can predict, a priori, that there will be interpersonal problems in the report area; I am predicting that if there are interpersonal problems, with regards to report writing, the supervisors will not tend to be aware of them.

Seventy-five percent of the supervisors stated that there may be some "few" problems with reports, but they were caused primarily by the inability of engineers to write clearly.

---

[4] John R. P. French, "Status, Self-esteem and Health," International Management Congress, September, 1963, CIPM, New York, 1963, pp. 735–39.

[5] Kay H. Rowe, "An Appraisal of Appraisals," *Journal of Management Studies*, Vol. 1, No. 1 (March, 1964), pp. 1–25.

The engineers held a different viewpoint. They believed that the problem with report writing was in the superior's inability to handle the situation competently. For example, 75 percent of the engineers believe that "my ideas get massacred," "no matter how you write, they'll rewrite it," "my reports get emasculated." Thus:

1. No matter how you write a report and how many times you write it and what you say, it's rewritten and rewritten and rewritten. So you learn to write a report, hand it in, and become like a machine, keep making the changes. The funny thing is, by the time they finish emasculating your report they come back to what it was before.

2. Well, the reports get cut up six times or so. They're very word-conscious around here. Anything that leaves the laboratory, they're afraid it might be misconstrued on the outside. They don't have any confidence in the engineer to report properly without being misconstrued. The joke of it all is that most of the reports are probably not read.

3. This is rather a pet problem with research. Sooner or later they find that they do not possess the ability to put into words the products of their reports unless they happen to be phrased in the pet jargon of their superior. So, as a result, I've seen reports, letters, and even memos written and rewritten as high as fifteen times. This impedes progress to a disastrous degree because when a man becomes disillusioned then he becomes irritated over the situation and progress begins to decrease.

4. My superiors more or less stomp on the reports. It's an ordeal for us to write them. Groups are now trying to write on both sides of the fence. Is this what the boss would like to say? Is this the way that he would say it? I'm afraid people spend so much time trying to write as the boss likes that they lose the essence of the report.

A final example where supervisors did not seem to be aware of their interpersonal problems with their subordinates was illustrated by the fact that 75 percent of the supervisors said that they strove to let the subordinates alone. They did not pressure them. On the other hand, 50 percent of the subordinates complained of too much dictatorship of research, pressure, and assignment of engineers to routine work.

To summarize, the superiors did not seem to be aware of some serious interpersonal problems with their subordinates. Also, the superiors' relatively low interpersonal competence was reported as the major cause for these problems.

Peer Relationships. Although I was not able to observe all the engineers and technicians in their everyday relationships, it is possible to predict from the fact that they hold values similar to those of their superiors that the engineers and technicians would also tend to have low interpersonal competence, although they may not be aware of this possibility. (It may be that, given the power structure in organizations, and given a general low interpersonal competence, the subordinate will tend to feel justified in focusing on his superior's limitations at the expense of his own.)

If interpersonal competence, as defined in this study, is low among engineers and technicians, I would tend to expect that their peer relationships should not go beyond everyday pleasantries. The same kinds of interpersonal problems that exist between the superior and subordinate should also exist among peers. The data support this hypothesis. Thus all the respondents were asked: "Do you know how your peers feel about you?" Sixty-seven percent of the supervisors, 55 percent of the engineers, and 73 percent of the technicians reported that they did not know how their peers felt about them. For example:

1. I don't know, actually. I don't know other people's impressions of me—and I hope it's favorable—but I don't think it's extremely unfavorable. I usually make efforts to be as good a person as I can be, but I don't know how people might judge my technical ability. As a person, I would guess that I get along pretty well with mostly everybody. I try to be cooperative and I know most everybody here does, too. I don't make friendships here that I carry outside.

2. I think that it is something you can tell, but never directly. But I think over the years I've developed a sense that tells me how things are going.

RESEARCHER: What is this sense? Could you tell me a little more about it?

It's hard to define. I think it's how they present themselves to you, how they react to your working with them or discussing something they have done.

RESEARCHER: Could you specify even further?

Maybe here again—to go back to the other thing I was talking about, in terms of making people feel that they are free—they are on their own. I think that, in knowing people, you know when to leave them alone and when to talk to them. It seems to me most people show you that they like you by leaving you alone and not pressuring you. Also, by not starting any fights; and, if you ask them to do something, they seem to do it.

Some Further Consequences of Low Interpersonal Competence

The Concept of Effective Leadership. Since owning, openness, and experimenting with feelings is low, and trust and concern for feelings almost nonexistent, if interpersonal difficulties arise it will tend to be difficult to discuss them openly. Under these conditions interpersonal competence tends to be considered irrelevant, and, if it exists, it would be suppressed. Also, under these conditions, it is understandable that the most effective qualification for leadership reported at all levels was technical competence. Thus 54 percent of the technicians and 44 percent of the engineers felt that an effective leader should be technically competent. When asked if interpersonal qualities were necessary, the same number responded with vague answers, such as "He should get along with people." When asked what qualities were necessary to get along with people, the responses tended to be that he should be "fair," "friendly," "let people alone," and "not upset people."

A substantial number of engineers (39 percent) said that they preferred a superior who was technically competent, who was articulate, and directive and controlling. These men implied that they preferred to be dependent.

> 1. First, I think he has to demand a certain amount of respect. You should want to please him, even though he disagrees with you. He comes through as a strong man, and you have to say, "By golly, maybe he was right."
> 2. I think to be an effective leader you must be able to talk at any level. I think you have to show that you're sure of what you're doing. This is required in order to create effectiveness. I think he should be critical of a person's work, but not overly critical to the extent that he demoralizes the person. This does happen on occasions. I think he should reassure the other people and discuss their projects on a friendly basis.

One way to account for both of these concepts of leadership is the low interpersonal competence of the individuals, plus cultural norms against the expression of feelings, and interpersonal risk taking. The most widely held concept of leadership is one of a leader who leaves people alone. The fundamental characteristic of this view is *minimum* interpersonal contact. As one engineer put it, "a supervisor who does not rock the interpersonal boat." The second concept of leadership is one of minimum subordinate responsibility and maximum superior responsibility for a relationship. Under these conditions the probability is quite high that if an interpersonal error occurs the superior will make it, and, in this culture, the subordinate will not tend to make it an issue. The interpersonal difficulty is therefore suppressed.

In view of the above it is understandable that 55 percent of the engineers said that management facilitates research by "leaving me alone" or by doing "nothing." If the superior would attempt to do something interpersonally, he would tend to cause difficulties. To put it in an extreme form, I am suggesting that interpersonal interaction among these respondents would tend to lead to interpersonal difficulties.

But if the supervisor does decide to "leave his subordinates alone," he may run a risk that he does not expect. On the one hand, as he hopes, most subordinates tend to interpret a lack of contact on the part of the superior as a sign of trust of them. However, we have also said that people, in this laboratory, tend to leave people alone because they are *afraid* to upset them. Subordinates may eventually begin to wonder if the superior is leaving them alone because he is afraid to upset them—and *not* because he trusts them.

Low Feelings of Interpersonal Psychological Success, Confirmation, and Essentiality. If the analysis above is valid, the interpersonal relationships tend to become even more impoverished in terms of emotions, risk taking, and concern for feelings and trust. If challenges and risks are practically nonexistent, then the probability for interpersonal psychological success will tend to be low. If people do not tend to be open with each other on the feeling level, then confirmation will tend to be low. Finally, if relationships remain on a relatively skin-surface level, feelings of interpersonal essentiality should be low. These feelings, in this culture, would feed back to reinforce the necessity for the concept of leadership just mentioned.

Also, if the members are to experience psychological success, it will have to be with intellectual challenges. Confirmation of the self will tend to be limited to technical aspects of the self. Thus feelings of essentiality will tend to exist with regard to the research and technical problems. These predictions will be explored in detail in the next section.

Some Consequences of Low Interpersonal Psychological Success, Confirmation, and Essentiality. So far I have suggested that the conditions above will tend to reinforce and emphasize the technical aspects of work. Also, since interpersonal risks are discouraged, psychological success will tend to be nonexistent and considered (by the participants) as practically not available. The members may strive, however, to do something about developing feelings of essentiality and confirmation. One symbol of the degree of essentiality and feelings of confirmation is the extent to which management gives things to the members. There may arise, therefore, strong predispositions on the part of the subordinates to ask for material (it is against the culture to ask for interpersonal) things that could confirm to them that they are essential. Some examples of such things are (1) space, desks, files, etc., (2) technical assistance, (3) equipment, (4) opportunities for further education, and (5) recognition through various types of prizes.

All members emphasized the importance of these factors. The finding relevant to this point is that although nearly 40 percent of the technicians and engineers stated that they needed more technicians, equipment and space, 46 percent of the technicians and 56 percent of the engineers said that the laboratory was well organized and well staffed with material services. The point I am suggesting is that the members, at all levels, should not tend to be satisfied with any given amount of any of these increments.

Observing various supervisory meetings made it apparent that a relatively large number of engineers and technicians was asking for more meetings "to get to know more about what each other was doing." Their superiors, in discussing these requests, were perplexed. They pointed out that anyone could go to anyone and ask him what he was doing. They also pointed out that any small group could invite another group to meet with it. Others pointed out that engineers and technicians complained that there were too many meetings.

It is interesting to note that where these meetings had been developed, the engineers and technicians have not been particularly satisfied. Could it be that in a culture that suppresses the open discussion of interpersonal issues the member will find it hard to be aware of, and to express his unfulfilled needs for, interpersonal essentiality, confirmation, and psychological success? He may tend to have feelings of wanting to interact and to talk with others but be unable to explain them rationally. But since the culture sanctions the intellectual aspects, the engineer expresses his unfulfilled needs in the interpersonal area by asking for interaction in the technical area.

Another important consequence is related to the difficulties researchers have in communicating with "outsiders." For example, the researcher must interact with line managers in order to obtain accurate data or to convince them to change their manufacturing procedures. This is a difficult task in itself because the researchers report that the line people tend to see researchers as meddling eggheads who tend to get the plants into trouble with their ideas. A relatively high degree of interpersonal competence on the part of the engineers and scientists would be useful in this difficult situation. Unfortunately, as we have seen, the researchers do not tend to have it.

It is not surprising, therefore, to learn that they reported (1) they had many difficulties in influencing plant people and (2) that most felt that it was the plant people's fault. Thus 83 percent of the engineers and 75 percent of the supervisors reported a lack of cooperation and trust between researchers, and plant people placed the fault largely on the plant people. For example:

1. The biggest problem, I think, is that the man at the plant feels that he will look foolish in the eyes of his boss if something new comes out that he hadn't thought of. Also, many people at the plants are afraid to change anything. If they upset things, then somebody will get on their ass. Also, there are people who try to create a sense of completeness in their plant by implying that everything that's being done in their plant is perfect, and this leads to a feeling of nothing's good that isn't invented in the plant.

2. Sometimes they resist because we don't have an adequate appreciation of the problems of the plant. In the case that I was familiar with, we worked very hard to develop a new process. Finally, we had it developed and we brought it to the plants. They fought it continually. They didn't even want to listen to us. It took a long time, before they calmed down, to see that what we had built for them was really helpful. Yes, I would say there's very

poor communication back and forth. Sometimes they fight us like hell and other times they get together—and they possibly get a fresh perspective on what we are trying to do.

I know in one case we asked for information from one of the mills and it took six months before they sent it to us, and what they sent us was really hastily done and poorly executed.

RESEARCHER: Do you think they realize that the information was not very useful?

That's probably why they sent it. That would keep us away for another six months. Yes, there are problems, I was in a group that took a product to the plant and we showed them that it was good, that it worked, and that it developed savings. But, as soon as we left, they seemed to avoid using it because they were afraid of difficulties that they might have. So we tell them to go ahead and try it and we'd correct the difficulties if they want; we'd go back and help them. But it takes a long time to move somebody in the plant.

I should like to close this section by citing one other factor that seems plausible enough to be worthy of mention.

Seventy-five percent of the research people report that there had been some "horning in" and pigeonholing of patents by the supervisors. In all cases, except one, I was unable to pin down actual examples to support these charges. When pushed for data, the researchers either said that they did not know of an instance or quoted a "very personal friend" who told them. For example:

1. Yes, I think there are problems of patents. I have heard of different kinds. For example, one of my friends here made a suggestion which could save the company thousands of dollars. He submitted his cure. He actually wrote up the project in outline form. Then he never heard anything about it. He waited and waited, until one day he asked his boss whatever had happened to the patent. His boss said that it was somewhere in the legal department in the home office. Finally he called the legal department, and they told him to take it easy, they were very busy, and that eventually he would hear about it. Recently, however, he heard through the grapevine that three supervisors have muscled in on his patent. Now that really is horrible.

2. There are quite a few instances in the labs here where ideas have been suggested and have gone through the patent group, and it has been discussed there and decided to be tabled. Within a short period of time, a year or so after, some other organization comes out with the very same thing as that. Then the people in the home office say, "Well, that's a good idea. Why didn't we think of

something like this?" You go back to the files and show them where it had been tabled for maybe six months or a year and they didn't think it was worth working on at that time. Now, this has happened to several people I know here at the lab.

The question arises: How much accurate information will the researchers in the laboratory obtain if their relationship among peers are (as suggested above) relatively skin-surfaced? Could it possibly be that rumors such as these have the function of express-ing pent-up feelings of hostility that may exist toward the superiors, and that fill in the interpersonal vacuum for confirmation and essentiality?

THE RIVALRY PROBLEM

During my research I learned of a rivalry between two key supervisors. Eighty-nine percent of the engineers and 92 percent of the supervisors described the rivalry as being "moderate" to "ex-tremely deep," with the majority choosing a position closer to the middle but on the side of the rivalry being "deep." For example:

1. Yes, I think there are rivalries in this laboratory and I think they depend on the personality of the people in the groups; and there are a lot of rivalries as far as space is concerned. Space is becoming a pretty big problem, and we're having less and less of it but yet we need more and more of it.

2. Yes, there are rivalries here. You see, the laboratory is divided into groups and subgroups, and the basic idea is very fine. One group is supposed to help another, and this is done by what they call service-type help. Now what happens is that if there is any rivalry between your group and mine, I can stall you from this particular work order if I want to. So you get mad at me and say "Well, the hell with you; I'll do my own piece of work that I've asked you to do." But you say, "No, you can't, because we won't let you buy the piece of equipment that you're supposed to execute this particular work for."

And so what you have, what it amounts to, is that different groups can't buy different pieces of equipment that they would like to get to speed some of their work. One reason is because another group has this piece of equipment and the other group is supposed to do the work for you, but they won't do it because they're too busy or they don't want it.

3. Yes, there are rivalries in this lab. For example, when one group has a semibreakthrough, not a complete success, but a

large enough success, there is inclined to be a little animosity between that group and another group. They are not doing the same exact projects, but their projects may be related. I have seen experts in one group asked to come in and consult on projects in another group, and in doing so, we have done it politely and in a gentleman-like way, but there is very definite feeling there.

RESEARCHER: Why? What is it that leads one side not to accept help from another?

Well, they'll accept it, but only with strong feelings. I think there's a feeling that these people are going into somebody else's back yard.

RESEARCHER: Could it also be a public sign of their failure?

In a way, yes. Actually, I think that basically this is what it is. It's a type of criticism of work that people have already done, and yet have not come up with completely successful answers. It implies that the other group has come up with a successful answer. This doesn't sit well at all. I'll say that there are rivalries here. In some ways, in some groups, cooperation is very, very poor. You get a service request, for instance, which requires the services of some other group in the lab, and we occasionally have to fight and raise hell to try to get the service. In general, I'd say though, there is good cooperation.

In this case, the source of the rivalry was apparently more related to the personalities of the members involved and less to the nature of organization. This conclusion seems plausible because the laboratory was new and expanding. It was still on its "honeymoon period." Consequently, space, funds, and openings for advancement were somewhat more plentiful than would be the case in an established laboratory. The supervisors said that there was little competition between the two divisions because each was relatively busy developing its own field and so far both had been quite successful.

However, interdepartmental rivalries, whether related to personalities or not, do become embedded in the emotions of people. This rivalry was no different except that the emotional involvement down the line was not very deep, probably because of the youth of the laboratory as an organization.

Every so often the researcher in the field is provided with an opportunity that he does not expect to see if his diagnosis fits reality. I could not predict a priori that a rivalry would exist in the laboratory. But once finding that it existed I attempted to predict that the parties should not be able to cope with the problem. More specifically, the people in the laboratory should not be aware of the rivalry or, if they were aware of it, they should report that they were unable to solve it. Since the former is obviously not the case, then the second prediction became the one to explore further.

It is clear that this prediction could not be field-tested by interviewing the subordinates of the supervisors where the rivalry existed. They would legitimately feel that they did not have the organizational authority or responsibility to solve the problem. Consequently, I interviewed the two individuals involved, their superior, plus one other organizationally equal supervisor. Let us begin with one of the three organizationally equal supervisors.

> Yes, we certainly do have some rivalries. I wish that you could have observed a two-hour meeting last week on space requirements. It was a two-hour meeting at the end of which we came out of the same door feeling that it was two hours wasted. Two hours of annoyance and frustration.
>
> RESEARCHER: What do you think can be done about it?
>
> It puzzles me. These personality problems are complicated. I wish there was a way to organize to eliminate these problems.
>
> RESEARCHER: Do you think it is having an impact on the technical effectiveness of the lab?
>
> If it is, only slightly. The lab is young and small. The people know each other and are contacting each other.

Turning to another, he too perceives the rivalry. He believes that it is having a negative impact on some projects but not on others.

> I don't believe that the rivalry is too disruptive, although it is distressing, and I hope by keeping gradual pressure—although I don't like to use the word pressure—but by making it very clear that to the extent that I can, every decision is an objective decision and it isn't based on any feelings other than "what are the facts," that it will gradually get better.

Thus one individual hoped for an organizational solution to ease the problem. The other believed that if those who were involved in the rivalry would be logical and objective, then the problem would eventually disappear. However, when he was asked how he would view an open exploration of the problem he replied that he had not tried that because it was hard to know how the men would react.

"You know," he continued, "this rivalry is a deeply buried thing. I don't think the two people involved realize how deeply involved they are. One of them is quite competitive, the other, for some obscure reason, impatient with authority as authority."

The supervisor's apparent unawareness of the incongruency between his diagnosis of the rivalry as being deep-seated and his solution that those involved should be objective and unemotional led me to infer that he was uncomfortable with the whole problem. He wished that these feeling issues did not exist and more so, that he did not have to solve them.

Turning to the two principals, they too were aware of the problem. Both were concerned but in different ways. One was unhappy about the other because in the long run he would suffer. On the other hand, the other was worried about all involved but especially about the organization as a whole. He felt that the rivalry would split the organization in half and make operations extremely difficult. For example, each one's department contained service facilities for the other. Already each felt that the other was purposely ordering his men not to cooperate. This perception was confirmed by some of the supervisors below, who felt it was wise not to cooperate too quickly; or, if they were in a bind, they thought highly probable that the boss would support them if they delayed the services longer than was promised. More important perhaps was the evidence that men across the two departments were not helping each other to solve research problems. Recently one group was accused of predicting that the other would fail and of asserting that only after the failure had occurred would they go in and bail the other group out. The other group denied the charge.

Like the first two, the third believed the problem was in the lack of objectivity and rationality shown by the others. "The trouble with——is that he is a very emotional fellow in these sort of things and he lets his emotions get the better of his reasoning."

Turning to the fourth individual, he described his working relationship with the third as "pretty poor." He continued:

I believe there is a barrier between the two departments. The fighting for responsibility and project money, all of this is building up and building up. Worse yet, if we are not careful we may develop a real operating rigidity in the laboratory. For example, his boys may discover a new property of —— and need the know-how that we have or vice versa. I have been in labs where it is like pulling teeth to get any help. This is already happening here.

RESEARCHER: Maybe I can be of some help during the feedback.

I wish you would. I've tried to reason with them. I haven't gotten very far.

RESEARCHER: How do you explain their behavior?

I don't know. I guess A feels he's getting what he wants. B never really tells me. He said you're doing a good job but don't get so emotionally involved with your people. He said you worry too much about them.

RESEARCHER: Do you believe that he wants to take action?

He hasn't done so. He's made no steps to do that. We haven't had a meeting of that kind in a hell of a long time. And this is what we should do. If we are all reasonable men with some semblance of logic it should work out.

Again we see a familiar pattern: The bewilderment of each side about the other's inability or apparent lack of desire to cooperate; the feeling of disillusionment as well as the ambivalent feeling that somehow a rational, nonemotional approach should solve the issue. The end result of this is best described by the comment made by one individual: "I think we are on a collision course, and no one seems to be able to do anything about it."

To summarize: Most of the engineers and almost all the supervisors believe that there was a rivalry between two key supervisors. A few believed that the rivalry was presently inhibiting work, while most said, if it did not do so now, it could in the future. None seemed to be able to develop solutions that they viewed as worthy of trying.

The situation was basically the same at the upper levels. Although each individual was aware of the rivalry, no one spoke about it openly and directly; they believed that it could be handled objectively and rationally. However, all admitted that, to date, all actions taken had not led to a solution of the problem. These conclusions are in line with our initial prediction that with relatively low interpersonal competence, individuals who are aware of interpersonal issues will not tend to believe that they can solve them in such a way that the problems remain solved.

The Confrontation

Apparently, sometime after his interview with the writer, one of the protagonists wrote a memorandum including a section on what he entitled the laboratory as an organization. In the memorandum he described the split but he did so in organizational terms. He wrote:

The Laboratory as an Organization

Although the technical accomplishments in 1963 are most encouraging my personal observation is that the lab as an organization presents a discouraging picture.
1. We function now as two laboratories.
2. The organization makes for building of a fence between two major parts. Chances are high that interchange of information will be further restricted in the future.
3. In some cases, the setting up of the two departments has had the effect of almost deliberate pitting one department against the other.
4. Actually, as a two-department setup, the organization does not go far enough. The authority to the department heads is actually on a string. Commitments are made directly for the departmental organization without previous knowledge of the department.

Summary

Our personnel are doing an outstanding job in the project work at hand. Developments from the laboratory will make a significant contribution to the company. In my opinion, however, the laboratory is on a collision course organization-wise. This can, in turn, adversely affect the performance and contribution of the laboratory to the company.

When the memorandum was received, it was decided to hold a session on the problem and invite the researcher to join the session. I agreed.

My strategy was as follows. As a researcher I wanted more corroboration that the executives would not be able to handle the problem to their own satisfaction. On the basis of my analysis I would have to predict that they would not talk about the personality and interpersonal aspects of the rivalry *even though each individual had talked to me about these aspects during the interview.*

Consequently, I decided to be an observer for at least the first hour of the meeting.

One member of the group attempted to describe the problem:

There is the general feeling that the organization (structure) is functioning to split the lab into two separate departments, that the flow of information is impeded between the groups and it is getting worse, and that the groups are competing against each other and not cooperating with each other.

The matter came up about a month ago, during a discussion of space allocation in the building and we talked about it a little bit at that time and then we agreed to get together and discuss it some more at a later date.

One of the individuals added:

Organizational charts can split labs. This occurs for a variety of reasons. I think the tendency in organization is that splits do occur, and therefore I think that as part of our function we should try to watch against splits and do everything we can to avoid them. I feel that our organizational arrangement was working in that direction.

The individual continued to describe the organization of the laboratory as a series of independent little research units decreasingly cooperating with one another. Moreover, budgets were becoming tighter and accelerating the tendency for splitting apart. The relevant point for this discussion is that the discussion was focused upon the organizational aspects. The organization was being described as the culprit even though all four participants had told the researcher that the main difficulties were interpersonal. This is in line with the diagnosis that interpersonal issues will tend to be suppressed.

One of the group continued the discussion by stating that budgets were necessary and important. He insisted that budgets did not split departments.

Another complaint lodged by one of the protagonists was that the number of meetings to discuss the laboratory as a whole had decreased; he showed how this had affected the technical progress in the laboratory. Exchange of technical information between the two departments had decreased to the point that one group did not know what the other was doing.

The other protagonist cut in to say that only last week his group had held a technical information meeting which was attended by hardly any of the men from the other department. The supervisor of that department admitted this was a shame, but said he felt that such a meeting was not the best basis for communication between the departments.

The rival supervisor agreed and added that he doubted if this situation was any different from that of other laboratories. This was accepted by the former, who added that he was trying to make it clear that the real problem in the laboratory was the absence of the desire for people to work with each other and cooperate. He then added:

> In my opinion formalizing the two departments within the lab is one of those things that has a natural tendency, if you will, to split apart and in that respect I think it is not good.

Finally he finished by stating that he was not finding the discussion enjoyable because he felt that it was bordering on personalities. But he was going through this for the sake of the organization.

Everyone supported the motive to have a more effective laboratory. Each pressed the other for *specific* suggestions. No one seemed to develop any that satisfied all concerned. The discussion continued for an hour and fifteen minutes. Finally, I decided that no one would discuss the important interpersonal issues unless I brought them up. I said, "If I understand the data, the people in the laboratory feel that there is rivalry between —— and ——; that it can become harmful, and that no one is able to do anything about it."

A: Now you've really said it.

B: Well yes, that's interesting. Speaking about budgets. . . .

and the discussion was again taken away from the interpersonal issues.

I suggested that B had taken the discussion away from the interpersonal aspects. B replied, "I guess that I did."

One of the supervisors then asked the other why he refused to cooperate with his department and why, at times, he was making trouble for his department.

The other looked surprised, "Who me? Why we always cooperate with your people."

> It is not so, and I can quote——who can give you many examples. Also, you've been trying to take much more space than you need.
>
> I have? Why it seems to me that it is your group who has been doing this.

The discussion continued with one supervisor asking if the other was not cooperating because he resented an organizational change. The other supervisor looked surprised and said that this was never a problem for him. He admitted that he had had difficulty since the change. "It was a situation that I could not cope with because I couldn't get you to talk or argue." He continued:

> Maybe it is a coward's way out. But I figure if I could define my area of work, I'd work like a beaver in that area. If I needed help from you, I'd ask for it.
> Well, that's one of the problems that we've had with you. We can get help from your group if it is the kind of help that interests you. But if it doesn't, then you can't get a whole lot of help from you. There have been many times that our people have tried to get help, to get something done. We were ready to pay for it, but the people tell me it is just like pulling teeth to get the help that they needed. You're a pretty clever guy, you know how to give the impression that you are giving help, the old lick and promise, when you are not really giving very much.

This comment led to a further exploration of the rivalry between the two men. Both worked very hard at clarifying the issues once they realized that each had incorrect impressions of the other and that each was behaving in an apparently noncooperative manner in order to protect himself. These discussions continued for several sessions and led to what the four top administrators have described as the beginning of a new and more effective relationship between the two supervisors.

The point of this description is not to suggest that the rivalry had been solved. The point is that the men resisted talking about the interpersonal dimensions of the rivalry problem. However, when they did, they began, according to their own admission, to work on the real issues. Also, according to their own admission, they began to develop more effective relationships.

OBSERVATIONS ABOUT THE TECHNICAL ACTIVITIES OF THE LABORATORY

The major objective of the laboratory is to produce new ideas that eventually enhance the financial and market position of the company. In the previous section I have attempted to show how relatively low interpersonal competence can lead to a situation of poor communication, little awareness of major issues, and rivalries that all seem to identify but no one seems to be able to solve.

That picture is only a partial one. The researchers are busy producing new ideas and products. A balanced analysis requires that we examine this aspect of the laboratory.

In making this analysis I am assuming that the laboratory has obtained technically competent researchers. Unlike the previous section, where I tried to diagnose the interpersonal competence, I had to accept the top laboratory management's view (and as we shall see, the researchers' view) that they do have a technically highly competent group that can be productive. I was unable to find any tests that could be used to measure the creativity and productivity of the researchers.

Although I may not be able to obtain independent evidence of the technical competence of the laboratory, it is possible to ascertain whether the researchers believe that they are obtaining adequate opportunity to utilize their abilities. As in the case of the previous analysis, the three key variables will be the degree of psychological success experienced at work, confirmation of intellectual aspects of the self, and finally feelings of essentiality.

Psychological Success in Research Activities

The first measure that we wanted was the kinds of satisfactions that the researchers experienced at work. The majority of the responses were related to the actual conduct of the research; the performance on the job. Thus 77 percent of the technicians, 93 percent of the engineers, and 100 percent of the supervisors said that their satisfactions were obtained in (1) producing new products that were useful and paid off for the company and (2) conducting research that no one had done before. For example:

> 1. It is extremely challenging, and it is challenging because no one comes to us unless they have tried to find an answer to this problem and have failed. These people come to us because they expect us to be able to do something that they have not been able to accomplish.
> 2. While in this work you're doing things that are new and different, so there's personal satisfaction in feeling that you've done something that hasn't been done before and that isn't in the literature so that everybody knows about it. You're really contributing something new.
> 3. Well, I think that the job in itself is satisfying. In other words, if we are able to do this, this project has succeeded where a lot

of other people have spent a lot of money and lost out. It is also satisfying to see a particular product which has a certain amount of potential. I like to be part of something and I'm really enthusiastic about it.

An indication of the potency of these views is obtained by examining the responses to the question, "Can you recall any satisfying experiences over the last few months?" The most frequent answer among the researchers was, "The research was successful and we obtained valid and useful results" (50 percent). The next most frequent reply was, "The research was successful but does not as yet lead to a practical application" (25 percent). The supervisors responded in the same manner to the same questions. On the other hand, the technicians expressed a lower level of aspiration. They found the sense of accomplishment as being satisfying no matter what was the accomplishment (42 percent). Twenty-eight percent of the engineers, 17 percent of the supervisors and 27 percent of the technicians could not recall a satisfying experience. For example:

1. Yes, in the early part of six months we started a project which has had many difficult hurdles to overcome. Now it might be another one of these projects where we're barking up the wrong tree, but it looks to me like it's really worth looking into and it looks very encouraging and that's what is satisfying to me.

2. I'd say one of the most satisfying experiences I have had is when we were able to put in a process in one of the plants and get it running much sooner and more effectively than the people in the plant thought that it was possible to do. I think it is quite an accomplishment. It went off with a few hitches, which is not of major consequence, and I think we saved the company unmeasurable tens of thousands of dollars because of lack of delay that might have resulted otherwise.

3. The last few months have been hard on me. They have been a period of learning the rules of the game as far as the new technology is concerned. I think only in the last few weeks have I been able to gain any satisfaction and that came from coming up with a few techniques that I think are more valid than the kind the group has been working with before.

Finally, I asked the respondents to estimate how much actual challenge they were experiencing on the job. The following table suggests that the majority of the engineers (researchers) and supervisors experience more challenging than not challenging or largely challenging work.

TABLE 2–2

PERCEIVED DEGREE OF CHALLENGE AND VARIETY IN WORK

	Technicians $n = 26$		Engineers $n = 36$		Supervisors $n = 12$	
	n	%	n	%	n	%
1. Routine and no challenge.....	8	31	4	11	1	08
2. Routine and some challenge...	9	35	12	33	4	33
3. Challenge with some routine :	4	15	6	17	2	17
4. Mostly challenge...........	5	19	14	39	5	42

From these data, it may be inferred that the degree of psychological success experienced in, and the feelings of essentiality about, the technical activities were relatively high.

The feelings of confirmation was inferred to be more difficult to obtain. For example, 72 percent of the engineers and 92 percent of the supervisors felt that it was difficult to evaluate their work. It took months to know if they were going to be successful. Only 15 percent of the technicians felt this way. Eighty-five percent felt that the effectiveness of their work could be measured relatively easily and quickly. For example:

1. I really don't know how you would measure it except by the number of reports that come out and the number of technical problems that get solved from various plants and the rate at which they're solved.
2. Well, the only real measure which could be applied, for instance, in this project is the yardstick that would have to be applied by a well-trained scientific director. He'd have to have access to the avenues that we are exploring, the approaches we're taking, and then he could tell if the effort was hard enough and was pushed enough. It couldn't be assessed by somebody who is not familiar with this type of work.
3. It takes time to measure the effectiveness of these studies. It is not too unusual to have to wait several months just to find out if we are on the right track.

From these comments we infer the already well-documented finding that research involves periods with varying degrees of uncertainty and ambiguity. It is not possible, therefore, for a researcher (engineer) to receive confirmation of his view of himself as a competent researcher in a short period. He must wait. The period of waiting can be frustrating and tension producing since it could be bringing the individual closer to success or to failure.

During this time the engineer may prefer to have a supervisor who can help him to cope with his tension and anxiety. If the analysis above is valid, then it can be predicted that the research supervisors will not tend to be too effective because allaying anxiety and enhancing confirmation are basically interpersonal, emotional activities. It is now more understandable why researchers prefer supervisors who let them alone. If one lives constantly under some internal tension, then it may be more desirable to be left alone than to be "assisted" by a supervisor who is not very comfortable in dealing with feelings.

It is also understandable why the supervisors cited "leaving their subordinates alone" as their most effective supervisory "skill." I put quotation marks around skill, because what skill is required in leaving people alone?

In this connection it is interesting to recall that most supervisors who said that they left the technically good men alone also said they tended to try to assist the poorer researchers. Is this further indirect support of the view being stated here? The supervisor must not feel too certain of his facilitative skills. If he were certain, then why not use them with the better men to help them become even better? Also, what is the probability that a supervisor with relatively low interpersonal competence will be of help to a researcher who is tense and defensive due to some failure?

Some Consequences of a Relatively High Psychological Success and Feelings of Essentiality and Confirmation on the Technical Level

Before I suggest some of the impacts of these factors, I should like to emphasize that the technicians do not obtain as much psychological success and feelings of essentiality as do the researchers. However, they obtain a quicker sense of confirmation than do the researchers.

One of the major influences of the above is to cause the people, at all levels, to value the technical activities of their jobs because these are the most satisfying.

I believe that the low degree of absenteeism and turnover among the researchers is also related to the same phenomena, but I do not have systematic data that suggest causal connection. I make the inference from the fact that many researchers remarked spontaneously that they enjoyed their work, could hardly wait to arrive at the lab, and some even said that they begrudged weekends.

Another result of this involvement may be the engineers' and technicians' relatively high evaluation of the laboratory and their apparent lack of desire for new policies or job changes. Beginning with the latter, 57 percent of the engineers and 31 percent of the technicians did not want any job changes. Forty-two percent of the engineers asked for changes that would take them away from present supervisors so that they could obtain more challenging work. The point is that the frustrations exist in areas where interpersonal relationships will have to be faced if changes are to be made.

Interestingly, 42 percent of the supervisors desired less paper and administrative work. Part of the cause of this problem may be the rivalry already discussed. If people are going to accuse each other of not being very helpful, then they will have to keep detailed records to prove their case.

Returning to the consequences of satisfying experiences in the technical activities, 46 percent of the technicians and 56 percent of the engineers reported that the laboratory was well organized. Only 17 percent of the supervisors agreed.

Sixty-two percent of the technicians, 67 percent of the engineers, and 75 percent of the supervisors did not have any new organizational policies to recommend. Nor did any of these groups need information about the laboratory that they were not being given (technicians 73 percent, engineers 67 percent, and supervisors 75 percent).

A positive picture was also revealed in the replies to the question, "Are there any long-range problems that you believe the laboratory is not now facing?" The answer was no (technicians 40 percent, engineers 33 percent, and supervisors 25 percent). Of those who replied yes, the majority were concerned with the laboratory developing too fast. They realized that all new laboratories have a honeymoon period and they wished that it would go through this period more slowly. A few were concerned about not enough emphasis on basic research. For example:

1. They're actually going to have a problem of space. I would say, financially, this company has backed the lab very well, but there's no question in my mind that we're going to have problems of space in the long-run future.

2. The way they're growing now I would say that one of the long-range problems I wonder about is whether they are growing too fast. You know there are a lot of people here from blank lab, as you probably know, and I hope they are aware of what happened at blank lab. It apparently grew too fast. Last year it looks like they've grown fairly rapidly, a lot of new groups. It's certainly quite a growth. I think we have to be very careful to make sure that we don't grow too fast. Also, I don't know if there is enough real basic research going on.

3. Well, yes, whether I'm qualified to have an opinion, I don't know. But I do see a long-range problem. It seems to me that too often we're on short-term projects which fail or succeed, but don't do anything for the future. I think, in my own field, we ought to have two programs. At the present time, we're always a little bit too late with short-term things and we aren't doing anything for the future.

Summary of the Results

I. *The Effectiveness of the Technical Activities of the Organization*
   1. The employees report a high degree of satisfaction with the technical activities of the enterprise. For example, they report a high degree of challenge, risk taking, feelings of essentiality and commitment in relation to the technical activities of their work.
   2. As a result there is a relatively:
      a) Low absenteeism and turnover,
      b) High positive evaluation of the organization by participants at all levels.
      c) Low desire to have one's job changed; to alter or add to existing policies.
      d) High satisfaction with wages.
      e) Few employees who feel that the organization is not facing up to its problems in the future.

II. *The Effectiveness of the Human Activities of the Organization*
   The results related to the human activities of the laboratory do not present as positive a picture as the technical side.
   1. According to the observations that were made of the supervisors' behavior, they tended to behave in varying degrees in such a way as to emphasize (*a*) concern for ideas and (*b*) conformity to their ideas.
   2. Openness to ideas is not very high and it is found primarily when a subordinate is trying to learn a superior's view.

3. Helping others, risk taking, trust, mistrust and not helping others are hardly ever observed.
4. The expression of feelings is suppressed (many times unknowingly).
5. The interpersonal competence at all levels is relatively low. The degree of interpersonal incompetence may be indicated by noting that the supervisors tended (*a*) not to be aware of all the problems unearthed by the research that they have with their subordinates, (*b*) when they are aware of them they are not able to solve them, and (*c*) most of the problem-solving strategies observed tend to make the situation increasingly worse.
6. There is a trend acting against cohesive interpersonal relationships among the participants at all levels.
7. Some consequences of the above may be:
    a) An increasing inability to solve interpersonal problems that can greatly influence the effectiveness of the laboratory. For example, the rivalry among certain supervisors between and within the departments.
    b) An increasing feeling on the part of the subordinates that they are not essential (as far as the human side of the organization is concerned).
    c) Decreasing experience of interpersonal relationships that build feelings of psychological success and internal commitment of the organization.
    d) Decreasing emphasis on effective leadership as being a leader who leaves people alone.
    e) Increasing overemphasis upon space, desks, files, technical assistance, equipment, prizes, etc.

I believe that these consequences will, over time, tend to get worse because the interpersonal competence necessary to alter factors II 1–6 is lacking. As the interpersonal difficulties become worse, they could reach a threshold above which the interpersonal difficulties will tend to inhibit the technical innovative activities and outputs of the laboratory. This prediction is partially illustrated in the next chapter and discussed more fully in Chapter 7.

CHAPTER 3

Organization B

OUR STUDY of Organization B focuses primarily on the executive committee and secondarily upon the department directors of one of the largest research and engineering laboratories in the United States. The laboratory had nearly 3,000 technical and nontechnical employees.

The top group contained ten members. Six had B.S., two M.S., and two had Ph.D. degrees. Twenty-five of the top research executives immediately below the top group were also interviewed. Five of them had B.S., eight M.S., and nine Ph.D. degrees and one had an LL.B. degree.

The Values of the Executive Committee Members

The first step was to infer the values that the executives held about effective human relationships. For this purpose the same open-ended questionnaire was used as in the previous study.

The results are presented in Table 3–1. The members, as a group, are predisposed toward the values inherent in the pyramidal structure. For example, they believe an effective leader directs and controls, that effective action is a function of rational behavior and of placing emphasis upon achieving the objectives. Almost all believe that interpersonal relations and emotionality lead to difficulties and should be suppressed; the problem of interpersonal relations and emotionality is not faced.

Another point of interest: Although most members state that interpersonal problems lead to ineffectiveness and thus should be suppressed, 60 percent say that interpersonal issues are the major

TABLE 3-1

VALUES OF EXECUTIVE COMMITTEE MEMBERS

$n = 10$
(*Expressed in Percent*)

1. *An effective leader is one who:*
   a) Is directive, controls, leads and
      inspires the men.....................................80
   b) Listens, integrates group wisdom.....................10
   c) Creates atmosphere for uninhibited
      discussion..10
2. *The best member is one who:*
   a) Is rational, objective, well versed in
      the topic...90
   b) Considers the group as a whole......................10
3. *The most serious blocks to program in a meeting are:*
   a) Emotional disagreements, subjective
      reactions...50
   b) Low interpersonal competence such as
      inability to listen, defensiveness, taking
      extreme positions...................................40
   c) Weak leadership.....................................10
4. *When disagreement erupts into personal antagonsims
   and hostile feelings, the best thing for a leader to
   do is:*
   a) Avoid dealing with the problem openly (use
      humor, table subject, adjourn meeting)...............70
   b) Take firm control over discussion...................30
5. *Most serious disagreements arise because of:*
   a) Low interpersonal competence (e.g.,
      narrow viewpoint, inability to admit
      errors, fear of losing prestige, biased
      point of view)......................................60
   b) Lack of understanding the objective of
      the meeting and the issues at hand..................40
6. *How much members trust each other is usually
   shown by:*
   a) Realizing limits of others and not violating
      them. Be courteous, disagree without hostility.......80
   b) Willingness to be open and frank....................10
   c) Willingness to leave details to others..............10

cause for serious disagreements and block the progress of meetings.

Following the theoretical framework described earlier, it is possible to predict that individuals who hold these values will tend to manifest the following pattern of behavior in their problem-solving and decision-making processes. The frequencies of the categories should be found to exist in the following order.

owning ideas
concern ideas
conform ideas
open ideas

TABLE 3-2

ANALYSIS OF OBSERVATIONS OF THE EXECUTIVE COMMITTEE

	1* n = 354		2 n = 167		3 n = 290		4 n = 315		5 n = 290		6 n = 142	
	n	%	n	%	n	%	n	%	n	%	n	%
own i. f.	289	82	131	78	222 1	77 003	244	78	233	80	114	80
concern i. f.	228	64	102	61	192	66	174	55	124	43	98	69
conform i. f.	100	28	44	26	55	19	66	21	75	26	36	25
open i. f.	44	12	30	18	63	22	50	16	47	16	28	20
ind. i. f.	19	05	14	08	25	09	63	20	80	28	7	05
antag. i. f.	7	02	7	04	16	06	12	04	11	04	1	007
n.h.o. i. f.	11	03		00	1	003	9	03	6	02		
h.o. i. f.	10	03	5	03	3	01	11	04	4	01		
own i–conf. i f.	62	18	31	19	33	11	19	06	68	23	32	23
own i–antag. i f.	5	01	2	01	7	02	11	04	11	04	1	007
open i–conf. i f.	4	01	1	006	3	01	2	006			1	007
open i–antag. i f.			3	02	3	01	2	006				

* Individual and group scores are considered as separate universes. All individual scores should approximate 100% and the same for all group scores. Thus n = 354 means 354 units on the individual level and 354 on the group level.

individuality ideas
antagonism ideas
not helping others to own ideas
helping others to own ideas

The frequency of feeling scores should be very small as should be the frequency of trust, mistrust, experimenting, as well as in the not owning, not open, not experimenting categories.

The frequency of the imbalance scores should be:

own i–conform i
own i–antagonism i
open i–conform i
open i–antagonism i

During the course of the research project, I observed six executive committee meetings over a period of three months. The results are presented in Table 3-2. We may conclude that as a group:

1. There is a high degree of *owning up* to ideas, of expressing opinions. However, the amount varies significantly among members.
2. The most important norm in the group is *concern* for ideas. The second most important norm is *conformity* to ideas. The third most important norm, whose frequency is half of conformity, is *individuality*.
3. Openness to ideas from others is relatively high when:
    a) A subordinate wants to learn the view of a superior.
    b) A presentation is being made by "insiders" or "outsiders" and some member needs clarification of a point.
    c) Some member wants to "lawyer" some other member or visitor.
4. *Antagonism* to ideas is low. The members rarely show discomfort (and never anger) toward each other (although they may feel it).
5. *Not helping others* is as infrequent as *helping others* and both are almost at the bottom in terms of frequency of occurrence.
6. *Under stress* (something that apparently rarely occurs) the *conformity* tends to go up but so does *individuality*. However, *individuality* goes down dramatically the moment the research director gives his view as to what ought to be done. (More about this later.)
7. Behavior that was hardly ever observed.
    a) Risk taking.
    b) Trust.
    c) Mistrust.
    d) The expression of positive or negative feelings.
    e) Overtly refusing to give one's point of view or overtly refusing to listen to someone else's point of view.

The meetings generated scores that were in accordance with the predictions. Thus *own i* was most frequent, with *concern i*, *conformity i*, *open i*, *individuality i*, and *antagonism i* following in that order. Also feeling (*f*) scores were extremely low as were the scores for trust, mistrust, helping, and not helping others. The frequencies of imbalance scores were also in accordance with the predictions.

The one exception to our prediction was the *individuality i* scores. In sessions 4 and 5 these scores became higher than *open i* scores, which was contrary to expectations. One possible way to account for the difference in session 4 is that the research director was not there. There is some evidence, to be presented below, that the members expressed more of their own opinions when the research director was gone. Session 5 was one in which a most difficult and controversial subject was discussed. Instead of the conformity scores increasing, as would be expected under stress, the individuality scores increased. An explanation for this phenomena will be offered below.

The next step was to develop predictions about how the members would view their group. The predictions would then be compared with the actual view of the members. These views would be obtained by interviewing each member. The interviews were semi-structured, lasting 45–90 minutes. They were all tape-recorded. The analyses were made from transcripts of the tapes.

Some Predictions from the Observations as to How the Members Will Feel about the Executive Committee as a Group

Based upon the observations, I predicted that the members, during the interviews, would characterize their group and its climate as one that tends to:

1. Discourage the expression of deviant points of view.
2. Discourage the expression of feelings.
3. Discourage risk taking and innovation.
4. Encourage conformity more than individuality.
5. Discourage the *overt* blocking or attacking of individuals *as well as* the helping of individuals. Any attacking or blocking that is to be done should be done diplomatically.
6. Discourage the discussion of issues loaded with conflict.
7. Discourage the discussion of important issues when they have not been cleared with the research director.
8. Discourage the development of trust and mistrust as group norms.

The Executive Committee, as a Group, Does Not Tend to Agree with the Predictions

Summarizing the findings, the majority of the executive committee does *not* agree with the predictions. *As a group* they report:

1. Feelings are expressed (60%) but
2. Not negative ones (90%) because
3. We trust each other and respect each other (70%), therefore
4. Individuality is high and conformity is low (60%).
5. If conformity becomes high it is only when we believe that the research director has made a correct decision. Then we must all agree because after all *he is* the boss (70%).
6. We help each other all the time (80%).
7. Issues loaded with conflict are not handled during the meeting for good rational reasons. They are:

a) We should not discuss emotional disagreements before the executive committee because when people are emotional they are not rational (70%).

b) We should not air our dirty linen in front of people who may come in to make a presentation (70%).

c) Why take up people's time with subjective debates (60%)?

d) Most members are not acquainted with all the details. Under our system the person who presents the issues has really thought them through (60%).

e) Prediscussion of issues helps to prevent anyone from sandbagging the executive committee (40%).

8. The executive committee climate or emotional tone is:

a) "Friendly," "not critical of each other," "not tense."

b) "The research director is in charge and he makes the decisions."

c) "Mutual trust," "warm," "congenial."

d) "Frank and no tensions because we've known each other for years."

e) "Rarely emotional; when it does happen you can pardon it."

How do we resolve the differences in point of view?

Some Apparent Contradictions during the Interviews

The data clearly show that the executive committee as a group did not support the a priori predictions. The question that arises is, why?

During the interviews and later as I read them, I became aware of what seemed to me to be important contradictions. The respondents were making statements that did not seem to be consistent. For example:

During One Part of The Interview They Said:		*Yet, Later (in the Same Interview) They Said:*
1. The relationship among the executive committee members is "close," "friendly" and based upon years of working with each other.	80%*	1. I do not know how (my peers) feel about me. That's a tough question to answer.
2. I have an open relationship with my superior.	70%	2. I have no direct idea how he evaluates my work and feels about me.
3. The strength of this company lies in its top people. They are a dedicated, friendly group. We never have the kinds of disagreements and fights that I hear others do.	70%	3. Yes, the more I think of it, the more that I think that this is a major weakness of the company. Management is afraid to hold someone accountable. They are afraid to say to someone, "You said you would do it, what happened?"

4. We say pretty much what we feel. 70%

4. We are careful not to say anything that will antagonize anyone.

5. The group discussions are warm, friendly, not critical. 70%

5. We trust each other not to upset one another.

6. We respect and have faith in each other. 70%

6. People do not knowingly upset each other, so they are careful in what they say.

7. The executive committee tackles all issues. 70%

7. The executive committee tends to spend too much time talking about relatively unimportant issues.

8. The executive committee makes decisions quickly and effectively. 60%

8. One of the big problems of the executive committee is that it takes forever and a day to make important decisions.

9. The executive committee makes the major policy decisions. 50%

9. On many of the major issues, the decisions are really made outside the executive committee meetings. The executive committee convenes to approve a decision and have "holy water" placed on the decision.

10. The members trust each other. 40%

10. The members are careful not to say something that may make another member look bad. It may be misinterpreted.

---

* The percentages represent the proportion of board members who manifested these apparent contradictions.

The apparent contradictions began to give me the impression that the members (as a group): (*a*) tended to be uncomfortable in talking about the weaknesses of the executive committee and the company; (*b*) were embedded in a human environment where it was not customary to explore issues of this type and where such information probably would not come up to them from below.

The next step was to return to the interviews for a closer look. I wanted to see if these impressions were valid.

A Closer Look at the Executive Committee Members' Responses

As I re-examined the interviews, I began to notice that a certain group of people tended to express the majority of the apparent contradictions illustrated above. Therefore, I wondered if there was not something these people had in common that would help to explain the contradictions among their views as well as the disagreements between their views and mine.

One conclusion from this analysis was that the executive committee could not be understood as a group. There were important differences in the preferences the members had about the kind of working relationships that they valued.

At the risk of oversimplification I should like to construct a continuum of these preferences. On one end will be Preference Pattern A and at the other end Preference Pattern B.

Preference Pattern A.   People who preferred Pattern A tended to be individuals who:

1. Did not feel comfortable with aggressiveness in themselves and in others.
2. Did not feel comfortable with the expression of negative or positive feelings in interpersonal relationships.
3. Did not tend to give overt feedback to others about the impact of their behavior.
4. Did not ask for (indeed gave cues to discourage) feedback from others about their own personal impact.
5. Perceived their competence to be primarily in the technical and not the administrative area.
6. Were therefore willing to accept dependence upon someone who they perceived to be competent in the administrative area.
7. Considered loyalty as being sensitive to the limits and desires of others, especially the leader (partially, I believe, with the hope that others might use the same concept in their dealings with them).

As one might expect, it was the members with Preference Pattern A who tended to see the executive committee as "friendly," "warm," "open," "risk taking," and "loaded with individualists."

Preference Pattern A tended to be dominant in the group. An indication of the importance of this pattern may be provided in the following way. When the members were asked, "Under what conditions does this friendly emotional tone change?" 90 percent replied, "Rarely," or "I can never recall such a case."

This may help us to understand that whereas in other groups the conformity and antagonism scores go up under stress, in this group only the *individuality* scores increased. Antagonism and aggression are not sanctioned and rewarded.

It is interesting to consider the possibility that with such an emotional climate, the members (unknowingly) prevent conditions from arising where their individuality is brought out. This jibes with one of the qualities of type A, namely, the predisposition to be dependent upon the research director for administrative matters. Thus if the research director makes a decision when he sees that the committee is looking to him for a decision, he may be perpetuating the subordinates' dependence upon him.

Preference Pattern B.   The members with Preference Pattern B tended to see the top group as "friendly," "not critical" *because* the members were "afraid," "uncomfortable with a good fight," "wanted everyone to love them," and "not very competent administratively."

Members who preferred Preference Pattern B tended to be individuals who:

1. Enjoyed aggressiveness in themselves and in others. Enjoyed a fight especially if they could win and not hurt anyone. (If they did hurt someone, they would not want to know about it because it would tend to upset them.)
2. Felt more comfortable with hostile interpersonal relationships and less comfortable with positive ones. (When they felt strong positive feelings toward their subordinates, they would tend to have a great difficulty in expressing these openly.)
3. Gave feedback to others about their impact (positive or negative).
4. Did not ask for feedback but gave cues that they could take it if it were negative. They would appreciate, but be uncomfortable with, positive feedback.
5. Perceived their competence to be in the technical and administrative areas.
6. Were uncomfortable with dependence on anyone for any reason.
7. Considered loyalty as being committed to a set of organizational policies and goals. A loyal member could be insensitive to others' feelings if it were in the interest of adhering to the organizational policies and goals.

Preference Pattern C.   Finally, there were a few members who seemed to be capable of behaving in accordance with the dictates of patterns A or B depending upon the situation. C is *not* in the middle of the continuum between A and B. C is on its own continuum because such individuals are quite comfortable with Pattern A or B. They tend to choose that pattern which they believe will achieve their objectives given the people, the problem, and the situation.

Needless to say that the preference patterns are ideal types. No one individual fits any one type. The same individual may manifest different amounts of each type. Indeed, the same individual could change his preferences as conditions varied. At the moment, all I am saying is that the members tended to be predisposed to one of these types while at work.

If this analysis holds up, then A's and B's views of the top group are consistent with their own preferences. For example, there is no doubt that the A's do see the executive committee as friendly and warm because it is made up of people who value such behavior (e.g., who do not express anger, hostility, deep disagreements, etc.). Also, they may honestly believe that the executive committee takes risks because the executive committee is taking as many risks as they are able to tolerate.

One more point. This analysis may help us to understand some of the reasons for the apparent contradictions described above. Almost all of the contradictions were found in interviews by members who preferred Pattern A. Most of these members began their interviews with replies that were in keeping with their values and their perceptions of the executive committee. Thus the positive, friendly, congenial aspects of the situation were emphasized.

As the interview continued, the questions became more probing and the executive committee members' responses correspondingly more concrete. The more the members described their situation in concrete terms, the more they may have begun to become aware that the situation was not as bright as they had pictured it at the outset. That the members were willing to contradict their earlier statements is evidence of their intellectual integrity.

A second possible reason for the members' reluctance to discuss negative views was related to the concept of loyalty held by most of these men. A member who preferred Pattern A tended to believe that it was disloyal to be critical of the organization. At numerous times during the interview I felt the members became uncomfortable when they found themselves saying something negative about the company.

Interestingly, this hesitation seemed to occur even in areas where the members directly involved were quite open about the difficulty of the situation. For example, a research manager had recently been appointed administrative head of all the research department directors. Since he had an excellent reputation for solving administrative problems, and for valuing highly the administrative process, I wondered if the research directors might not have some questions about his appointment. Moreover, his new position interposed another layer of authority between the department directors and the executive committee. I decided to ask the executive committee members what they thought the impact of the new appointment would be on the department directors.

The executive committee member involved and the few who preferred Pattern B quickly agreed that the department directors probably would question the logic of the new position. For example:

> Yes, definitely, you can sense this [resistance], and this is the one reason I have been approaching my relationships with the department directors carefully and cautiously. For example, one fellow said, "Well, when I get all through you know there is too much bureaucracy over the research departments." Now I don't know completely what he means by this, he didn't mean just me. But, what he exhibited was a misunderstanding of what we are trying to do. Another fellow approached this at arm's length. He said, "Well, now you know when we reported to ——, we just touched base with him on certain things. Will this new relationship be the same?" I said yes and even more so.

This executive committee member not only was willing to speak about these difficulties, but he had developed several strategies of action.

On the other hand, the executive committee members who preferred Pattern A tended to play down any possible difficulties when they discussed the question during the interview. "No, I don't see any difficulties," or "No, I don't think that we will have any trouble. What you must realize is that we have a fine group of people here."

The Staff Subordinate Problem

As one might predict, each executive committee member tended to obtain as staff subordinates men who had the same preference pattern as they did. In many cases (especially those who had Preference Pattern A) the staff subordinates were not as effective as expected. The crown princes were not as effective as their superiors. Typical quotations were:

1. Many staff subordinates do not have enough drive.
2. Not enough tendency to innovate. They are followers.
3. The staff subordinates always go along with the status quo.

4. It now looks as if most of the executive committee members did not want strong staff subordinates because they were afraid that they would have to spend too much time convincing them.

5. The staff subordinates are amazingly like their bosses. They even take on the mannerisms of their bosses.

Another factor that may have coerced each executive committee member to appoint a staff subordinate similar to him may be his need for support against the other staff subordinates. For example, if A and B did not really respect each others' preferences, then a need might arise in each executive committee member to have a staff subordinate who confirmed to him that his leadership style was the most effective one.

Moreover, any interpersonal conflicts among the executive committee members could lead the staff subordinate to take on more of his superior's mannerisms. For example, if a superior predisposed toward Pattern A had a difficult session with a superior predisposed toward Pattern B, he might come to his office and without thinking as to the impact, say, "Boy, so and so is certainly a difficult person. Why must he be so aggressive and loud?" Such comments, if heard by the staff subordinates, could give them cues as to how they ought to behave in front of their superior.

The Subordinates' View of the Executive Committee

One of the major themes of the analysis has been that the group norms are such that they encourage an overoptimistic view of the executive committee and discourage feedback to it of negative information. This, in turn, acts to reinforce the original picture.

However, if the analysis is correct and the executive committee has the characteristics that we suggest, then the subordinates should perceive the limitations of the executive committee, because they should experience them as inhibitors of their successful operation. I would predict, therefore, that they should evaluate the executive committee as low in risk taking, openness to uncomfortable information, and high on conformity, etc. The only exceptions should be the subordinates who themselves are highly predisposed to Pattern A. They should find it personally difficult, and organizationally disloyal, to be critical of the executive committee, even to the researcher.

Twenty-five key executives just below the administrative level of the executive committee were interviewed. They were asked to rate the executive committee as low, average, or high in terms of five qualities. These were:

1. Openness to uncomfortable information.
2. Risk taking.
3. Trust among members.
4. Capacity to deal with conflict and emotionally laden problems.
5. Conformity.

The results are presented in Table 3-3.[1]

The subordinates tend to perceive the executive committee as being low in openness to uncomfortable information, risk taking,

TABLE 3-3

How Would You Rate the Executive Committee	Low		Moderate		High		Don't know	
	n	%	n	%	n	%	n	%
1. Openness to uncomfortable information..	12	48	6	24	4	16	3	12
2. Risk taking.........	20	80	4	16	1	04		
3. Trust..............	14	56	9	36	2	08		
4. Conformity.........			2	08	23	92		
5. Ability to deal with conflicts...........	19	76	6	24				

trust among members, and capacity to deal with conflict issues, and high in conformity to the research director.

Another check of their view on the last two qualities was obtained in asking them, "How do you think the executive committee handles conflict?" Sixty percent replied that "feelings are carefully guarded," "no one speaks up." Forty percent added that conflict issues were usually solved by the research director. For example:

1. I've never known the executive committee to have conflict. They're very careful not to have conflicts during the executive committee meetings.

2. I've never seen the executive committee get into a real conflict situation. It's my experience that if there is a difficult issue to be discussed, the research director would make sure that it was

[1] The majority of the positive evaluations were made by subordinates who were predisposed toward Pattern B. Since the subordinates were interviewed primarily about their reactions to the executive committee, not enough data were obtained to make inferences about preference patterns with confidence.

discussed much before it ever gets to the executive committee.

3. Not very well. You can see that in the problem of stopping major projects that are dead. You have to say, well, now look fellows, this is the way it is going to be. We're going to knock so many dollars off. They never come up with the old baseball bat and the iron fist. So you go through all kinds of juggling for months. They'll delay and delay and delay such decisions.

Openness

1. I think they get awfully confused by this. I think that they want things to be essentially black or white. I don't think they feel comfortable where there is anything contradictory.

2. I think they are receptive. I mean it is not taboo to talk about difficult things. It is not too bad, I guess.

Risk Taking

1. The executive committee never takes risks if they can help it.

2. Risk taking is extremely low.

3. After being with this company for a long time I would say that the executive committee makes sure that no real risks are taken.

Trust

1. Recently there has been a considerable degree of mistrust because few of them felt secure. They didn't know where they stood with the research director. I think very few of them do today.

2. I suspect that about half of them could cut each other's throat.

3. Trust is quite good. They seem to know each other well. I have never seen them upset each other.

4. I would say average—no, it is not real high. I think they are all fine now, but there are instances where some action was taken that can be interpreted as mistrust of each other—at least this is how other people read it.

Conformity

1. I think they are all conformists.

2. I would say there is a high degree of conformity to what the research director wants.

3. In my experience if these people have strong feelings on a subject they will voice them.

4. I think the members will express their view openly, but, once the research director makes a decision, the rest is academic. Eventually they all go along.

Conflict

1. I think this company in regard to management has run away from conflict. A couple of things that have been a great disappoint-

ment to me on this executive committee . . . and I think that what made them run away was the element of conflict. They just didn't want this.

2. I have felt that the research company for years has been extremely cautious. They want to avoid conflict at all costs. I think this is hurting us.

3. The executive committee will not allow conflict to persist. They will get a compromise in a committee way.

Data consonant to the above were obtained in response to the question, "How would you characterize the climate or tone of the executive committee meetings?" Fifty-two percent responded that the members seemed relaxed and friendly because one man was "running the show" whereas 32 percent attributed the same qualities to the fact that the members were "nice fellows who hate conflict." For example:

1. They seem to work well together and they also work well with the people who come up before the executive committee. I don't mean to say that they all agree because they don't; they often express different points of view, but eventually they all get together and arrive at a solution without any bitterness or strong dissent.

2. I have not found, the few times that I have been before the executive committee, that there is real debate. You get the feeling that there is—well, that this issue has probably been settled before or at least all the people that count have been hit before. Maybe that's the way to operate, but I don't see any genuine open decisions with rare exceptions.

3. I think its terrible. The reason I think that is that I get the feeling that the executive committee members are demotivated almost to the point that sometimes I get the feeling that they don't give a damn. I get the feeling that their function, their responsibility, their power has been taken away from them to the point that they figure, "All right, let —— or —— run this damn place."

RESEARCHER: I gather you get the feeling that they have withdrawn.

Yes, they have withdrawn. For example, the other day one of the executive committee members professed that he did not know the function of one of those new committees. He honestly told me that he didn't know what the hell it meant, and he said would I please explain it to him. I don't know whether this was an act or what, but that is the kind of episode that convinces me that he must be withdrawn.

Further supportive data were obtained from the interviews with 50 assistant managers and senior researchers. These individuals were situated at least two levels below the top executive research group. Nearly 65 percent felt that the top group did not understand their department's problems. Nearly 75 percent rated the top group as low in risk taking and 50 percent as high in conformity. Only 1 percent rated the top group as high in risk taking, and none rated it low in conformity. The majority of the remainder felt that they did not have adequate contact with the top group to rate it on conformity.

This points up to the fact that the ratings given by these research supervisors and senior researchers were based more on hearsay and less on actual contact. Thus the impact of the top group upon these levels may be as predicted, but the reason may be more related to what these levels hear from other superiors or infer from policies (or lack thereof) than to direct contact.

How Do the Subordinates Develop Their View of the Executive Committee?

The subordinates tend to experience the executive committee in the same way as predicted by the analysis. Why is this so since the executive members (a) view themselves differently (b) presumably try to behave accordingly to their perceptions, and (c) are constantly developing communication and executive development programs that emphasize risk taking, openness, etc.?

I do not have any direct data to answer the question. However, there are a few pieces of data that seem to fit together into a coherent picture. Such data are, of course, not proof, but the development of a reasonable hypothesis to be tested.

The subordinates, realizing the difficulty and complexity of the issue, tended to spend much time in developing the proper approach to take before the executive committee. The presentations were rehearsed several times in order to see that all the relevant information was included in such a way as not to upset anyone. It would not be an overexaggeration to say that the subordinates brought a knotty issue to the executive committee with a feeling of happy suspense, wondering how the executive committee would react and what it would do in response to what they saw as their little administrative bombshell.

However, most of the subordinates missed the important interactions among executive committee members *before* the official presentation was made. The reader may recall that the executive committee had a practice of discussing knotty issues outside the executive committee meeting. The sequence of events usually was that a subordinate would take the issue to the relevant executive committee member and make a pre-executive committee presentation. The executive committee member would then agree that a presentation to the total executive committee was necessary and set a date.

Before the meeting the executive committee members centrally involved would visit the other members individually to inform them of the problem, obtain their views, and slowly overcome any important resistances. This process would continue until all the issues were substantially resolved or (and this rarely occurred) until the sides were so clearly drawn that the next step was for the research director to make a decision.

These discussions would not only result in the difficult issues being resolved but the element of surprise and emotion were also greatly reduced. These discussions were not usually described to the subordinate. All he was told was that the "way had been cleared."

The subordinate arrived at the meeting quite involved emotionally. He not only wanted to see what would happen to the executive committee. More important, he realized that his organizational function was at stake. If he upset the executive committee, they might never forget it. An indication of how important executive committee presentations were to the subordinates is that during the interviews 84 percent reported that they liked going up before the executive committee because it helped in becoming visible and going up the ladder. For example:

> 1. I think the reason why people like to go up is it gives them a chance to be visible before the executive committee, and after all, these are the people who are going to make the decisions. Also, from my point of view, it's good discipline to get my subordinates to really think through what we're doing and why.
> 2. Oh, I would say most of the people like going up before the executive committee because of the prestige involved in it. They are all aggressive guys who take pride in their professional ability, and I feel they like to go to the executive committee, and they like to make presentations to them. And I think they like to expose themselves so that the executive committee can get to know them. As a matter of fact, I tend to bring in the younger guys, the

younger men, in order to give them an impression that they are quite important.

During and after his presentation the subordinate might be surprised (if this is his first major presentation) that none of the obvious knotty issues were discussed, no emotions developed, no sticky questions were asked, no embarrassing comments made, no major policies issues explored. Yet the executive committee was to make a decision based upon that discussion. The decision might then be made while he was present or immediately afterward. However, in any case he usually left bewildered as to how this was possible. He soon learned when he started to ask others that the decision had been largely made before the meeting. If so, he wondered, why have the presentation? Why go through motions? Are these men joking? If not, are they really busy? Is the executive committee truly an executive committee?

The subordinate could receive two kinds of replies. If no decision seemed to have been made, he could be told that he had misunderstood the objective of the meeting. The objective was to brief the executive committee so that it could think about the issues. This type of reply may partially explain why 52 percent of the subordinates said that they wished that the executive committee would differentiate more clearly between briefing sessions and decision making; between operations and long-range policies.

If a decision had been made with minimal discussion and/or with the exploration of the less difficult decisions, then the subordinate was usually told that a tradition had been developed that outlawed deep disagreement, open discussion of knotty issues, embarrassment, conflict, etc. The unintended impact of both approaches upon the subordinate may be great. Thus 52 percent reported views similar to the following:

> 1. I'm afraid that I really cannot divorce my feelings from the matter of personality. I know the executive committee people pretty well from various contacts, semisocial in the sense of organizational functions, technical meetings, etc. In my last couple exposures to the executive committee, I wound up with the feeling that it is a collection of people who are sort of a classical type here in our company. I have a feeling that there is missing any really dynamic expression on the part of most of the people who are in it. I get the composite feeling that these people are running a little scared. I admit it was conjecture on my part, and I'm reading into

this, of course. But you asked me about my feelings and that's how I feel.

2. Every time I leave the executive committee I get the feeling that this is pretty much a deadly affair. And are these people the ones who are running the organization? If they are, well, not counting all, but collectively, they are not a very inspiring group when they function as a unit.

3. I think that the executive committee talks a lot about issues not pertinent to them. Most of the decisions that they make should be made down the line. . . . Also, it is a stupid thing to bring up something to the executive committee if the research director is not there, unless you want to hash things around and get general opinions.

Obtaining an answer, I might add, was a long and difficult process. Such matters were not easily discussed. However, as the light began to dawn on the subordinate, and given his desire to be advanced and to get his decision approved, most of them may have decided to play the game. This resulted in their coming to the executive committee *expecting* minimal conflict, discussion, etc., on knotty issues. With this expectation they began to worry mostly about the reaction of the research director. For example 80 percent said that they judged the effectiveness of their presentation by the behavior of the executive committee. Also, they began to worry whether they had made their first presentation (pre-executive committee) carefully, because that was the critical presentation. Finally, as one man said, "I began to realize that the important skill is to make a presentation which brings forth harmless questions and does not generate any long discussion that could easily get out of hand." Some typical examples:

1. The main thing is the research director. If he's happy then you have succeeded; if he's not then you have failed. The main way to judge your success is by the questions people ask. If they asked questions which suggest that they are following you, then you get the feeling that you're doing all right.

2. During the executive committee session I'm really only concerned about my impact on two or three people. The balance I wouldn't care what impact I had. And this is normal in any group. You pick out selective individuals you're trying to get a feel for and you communicate to them.

RESEARCHER: Who would you say is the key person?

The research director, no question about it.

3. I think that by the outcome of the discussion if you are going

along at an executive committee meeting and you hit an area of controversy in which everything falls to pieces because everybody is trying to solve a problem, then you may not have done your best job of trying to steer the thing into the right channels, as opposed to going through quite smoothly, having it come out so that even though the answer is no, you feel that you have at least steered the thing right. It is when everything falls apart in a discussion that you usually feel that you have not done a good job.

Given the norms in the organization against saying anything negative or embarrassing, it is not too difficult to predict that the individual will not tend to explore these feelings with the executive committee members. Indeed, if he communicates anything up the line, it will be positive information. Consequently, the strength of the feelings that the subordinates had about the executive committee, should come as a surprise (and indeed they did when they were fed back to the executive committee).

In order to give the reader a clear view of the dynamics of the executive committee's decision-making processes, I should like to include some anecdotal descriptive observations. They point up the dependence upon the research director, the hesitation to disagree openly with him, and the relatively superficial discussion of a major issue.

Two Examples of Decision Making during an Executive Committee Meeting

One of the major administrative decisions made while I was observing the executive committee was the establishment of several top management committees to explore basic long-range problems of the organization.

As was customary with major decisions, this had been discussed in private by the research director with the various members of the executive committee. The research director began the meeting by circulating a draft of the announcement of the establishment of the committees as a basis for discussion.

Most of the discussion was concerned with raising questions about the wording of the proposal.

"Is the word *action* too strong?"

"I recommend that we change 'steps can be taken' to 'recommendations can be made.'"

"We better change the word 'lead' to 'maintain.'"

As the discussion seemed to come to an end, one research executive said that he was worried that the announcement of these committees might be interpreted by the people below as an implication "that the executive committee believes that the organization is in trouble. Let's get the idea in that all is well."

There was a spontaneous agreement by all research executives. "Hear, hear!"

A brief silence was broken by another research executive who apparently was not satisfied with the concept of the committees. He raised a series of questions. The manner in which it was done was interesting. As he raised each issue, he kept assuring the research director and the group that he was not against the concept. He just wanted to be certain that the executive committee was clear on what it was doing. For example:

"I'm not clear. Just asking."

"I'm trying to get a better picture."

"I'm just trying to get clarification."

"Just so that we understand what the words mean."

The research director nodded in agreement, but he seemed to me to begin to become slightly impatient. He remarked that many of these problems would not arise if the members of these committees took an overall company point of view.

A research executive said (laughingly): "Oh, I'm for motherhood too!" After everyone laughed, the research executive became completely serious and said in effect, "All kidding aside, I think that it is difficult for an individual who is responsible for a particular department to take an overall point of view." Interestingly, he and other members tended to have difficulty in maintaining an overall point of view during their own deliberations. One research executive said, "I'm neutral on your problem. You might say that your man on the bench would like it—but I don't know. It doesn't bother me—it is not in my area." (He laughed.) Another research executive (laughingly) chided him for not having an overall point of view.

I developed the impression that the proposal was the research director's personal "baby" and that the executive committee members would naturally go along with it. The most responsibility that some felt was that they should raise questions so that the research director would be clear about *his* (not their) decision.

The proposal was tabled in order for the written statement to be revised and discussed further during the next meeting.

At that meeting the decision-making process was the same as the first. The research director circulated copies. During this session fewer research executives asked questions. Two especially pushed (with appropriate care) the notion that the duties of one of the committees were defined too broadly.

The research director began to defend his proposal by citing an extremely long list of examples indicating that in his mind "reasonable" people should find the duties clear. This comment and the long list of examples may have communicated to others a feeling that the research director was becoming impatient. When he finished, there was a lengthy silence. The research director then turned to one of the research executives and asked directly, "Why are you worried about this?" The research executive responded and quickly added that as far as he could see the differences were not major ones and that his point of view could be integrated with the research director's by changing some words.

The research director agreed to the changes, looked up, and asked, "I take it now there is common agreement." All research executives said yes or shook their heads in affirmation.

I began to wonder about actual depth of the commitment of the executive committee members to the idea. During the interview, I asked them about their views of the proposal they had approved. Half felt that it was a good proposal. The other half had reservations ranging from moderate to serious. However, being loyal members, they would certainly do their best to make it work.

These data help us to see more clearly how the subordinates develop the view of the executive committee members as being dependent upon the research director, being careful not to disagree with him, and limiting discussion to the less important aspects of a decision.

The second example is related to a budgetary issue. The budgetary experts warned the executive committee that the number of research projects already submitted for approval, if approved, would lead to the contingency fund being used up with ten more months to go before the end of the fiscal year.

The relevant executive committee member immediately asked for permission to make a presentation to the executive committee.

At this point, it is difficult to piece together exactly what happened. As far as I can ascertain, someone notified the staff subordinate of each relevant executive committee member that his overall research budget was to be reviewed and that he (or his superior) should be prepared to suggest what projects could be cut from the budget.

This was not the view of the research director when the executive committee meeting began. He believed that the reason the budget people were making a presentation was to ask the executive committee for overall policies to tell them what to do if such a state of affairs occurred again.

The meeting began with the budget representative making his presentation. After he finished, the research director made some corrections in his presentation, which, from the research director's view, implied certain guides or rules. The research director then suggested another policy move which resulted in an accounting shift of funds, thereby giving the contingency fund almost the total amount it had lost. The problem seemed solved.

The research director then reminded everyone that he assumed all the projects had been cut to the bone and only the best ones were being included in the budget. One research executive assured him that it would be impossible for him to cut his research budget any further. The others, not only assured him, but actually added several hundred thousand dollars of new projects which "just came up to them and were urgent."

At the end of the meeting I interviewed some of the participants. The research director felt the meeting had succeeded because he had given the budget people a guide with which to operate. Two of the research executives were very pleased that none of their projects was cut. Another was pleased, but wondered if the research director had made a wise move. The two staff subordinates were quite surprised at how smoothly it all went.

The administrative staff people were startled, however. They had expected that their sound of financial alarm would bring pressure for budget cuts which some felt were long overdue. For example:

> 1. I think we stirred them [executive committee] up a bit and shocked them so much that they were finally forced to make a decision. The research director's solution surprised me. Also, I thought he should have questioned the budgets more.

RESEARCHER: Do you feel they were padded?

Well, to be honest with you, hell yes. Not only do I think that they were padded, but I would say, hell yes. I don't understand how the research director could do what he did. I guess he's got to live with these people, and it's not easy for him to stand up to them. If I were in his shoes, I think I might say, O.K., if you think you've pared down your budget, let's see. I guess this would have made the others angry and the research director didn't want this.

Another said:

2. Yes, I was somewhat surprised that he did not push the issue. I decided that he felt that the executive committee was not the place to push it. The way we work, he'll probably talk to each man individually.

RESEARCHER: What impression does this leave you about the function of the executive committee meetings?

Well, as I told you before, executive committee meetings are not held to solve important issues. I guess in this one we sort of violated practice by asking the executive committee to do some work in the meeting which is usually devoted to ritual. So the research director took over and ran the meeting. Again I expected this, because I did not expect the executive committee, as a group, to resolve the issue.

3. I don't think he (research director) went aggressively as he should have down each item and really carried the ball. Why he accepted all those requests without questioning them more aggressively, I don't know.

For reasons that are not quite clear to me, the research director reversed himself a few days later. One research executive suggested it was he who convinced the research director to reverse his stand. Another said it was he who cautioned the research director to reverse himself.

The reversal pleased the staff people. The issue immediately arose as to who was to ask the research executives to cut their budgets. The research director decided that the budget representatives should meet with the various research executives or their advisors to begin to consider cuts. Interestingly, in three days each research group added to its list of priority research and cut a few projects which, for administrative relations with the rest of the corporation, could not be cut.

The administrative staff people were beginning to feel frustrated. First, none of the research executives seemed to be willing to give them a definite list of projects to cut. "They are quite good about adding to the list, but it is very difficult to get them to cut anything. In fact, every day I get telephone calls with new additions to the budget."

The difficulty seemed to be that the group that had been asked to collect information from the executive committee was composed of people with much lower status.

The Subordinates' Relationships with the Executive Committee

The next step in the analysis is to see if any relationships can be found between the executive committee's internal dynamics and their relationships with the subordinates.

The majority of the subordinates perceive the executive committee as getting into too many everyday operating activities (60 percent); as moving too slowly in making a decision (48 percent); as not representing adequately the subordinates' view (72 percent); and therefore as not being facilitative to the subordinates (50 percent).

Some typical statements are:

1. As I said before, I still do not know what the executive committee responsibilities are. If I were they, I would want to review them and see if they are not getting too many things that should be decided at the lower levels. In my opinion an organization should pick good men and let them alone.

2. In general I think the impact of our executive committee is to prevent change. They don't actively stop you, but they, in effect, make sure that you don't change this organization very much. By not actively encouraging change and by going on as we always have, they inhibit change that way. I should add that if you don't want to do anything different in this company, there is no problem; you should get along very well with the executive committee.

3. One thing that I can think of is sometimes I think in setting the general policies they overlook the facts and the realities of the lower level. I can think of one very specific situation where I think the company is moving in absolutely the wrong direction. But there is no way of getting this point across to them; that is, to the executive committee or the powers that be in this company. In this company if you have an idea that isn't popular with the executive committee, I think you'll find that it is very difficult to get the executive committee to consider it.

4. I don't feel that our point of view is well represented. In fact, I would say that it is much more poorly represented now than when we were reporting directly to a research executive. At that time we

felt that he was our spokesman at the executive committee. Now we have one man who is supposed to represent all departments, and I would say that I don't see anybody representing our point of view at all.

It is interesting to speculate on these views. Why is it that the executive committee remains on the operating level? The research director (and a majority of the subordinates agree with him) has tried very hard to keep the executive committee away from everyday operating procedures. Indeed, the research director reported to the writer that one major frustration of his was the executive committee's apparent inability to make decisions at the policy level and to suggest administrative innovation. One possibility (and this is speculative) is related to the dependence of the executive committee members upon the research director. As was mentioned above, they behave in such a way that he has to make the decisions. Interrelated with this reason, is the research director's belief that he *does* make the decisions. He does contribute heavily to the *conformity i* scores. Thus he may want to have an executive committee that makes decisions, but he does not always behave in this manner. Interestingly, 80 percent of the executive committee members speak very highly of the research director as a man who is not afraid to make decisions and to develop effective relationships with the corporate board. It may be that the executive committee members like him because he is doing what needs to be done and therefore protecting them from taking the responsibility.

It may be, therefore, that the research director wants the executive committee to make decisions, but the committee does not seem to accept the responsibility. If so, then it would seem necessary that the research director raise this as an issue of the executive committee's and his effectiveness. But, to do so would be to violate the norms. "It might upset people," stated the research director and besides, he continued, "You have to have patience with these people."

To summarize, I believe that the executive committee members (since most prefer Pattern A) desire to be dependent upon the research director for administrative matters. The research director behaviorally fulfills this need because he *does* make the decisions. As a result the executive committee deals primarily with operating procedures, which makes the subordinates feel that they are being dominated and dependent. Thus the internal dynamics of dependence upon the research director are spread to the executive committee–subordinate relationships.

Another resultant of the internal dynamics of the executive committee upon the subordinates may be found in the case of the organizational changes discussed previously. The executive committee members established three major committees because most of them felt that the research director wanted them. Although half of the executive committee had questions about the effectiveness of the organizational changes, their views as loyal executive committee members did not permit them to raise these questions.

The research director, on the other hand, wanted the committees in order to give the subordinates greater influence in the organization. He felt that if these committees did indeed help bring up long-range issues, the executive committee would have to deal with them. However, the subordinates rarely expressed such an interpretation of the move. They saw it as "new and unneeded bureaucracy," "going to a committee form of management" (76 percent). Only 20 percent thought it was an excellent move. Why?

First, the 20 percent who liked the move were primarily staff people who had helped the executive committee to draft the plan. Also, they wanted these committees because that meant that the administrative process was no longer to have second-class status.

1. Frankly, I'm very skeptical about these new committees. However, I don't think there is much we can do about them because I hear they're the president's pet project. Now don't get me wrong, the motives and the objectives are fine. I realize that our corporation is the greatest committee company that was ever invented, and its reasonably successful record says that it must be a workable scheme. However, I tend to react a little bit adversely to permanent committees that try to get into decision-making functions. I tend to think committees are good for information gathering and nothing else.

2. I think the new organization makes a lot of sense. It makes sense to have a research executive who is not responsible for the administrative details but is concerned with the scientific aspect.

3. Sometimes some of us wonder whether all these organizational changes aren't made to hide a fundamentally weak executive committee. A lot of us feel strongly that the way the research director handles himself in concentrating on the diplomacy and in the relations of the business is great. This is what our company has lacked,

and we need it, and his outward-looking atmosphere is something that we're missing. However, none of us think that the way to run a company is to have a lot of committees who overlap each other anyway.

4. Well, let me say first that the new committees came as a complete surprise to me. In fact, I'm not sure whether they have been communicated down the line. I don't understand why all the secrecy about it. These are new committees, and I think I'd better hold judgment until we see how they work. Frankly, I'm not sure how in the world these committees are going to work. I participated in one, and watched another committee, and already I can see that they are going beyond the stated purpose. They are overlapping. We're discussing in our committee what the people are discussing in the other. I hear that in the other committee during the first meeting the man in charge said the sky's the limit as far as discussion is concerned. I would say that my prediction is that they're going to find out that these committees greatly overlap.

The last comment indicates two problems connected with the decisions to form the committees. First, the men who were especially to profit from the move were never asked to cooperate in planning the move. And, in this milieu it is difficult to see how they could be invited, since one objective of the committees was to induce the executive committee members to give away some of the power they had exercised. This would be a touchy issue and could not be explored openly with the executive committee, let alone with the subordinates.

The second problem was that the executive committee never fully discussed the scope of the committees. Again, I suspect they did not do so because such a discussion might bring up the difficult issue as to why their scope of responsibility was being changed. As a result, the charters of two of the three committees overlapped.

Probably the most important reason why the subordinates did not have positive feelings about the new committees is related to their perception of the executive committee members' (unintended) tendencies to suppress difficult issues. If the overwhelming majority of them felt that the executive committee members were afraid to be open, to take risks, to deal with conflict, then why should they be hopeful about committees administered by executive committee members? They expected them to become "briefing sessions," "propaganda platforms," "opportunity for us to get things off our chest but not for action." I should predict that even if these committees did somehow develop open communications and truly difficult issues were aired, the members would still have to refer them to the executive committee. At the moment, they should feel that this would mean further delays.

Another problem that existed between the executive committee members and their subordinates was that few of the subordinates (68 percent) felt that they were given any direct information about their effectiveness. The 32 percent who did report that they knew where they stood all came from one unit which reported to a superior who preferred Pattern B. Moreover, 80 percent said that there was no legitimate way to inform their superiors how they (subordinates) felt about them. The 16 percent who felt that such an opportunity existed again came from the same unit. Some typical statements were:

1. No, I really don't know how he feels about me. Oh, I get indirect signs once in a while.

2. The only way I know how he feels about me is that I seem to be getting raises.

3. No, I don't know how he feels about me. How do you find out about these things—can you go up to a fellow and ask him?

4. I know how he says he feels. He's extremely open about this day by day.

RESEARCHER: And does he have any idea how you feel about him?

Oh, I'm just as open with him. I think we have a very open relationship. I have never seen or experienced in my career a relationship that is as complete trust and open as this one. I think we think alike, and I have no hesitation to pass any information out to him.

RESEARCHER: If I hear you correctly I gather you're saying it's been your experience that you can disagree with him.

Oh, I never disagree with him and hide it. In fact that would be the worst possible thing you could do with him. If you work with him, you learn right from the beginning that the best thing to do with him is to level with him.

It is interesting to speculate why about the same number of executive committee members reported that they were not given direct data about how their superior felt about their effectiveness. This again may be an indication of how the internal dynamics influences the organizational dynamics. Given the executive committee's norms, the executive committee members did not tend to expect direct feedback from the research director. Indeed, as has been shown, he sensed this and was very careful not to upset them. As a result the executive committee members came to believe, "It is proper for a subordinate not to receive direct feedback from the superior." Consequently, this may have taught the executive committee members not to give direct feedback to their subordinates.

One may then raise the question if executive committee members would not also tend to promote men with whom they were most comfortable. As we have seen during the discussion of the staff subordinates this was, in fact, the case. This tended to result, therefore, in subordinates behaving toward their subordinates in the very way they were critical of their superiors for behaving. For example, 80 percent of the immediate subordinates of the executive committee replied that they would deal with conflict by hiding, suppressing their feelings. For example:

> 1. Well, I certainly would not try to solve the problem on the spot. I think I would talk to the people individually and then hold a meeting. I don't think people should get emotional. Damn it, when they get emotional they just don't get anywhere. And of course, after it is all over, I send a written memo to them to make sure they really understood the problem and ask them for the resolution and ask them to sign this paper. In some sections, a few I might say, I think I would handle the disagreement openly. In others, I just kind of smooth things over and work my own way in the background.
>
> RESEARCHER: In your experience which would you say is more typical?
>
> Well, I think it is typical here to stay away from too much conflict.
>
> 2. I usually let them blow off steam and if it involves several departments I'll ask each of the directors to appoint somebody to work together at the lower levels to see if they can iron it out.

Although we did not collect data on the subordinates, if we assume, for a moment, that as a group they had similar predispositions and therefore as low interpersonal competence as did the executive committee, then it is understandable why 64 percent decided that the best way they could facilitate the work of their subordinates was to leave them alone. However, as was pointed out in the first case, such a leadership practice had an unintended consequence. In this culture, leaving people alone was also the proper way of dealing with difficult people. Thus the absence of the supervisor could be interpreted as a sign of trust or mistrust;

difficulty or no difficulty. Probably the technically competent men would not be as threatened by this because they would obtain confirmation as a result of their work. However, this would not tend to be the case for the less technically competent men. Again, we would predict that it would be they who would push for the hygienic factors of more meetings, etc.

Summary of Results

1. The top executive group, as predicted, held the pyramidal values. Predictions were then made about how the categories would rank in frequency of occurence given the values held by the top executive group members. These predictions were largely confirmed.
2. However, the predictions that the top executives would report that their group norms did *not* encourage such behavior as openness, risk taking, and innovativeness were not confirmed.
3. An analysis of the top executive interview protocols resulted in some theorizing that the majority of the members held certain predispositions which prevented them from realizing their group's weaknesses.
4. Predictions were then made that if the researcher's diagnosis was valid, then the subordinates immediately below the top group would view the group as low in openness, risk taking, trust, expressing feelings, and capacity to deal with conflict, and high in conformity. These predictions were largely confirmed by the responses of the immediate subordinates during extended interviews.

CHAPTER 4

Organization C

THE THIRD and last of the studies upon which this book is based deals primarily with the board of directors of an organization whose output is described as innovations in management practice. The firm consults in a wide array of managerial activities. The board is an internal one and, at the time of the study, had five members. All the stock was owned by the board members.

Instead of observing the board members during the meetings, a different approach was taken. The board tape-recorded its monthly meetings and sent them to Yale for us to score them. The plan was to see if it was possible to analyze five months of board meetings "blind." Also, instead of interviewing the members individually, the plan was to present the board with the analysis and tape-record their spontaneous reaction.

The board accepted the proposal, and the project began. Although the values of the board members are presented first, they were not collected in that order. Data about the interpersonal values of the executives were obtained after the diagnostic phase. This was necessary because if the researcher knew the values that the men held, it might bias his observations and scoring of the meetings.

The Values of the Board Members[1]

All but one member believed that the effective leader was one who directed, controlled, and inspired loyalty of the men. All the

---

[1] The members completed the same open-ended questionnaire as was used in Organization B.

members reported that the best executive is one who is rational, objective, unemotional, and expert in his activity. Finally, all but one of the directors reported that when disagreements erupt into personal antagonisms and hostile feelings, the best thing for a leader to do is to "switch subjects," "table the discussion," "ask people to keep personalities out of the discussion" and "be reasonable people."

Following the theoretical framework described earlier, it was predicted that the following pattern of behavior should be manifested by the members during their board meetings. The categories should be found to exist in the following order of frequency:

owning ideas
concern ideas
conform ideas
open ideas
individuality ideas
antagonism ideas
not helping others to own ideas
helping others to own ideas

If the *conform i* and *concern i* are reversed in frequency, then the members should report that there is a high degree of competition within the group, especially among the most active participants. Whether the source of competitiveness was "in" the personality, small group, or organizational factors (or all three) could not be predicted a priori.

The frequency of the feeling scores should be very small, as should be the frequency of trust, mistrust, and experimenting, as well as that of the not owning, not open, not experimenting categories.

The frequency of the imbalance scores should be:

own i–conform i
own i–antagonism i
open i–conform i
open i–antagonism i

The Results of the Observations

The results of the observations are presented in Table 4–1. Seven, instead of five, meetings were scored and the time period was extended from six months to a year. The reasons for the

TABLE 4-1
Frequency of Categories

Category	Session 1 (n = 160)*		Session 2 (n = 210)†		Session 3 (n = 170)‡		Session 4 (n = 170)		Session 5 (n = 170)		Session 6 (n = 170)		Session 7 (n = 115)	
	n	%	n	%	n	%	n	%	n	%	n	%	n	%
own i	109	68	153	73	122	72	122	72	124	73	114	67	86	75
conform i	88	55	99	47	87	51	65	38	100	59	85	50	48	42
concern i	43	27	59	28	46	27	32	19	49	29	53	31	45	39
open i	29	18	32	15	32	19	—	—	26	15	32	19	22	19
individuality i	18	11	32	14	12	07	2	01	—	—	8	05	—	—
antagonism i	—	—	15	07	15	09	63	37	10	06	22	13	20	17
n.h.o. own i	16	10	13	06	—	09	32	19	20	12	17	10	9	08
not open i	—	—	—	—	—	—	15	09						
own f	13	08	4	02	3	02	2	01			2	01		
concern f	5	03	2	01	2	01	2	01						
Imbalance Scores														
own i–conform i	34	21	40	19	29	17	46	27	58	34	58	34	32	28
own i–antag. i	6	04	13	06	8	05	29	17	8	05	19	11	18	16
open i–antag. i	3	02	2	01	2	01	12	07	2	01			1	01
open i–conform i	14	09	17	08	12	07	39	23	5	03	7	04		
own i–mistrust i	2	001	2	001	—	00	8	05						
open i–mistrust i	—	00	—	00	—	00	2	01						

* It should be kept in mind that individual and group scores are considered as separate universes. Thus all the individual scores should approximate 100% and the same for all the group scores. Thus $n = 160$ for the individual and another $n = 160$ represents the group score.
† The figure 210 means that many units were scored on the individual and group level. (Total, 420.)
‡ Total $n = 340$.

extension (beyond the obvious value of obtaining more data) are presented below.

The first conclusion is that the predicted pattern was observed with the exception of the fourth meeting. Thus *own i* was most frequent, with *conformity i, concern i, open i, individuality i,* and *antagonism i* following in that order. Also, feeling scores were low as were the scores for trust, mistrust, and helping and not helping others. The frequencies of the imbalance scores were also in accordance with the predictions.

Since *conform i* was significantly more frequent than *concern i,* it is predicted that subsequent research should uncover a situation of competitiveness among all or the most frequent participants. As we shall see, evidence was uncovered subsequently in agreement with the prediction.

Session 4 was significantly different from what was expected in several ways. The major differences were (*a*) that *antagonism i* was the third highest score, (*b*) *that open i* was extremely low, and (*c*) *not* helping others was unexpectedly high.

The day the tape was received at Yale, the chairman of the board telephoned to "warn" the writer that a tape would arrive for which the group wanted to apologize. "It isn't like us," "extremely poor," "too emotional," "things got out of hand," and "thank God we don't have many of those" illustrate the view taken by the chairman. The quantitative pattern did show a significant difference. It was decided to expand the number of sessions to be observed beyond the five originally scheduled, in order to see if the pattern would return to the expected state and remain relatively constant. The data in Table 4–1 suggest that this did occur.

Although the data are in line with the expectations, it should be made clear that, to date, the theory provides no way to predict a priori when a group's pattern will enter a state of disequilibrium. An analysis of the tape suggested that part of the problem was the subject discussed. It was a subject which involved the organizational and personal security of the majority of the board members.

It may be possible to develop knowledge about the conditions under which disequilibrium will tend to occur. Some examples would be discussions that involve altering significantly (1) the objective of the organization (or any subunit), (2) the degree of rationality to be used, (3) the amount and nature of rewards and penalties, control, and authority.

Another possibility is that any discussion designed to discuss those topics that are typically considered not discussable would tend to lead to disequilibrium. Some examples would be (1) interpersonal relations, pent-up feelings, (2) the need for conformity, (3) the necessity for mistrust, (4) the existence of organizational defenses such as management by crisis, through fear and detail, interdepartmental rivalries, and the distortion of data sent to the upper levels.

Also, disequilibrium may occur because of particular personalities, or because of the level of pent-up feelings due to tension and frustration that exist among the members, or any subset of members, which reaches the breaking point. But, what is the breaking point? How does one operationally define it? These remain as unanswered questions.

One possible way to begin to understand this problem would be to hypothesize that the imbalance scores are indications of the pent-up feelings. The greater the pent-up feelings, the greater the need to aggress against those perceived as causing the problem. But, aggression is a feeling (which is suppressed) and one whose expression goes against the value of group loyalty. Consequently, if it is to be expressed, it must be done guardedly. The imbalance behavior may be a safe way to express these feelings. Such behavior creates difficulties for the receiver, but gives the sender a way out. If the receiver complains about the "minus" aspect (a possibility which is not highly probable because of the value against the expression of feelings), then the sender can deny the "minus" and emphasize the "plus."

The Reactions of the Board Members to the Feedback of the Results

Having made the analysis above, predictions were made about how the members must feel about each other and the group with respect to certain qualities. For example:

1. Since *conform i* is high, the members should report a high degree of competitiveness within the group. People should report the need for a strong predisposition to be articulate if they were to succeed in the group.

2. Since *conform i* is high, *trust i, helping others,* and *experimenting i* are low, the members should report that they do not feel that they can be (in this group) as innovative as they are capable of being.

3. Finally, since a substantial proportion of the *conform i* scores was attributed to the chairman, the members should report that they are dependent, at least, upon the chairman.

The feedback session was taped so that inferences could be made from the tape content. Although this exercise does not constitute a test of the hypothesis, it, coupled with other similar anthropological substudies, helps to give us added confidence in the findings.

An analysis of the tape shows that all the members stated that effective executives are able to be articulate and "sell" their ideas. "If you can't get up, say something in a convincing manner, you know, sell it, then you're not going to get far around here."

"Not being heard as intended," "cliques getting together to ride their favorite hobby horse," "lawyering" were so often mentioned by the executives that, as one said, "They're so much a part of life around here, that I wouldn't know what the hell to do without them."

Regarding the qualities of trust and innovativeness, the discussion was also in line with the expectations. For example:

A:[2] I would think that each of us is in some group that is far more creative than we are when we are together.

B: In my judgment that is true. I can only speak for myself. I'll try to answer it as honestly as I can. I do not feel that I can be very creative in this group. Indeed, I'll say, I'm associated with a group which, in my opinion, could be far more creative than it is.

D: It would seem to me that to the extent that I have any creativity at all, it is never expressed in this group.

C: I think that when we meet, there is always a tendency for our contributions to be critical. As a result, the person who is doing the creating is wary. He cuts off [his new ideas] before he has gone too far. It isn't long before he loses his confidence in pursuing a new line of attack [on a problem].

E: Moreover, it seems to me that we spend four to five hours doing what ought to be done in an hour.

C: I always feel in these meetings people aren't really trying to be open or to help. Hell, I wouldn't come to this group to explore a new idea.

---

[2] Letters represent individuals.

B: I agree about the lack of creativity or whatever else you wish to call it. But, I do not agree that the problem is lack of openness. I think we're too candid. There are a lot of things that are said that might well not be said.

A: I agree that we don't tell our true feelings, but I'm beginning to think that we should.

B: I for one would never think of coming to this group with a very important idea without having presented it elsewhere. In other words, when I come out with a brand new idea, this would not be the best place.

You made the point that we tend to ask questions which try to prove our own point of view. I agree.

C: Yes, and it isn't long before you realize that people are asking questions in order to "lick" you.

Later on during the meeting, that problem of dependence upon the superior and his management by detail was brought up. For example:

B: Now my own experience has been sufficiently frequent to know that my judgments will differ from yours. And, if I want to do the good thing, I'd better find out what your judgments are. . . .

C: Now I know (to A) you don't see it that way, but I agree with what B just said.

A: I don't understand that. Thousands of things go out the way I think they shouldn't go out. I say nothing because . . . [cut off]

B: How long do you say nothing? Do you really think there are any significant criticisms that you don't get out within a week of the time that you registered your criticisms?

C: I don't know to what extent this is the experience of others. The way in which he expresses his point of view to me, on anything that is relevant to my work, happens not to be the way which will encourage me to state my point of view.

B: I am struck by the fact that for an articulate person (as I viewed myself), there is probably no one I've ever known in life to whom I can express myself less clearly than to ——[superior]. I am frequently disappointed at the dismal way in which I manage to say things and how poorly I did in saying what it is I really meant to say.

Later the lack of faith the superior had in the subordinates to stop "dead projects" came out.

A: What safeguard is there then? Just suppose the forward movement wouldn't get moving, how long would it go and what would be the time that inefficient projects were stopped?

B: Look, I disagree with you. I think we have enough common

sense to stop them. But we don't because we know you'll step in when you think it's necessary. If you really gave us the responsibility, we'd stop them.

A: I wonder. The poor projects don't seem to stop. They keep going. There is a lack of control, isn't there?

C: I doubt what we need is more control. . . .

B: In fact, I never know what to make of your memos. You're so damn worried about the details. I'm never sure that the purpose of your memos isn't to make somebody foolish or feel foolish.

The Subordinates' View of the Board

As in the case of the previous study, I hypothesize that the board members tend to use the same pattern of behavior with their subordinates as they do with each other. If this is valid, then the subordinates should report that as a result of the impact of the board, they experience that:

1. They are controlled by the board's behavior. They should experience feelings of binds due to the imbalance behavior of the board members.
2. The board does not tend to encourage innovation and change.
3. The board tends to place them in situations where they are competing with each other.

The top 18 executives just below the board were interviewed. The objective of the interview was to help develop a total organizational diagnosis of the factors that inhibit and facilitate their effectiveness. No mention was made of the state of the board study other than that it was progressing and that this next step was a natural sequence in the process of understanding the total organization.

The major topic headings covered in the semistructured interview were (1) perceived job satisfactions and dissatisfactions, (2) perceived pressures and fulfillments, (3) perceived organizational strengths and weaknesses, (4) long-range corporate objectives, (5) respondents' perceptions of their managerial strengths and limitations, (6) the perceived quality of his relationship with superiors, peers, and subordinates, and (7) their assessment of the degree of creativity and innovativeness of the organization as a whole.

The results of the interviews are presented below. The framework for presentations was relatively simple. The results were organized into two categories. The first category included all the factors that the executives reported as factors that tended to *facili-*

tate the effectiveness of the organization. The second category included all the factors that tended to *inhibit the effectiveness* of the organization.

Factors that Facilitated Organizational Effectiveness

I. *Minimum pressure from my immediate superior.*

$n = 18$

a) I have as much or almost as much leeway from my superior to do my job the way I believe it should be done.......77%
b) I have inadequate or no leeway from my superior..........33%

Some examples of quotations that illustrate the statistics.

1. Within the organization, I think that I am given a fairly large degree of leeway; I'm given a fairly free hand. I don't think my restrictions are very great. If they are, I've gotten so used to them that I'm not conscious of them any more.

2. There are limitations, but I think that the leeway, except for the limitations, is very great. And I think the limits are necessary limits.

3. Leeway—not a damn bit. Zero. They don't want you to make any important decisions around here.

II. *Intellectually challenging and satisfying work.*

a) My work is challenging, intellectual work with plenty of variety and intellectually challenging people................67%
b) My work is challenging because I have to deal with people....33%

For example:

1. I find it a very stimulating experience being with the kind of people I am with and doing the kind of things that I do. It is a challenge. It has all the elements of problems, mistakes to be avoided, victories to be won.

2. Oh, I think the greatest satisfactions of all come with this job. Certainly for a person like myself. There are very few things in this world where what in essence comes out is yourself.

3. If you are a professional, you take satisfaction in having done a particular job well. I would not consider that our programs are the most important thing in my life or the reader's life. However, I think that they are well worth doing and well worth doing well and therefore, I derive great satisfaction out of doing this kind of work.

III. *Minimum internal departmental rivalries and fighting.*

a) Frictions exist primarily *among* departments.............67%*
b) Few or no frictions exist *within* departments.............67%
c) Few frictions anywhere...................................17%

* An asterisk indicates individuals reported more than one answer. Therefore, total percentage will be higher than 100%.

For example:

1. Yes, I doubt if there is much openness say between us and sales, or the business group. Some people say we should improve communications with the business office. "Why?" I ask. Every time I call, they either deny my request or ask me to wait five days.

2. Meetings may be guarded in other departments, but not in ours. There is no premium placed in holding back. There is no benefit in holding back and not asserting your point of view. From what I hear, this is less true in other departments.

3. I think there are fairly many of them. I do not think they are terribly apparent. I am certain that they are even at the very highest levels, but everyone is quite gentlemanly about it all. I don't know how to say they're handled except it is not out in the open.

4. I would say we try to solve problems by peaceful means. Unfortunately, these means don't work as often as we would like. I'm all in favor of peaceful means because certainly I don't really think anybody hates anybody else. It just seems as though when one peaceful means doesn't work, you try another and well, when that doesn't work, you say to hell with it.

IV. and V. *Minimum overt or covert competition for promotions and adequate wages.*

    a) Very little fighting for upward mobility. There is not much opportunity for advancement. We are professional and small. My main desire is to earn good wages (which, for the most part, I do)...................................100%

For example:

1. This is not a very big company. Being realistic, there are not too many opportunities. You may split a few jobs up. But, there is a limit to this. There aren't that many openings.

2. That's not an easy question to answer. I suppose we all look forward to the day when we can be an officer of the company. I would guess that if I were asked, I would say I would like to go to the top.

3. Everything here is more or less fixed. There is only a certain limit as far as promotions. There is only one guy who can be the boss, and if he refuses to leave or die, then you cannot go anywhere.

VI. *Deadlines (inherent) in work.*

    a) It is challenging to be able to produce intellectually sound material and do it within a deadline....................61%

Factors that Inhibit Organizational Effectiveness

I. *Organizational crises and ambiguity.*

$n = 18$

    a) Unilateral, conformity producing policies; unpredictable swings in policies....................................100%

For example:

1. I think there is very little question about it. This company is run with little worry about how other people react. I think people question whether top management knows ahead of time what they are really doing.

2. Well, that's a good question. Have you ever seen an organizational chart in this place? Well, when you do, don't believe it. I know several jobs that are on the chart, and they do not reflect the facts.

3. I would say our top management tends to be arbitrary. They set goals that are unrealistic. They supervise in a negative manner. A man who is constantly criticized for his operations is not stimulated. I think the people, at my level, operate under negative supervision. I believe that if we had the climate of years ago, we would grow.

4. Management by swings. One day it's one thing. The next, another. And to make it more interesting, the changes are slowly leaked out (usually to the people least affected). It takes six months to realize the whole organization has been changed.

II. *Interdepartmental rivalries.*

    a) Departments do not cooperate with each other as well as they should...67%*

    b) Departments did cooperate with each other..............17%

---

* The interviews were semistructured, and thus individuals had the option not to react to certain categories.

For example:

1. I'm afraid that trust is not very high. I think you decide whom you can trust and draw your lines accordingly. I think there is a certain alignment among divisions.

2. Well, I wish I knew. I'll call someone and we'll decide on a course of action. Then, later I'll get a memo asking me to explain it. What the hell!

3. I would say (within the group) trust is very high. On the other hand, look, you can't be square about it either. You have to realize that there are politics going on and you've got to realize sometimes that somebody has got a knife out for you in one way or another. Also, there are a lot of departmental rivalries.

III. *Lack of innovation and creativity.*

    a) We are not as innovative as we are capable of being.........83%

    b) We are not at all innovative...........................17%

For example:

1. I don't think we are very innovative. At least not in the recent years. I think, in being honest with myself, I think that I have been

here long enough to know what is not going to be approved. so I never bother recommending it anymore. I don't think that it is that serious that we do not have it.

2. Innovation—very close to zero. Why? First, because the organization—the officers—do not want it to grow. There is little willingness to plow back earnings into growth. There is a policy of the top to be so hard on a new idea, no matter where it came from, that after years of being knocked down and seeing other people knocked down, people have stopped suggesting things.

3. Innovation is our business, and its lack of prosperity and progress in the last ten years is in direct proportion to its decreasing innovation.

I guess that after a certain number of times the organization soon learns that it is not worth wasting time trying to be innovative.

4. I think we are ossified.

IV. *Superior's lack of authority.*

    a) My superior has less leeway than I do.................67%
    b) My superior has adequate leeway......................17%

For example:

1. I often wonder exactly how much my boss can really get done in this organization. Sure, he goes to meetings with the board, but I doubt if he has much influence. When you get right down to it, he can't change their minds.

V. *Pressures from managerial controls such as financial controls.*

    a) Budgets and the business office are beginning to run the company rather than being our servant.....................67%
    b) Budgets and the business office are not a problem. Indeed, they are helpful.......................................17%

For example:

1. We've been fighting the battle of the automatic monsters for at least two years, and the results have been less than satisfactory. They're like a separate corporate enterprise. You can complain, you can get mad at it, but it doesn't seem to do a hell of a lot of good.

2. The problem, as I see it, is that the tail is wagging the dog. If we want to make a change, we can't because they can't handle it.

VI. *Unilateral work deadlines.*

    a) Unexpected deadlines caused by top management or interdepartmental problems...............................67%

For example:

1. Nothing burns me up more than to have a job almost finished and to find out that there has been a change in attitude from above.

2. Then there is the ——— department fighting the ——— department. Each worries about its own problems and interests and says to hell with the other. And I don't think you'd get anywhere by getting them to sit down and listen to one another. We've tried it, and in a half an hour they're at each other's throats.

In examining the data, several conclusions merit emphasis. They are: All factors except one that the executives reported as facilitating organizational effectiveness were primarily related to the satisfactions intrinsic to their work: the adequate pay, minimum interpersonal problems *within* any department, as well as minimum competition among the individuals, within each department, for promotions.

The only other factor that was reported as facilitating organizational competence was the minimum pressure and freedom from the immediate superior to do one's job the way one saw fit. In order to understand fully this factor, it should also be kept in mind that 67 percent of the executives reported that their superiors had little significant influence with the board and that they (executives) wished that they could influence more frequently the major long-range policy decisions. Although the immediate supervisor may be more "employee-centered," this does not decrease significantly the pressures that the executives reported that they experienced coming from the board. Nor is it very comforting for them to realize that their "understanding" superiors do not have as much influence as they (the subordinates) wished that they had. This lack of influence by one's superior caused concern with the subordinates because they felt that the superiors were not able to obtain for them what they needed to do an effective job.

Finally, it is clear by the comments made by the subordinates that they assign the greatest proportion of their difficulties to the behavior of the board. They do not seem to report that the organization per se is at fault for such factors as low innovativeness, conformity, and lack of authority.

The Blindness of the Board to Its Impact upon the Subordinates

This board tended to be blind to its actual impact upon the subordinates. In this section I should like, by using the theoretical framework, to explore some possible causes of the blindness. In doing so, I shall focus on three frequently mentioned practices of the board that the subordinates disliked. They are (1) constant changing of organizational charts and keeping the latest versions semiconfidential, (2) shifting executives from one department to another without adequate discussion with the other executives involved and without clearly communicating the "real" reasons for the move, and (3) developing new departments whose goals and products ranged from overlapping to competing with already existing departments.

In order to understand these practices, it is helpful to recall that the board members strongly believed that effective interpersonal relationships tend to be (1) those human relationships that lead to the achievement of the objective, (2) those that emphasize rationality and de-emphasize emotionality, and (3) those that provide direction, control, and appropriate rewards and penalties.

These values, I believe, can help to account for the board's behavior. For example, the board members' reasons for the lack of communication of changes varied in detail but not in substance. Most of them were based upon the value of de-emphasizing activity that could lead to emotional difficulties. This was hidden from themselves by the rationalization that the subordinates were not interested or were too busy. Reasons for the lack of full explanations of changes to the subordinates were, "In order not to get people upset"; "If you tell them everything, all they do is worry and we get a flood of rumors"; "The changes do not *really* affect them"; and, "It will only cut in on their busy schedule and interrupt their productivity."

The void of clear-cut information from the board was "filled in" by the executives. Their explanations ranged from, "They must be changing things because they are not happy with the way things are going," to "The unhappiness is so strong they do not tell us," and "Their unhappiness is due to their own ineffectiveness, and they do not dare admit it."

Even the executives who profited from some of these moves reported some concern and bewilderment. For example, three executives reported instances where they had been promoted over some "old-timers." In all cases they were told to "soft-pedal the promotion aspect" until the old-timers were diplomatically informed.

Unfortunately, it took months to inform them, and in some cases it was never done. The situation was "solved" because the old-timer, who sensed the true state of affairs, left the organization. Interestingly, these practices created some anxiety among those who profited because as one man said, "If they do it to him, why won't they do it to me some day?"

In terms of our categories, the board's behavior tended to add to the norms of antagonism, mistrust, and conformity as well as not owning up to and being open about one's behavior.

Another practice of the board that produced difficulties in the organization was the increasing intervention into the detailed administration of a particular department when its profit picture looked "shaky." This practice was, from the subordinates' view, in violation of the stated philosophy of decentralization.

When asked, the board tended to explain this practice by saying that it did this only when it had doubts about the department head's competence and then this was always done in the interests of efficiency. When they were alerted about a department that was not doing well, the board members believed that the best reaction was to "tighten controls," "take a closer and more frequent look," and "make sure the department head is on top of things." The board members quickly added that they did not tell the man that they were beginning to doubt his competence so that "he would not become too upset." Again we see how the values of de-emphasizing the expression of negative feelings and the emphasizing of controls influence the board's behavior.

The department heads, on the other hand, reported different reactions. "Why are they bothered with details?" "Why do they not leave me alone?" "Don't they trust me?" "If not, why don't they say so?" These questions illustrate the impact this practice had upon the executives which, in terms of our categories, was to produce more *conformity, antagonism, mistrust,* and *fear of experimenting.*

Still another board practice was the "diplomatic" rejection of an executive's idea that was, in the eyes of the board, "offbeat," "a bit too wild," and "not in keeping with our mission." The reasons given by the board for not being open about the evaluation again reflected adherence to the pyramidal values. For example, "We do not want to embarrass them"; "If you really tell them you might restrict creativity"; or, as another put it, you might "raise unpleasantness."

This practice tended to have precisely the impact that the superiors wished to avoid. The subordinates reacted by saying (to each other or to themselves), "Why don't they give me an opportunity to really explain it?" "Why are they afraid to discuss it?" "What do they mean when they suggest that the 'timing is not right,' or that 'funds are not presently available'?" In terms of our categories, in addition to reinforcing the norms of conformity, antagonism, and mistrust, there is also the reinforcement of rejecting experimentation. It is understandable that the executives reported that they did not feel free to be innovative.

One of the most crucial consequences of the board's activities was the lack of predictability or consistency as to when the board would manifest some imbalance behavior. The subordinates were in a situation comparable to the dog that Pavlov was able to make neurotic by first conditioning it to a particular sequence of events, and then changing the sequence arbitrarily and without consistency. Similarly, the executives developed what they believed to be a stable pattern of relationships with the board only to find one day that they were no longer operative.

Diagnosing the Subordinates' Values

One way the subordinates adapted to the board was to take on similar behavioral patterns. For example, they tended to de-emphasize openness and risk taking and emphasize conformity and playing it safe. This led me to hypothesize that the subordinates would tend to hold values about effective interpersonal relationships that are similar to those held by the board.

The same sentence completion questionnaire given to the board was filled out by each subordinate. The results indicated that the subordinates, as a group, did hold values that are similar to those held by the board.

Table 4-2 indicates that the members believed group problem solving was effective (1) when objectives were clear and people were rational (not emotional); (2) when the leader directed and controlled the groups including, (a) suppressing emotionality or (b) dealing with it on an intellectual level; and (3) when the group contained members who (a) had technical abilities and knew the intellectual content well, (*b*) were motivated to contribute, and (*c*) exhibited minimal "mistrust," "insecurity," and "stubborness."

In connection with the replies in number VI, it was the first time that mistrust, insecurity, etc., were mentioned more frequently

TABLE 4–2

RESPONSES TO VALUE QUESTIONNAIRE BY THE EXECUTIVES

$n = 18$

I. *Group problem-solving discussions are effective when:*   *n   %*
   1. The agenda and objectives of the meeting are clearly defined............13 72
   2. People are rational and do not play politics........................10 55*
II. *When a deep disagreement occurs, the best way for a leader to handle it is to:*
   1. Deal with it on an intellectual level or avoid it (e.g., cut it short; switch subject; call off discussion)..16 89
   2. Deal with the disagreement openly................................ 6 33
III. *When the disagreement erupts into personal antagonisms and hostile feelings, the best thing for a leader to do is:*
   1. Deal with it intellectually or avoid it (e.g., go to another subject; adjourn meeting; have a cooling-off period; redefine objectives).........15 83
   2. Deal with it, but not completely openly (e.g., meet with antagonists separately and try to discover basic disagreements, etc................... 8 44
   3. Deal with it openly... 1 05
IV. *The effective leader (of a decision-making group) is one who:*
   1. Is in constant control over people. Understands what he wants from group and makes the decisions....................................16 89
   2. Is objective, has the technical abilities, knows the facts............... 7 39
   3. Is in control but he attempts to encourage expression of all viewpoints; maximizes communication within group; establishes and maintains frank and objective atmosphere...................................... 7 39
V. *The best member is one who:*
   1. Knows field well; has technical abilities; willing to accept goals of group; capable of accepting decisions of others...........................12 66
   2. Feels responsibility to contribute to decision making; is open to new ideas... 8 44
VI. *The most serious blocks to progress in a meeting are:*
   1. Mistrust; insecurity; closed minds and stubborness; not listening.........23 128
   2. Lack of clear-cut objectives; unclear goals and rules of meeting.........14 77

* In some cases more than one reply was given, and thus the total is beyond 100%.

than "clear-cut objectives." This may result from the apparent high degree of insecurity (personal and organizational) manifested by the 18 executives in their peer relationships. However, if we can believe the interview data, then this possibility was not very probable since a large majority mentioned (in the interviews) that there was little "within group" friction. However, in addition to their relationships with the top, they could be referring to the intergroup conflicts that were high.

Diagnosing the Subordinates' Behavior

According to the theoretical framework, the 18 executives should behave toward their subordinates in a manner similar to that which the board manifests toward them. The one exception should be that *concern i* should be more frequent than *conform i* because, according to the executives, there is a minimum competition within each group.

Almost all executives agreed to have two different meetings taped. In one meeting they were the formal leaders, in the second they were peers or subordinates.[3]

The results are presented in Table 4–3. They are consonant with the predictions in 11 out of 15 sessions analyzed. In four cases the *conform i* scores are higher than the *concern i* scores.

Let us examine the four exceptions. In three of the sessions where conformity was higher, one or more board members attended. Recalling again the interview data, it is plausible to consider the possibility that when the board members were present, they tended to create the need for the subordinate members to compete. This would raise conformity above concern. Also, their presence in the meeting could raise the conformity scores by their own behavior.

It is interesting to note that no board member was present in any of the sessions (except one) where concern was below conform. In the one session where concern was higher than conform, and the board member was present, the session occurred *after* the board had undergone two change sessions (which are discussed in the next chapter).

There is one further problem that needs to be explained. Although sessions 7 and 8 fit the hypothesis, they should not, since in both cases a board member was present. Again, some *ad hoc* theorizing may help to explain the discrepancy. Board member A was in each session (7 and 8) with one of his subordinates. An analysis of his scores shows that A's behavior accounts for most of the conformity scores and all the imbalance scores (excepting one unit of *open i–conform i*). The reason that concern is higher, therefore, is

---

[3] It was not possible to obtain a larger sample of meetings for reasons to be mentioned in the section on change.

that the subordinates manifest little conform behavior. They constantly behave with a concern to A's ideas. The subordinates in each case probably did not feel free to produce conformity for their superior and probably felt minimal competition, since they were alone with him during the meeting.[4]

With the exception of session 3 (and the difference discussed above) the pattern in the remainder of the cases was as predicted at the outset of this chapter (and as found to exist for the board). Interestingly, session 3 was an extremely threatening one for many members. Board member B announced some major changes in the organization. The reaction was violent, and the result was a high antagonism score plus exceptionally high imbalance scores.

We note that session 12, which did not have high conform and imbalance scores, was also run by B. The session was one where he was discharging two key executives. Although B (as we shall see) was a highly volatile person, he was not so during session 12. This session also occurred after the change sessions began.

Finally, we note that the frequency of the imbalance scores ordered themselves as predicted, with the exception in sessions 3, 9, 11 and 13. Their *open i-conform i* was higher than *open i-antagonism i*. According to our view this should have been reversed.

We again turned to the raw data and found that in sessions 3 and 4, all of the *open i-conform i* scores were attributed to board member C. He, as we shall see, was the major contributor of the *open i-conform i* scores in the board analysis. We cannot account for session 11 except to say that in all other sessions where any *open i-conform i* scores were found, they were attributed to subordinates of C. The small number of cases, however, makes this only an interesting finding, to which we can attribute little weight.

To summarize, from an admittedly small number of tapes certain regularities did appear. The 18 executives, as a group, tended to be slightly less conformity-producing than their supervisors. However, they were relatively the same in not dealing with feelings and with the amount of imbalance behavior they produced. Finally,

---

[4] These data suggest a limitation of an observational approach. One could argue that the subordinates were conforming in that they were keeping their mouths shut. Such conformity would not be scored because since it is covert, it is not observed. One way of offsetting this limitation is to analyze and note the frequencies of conformity scores for each individual. If one or a few dominate, one might then infer conformity.

TABLE 4-3
Analysis of Executive Behavior*

	1 n=145		2 n=100		3 n=175		4 n=85		5 n=105		6 n=140		7 n=100		8 n=55		9 n=100		10 n=90		11 n=120		12 n=75		13 n=125		14 n=100		15 n=40	
	n	%	n	%	n	%	n	%	n	%	n	%	n	%	n	%	n	%	n	%	n	%	n	%	n	%	n	%	n	%
own i	83	57	66	66	106	61	56	66	77	73	98	70	76	76	44	80	74	74	58	65	93	78	47	63	89	71	73	73	28	70
conform	67	46	24	24	66	38	28	33	54	51	64	46	34	34	20	36	35	35	44	49	68	57	18	24	32	26	39	39	9	23
concern i	70	48	75	75	46	26	57	67	38	36	75	54	49	49	31	56	63	63	45	50	46	38	43	57	72	58	53	53	31	78
open i	17	12	18	18	30	17	15	18	10	10	23	16	14	14	8	15	22	22	13	14	24	20	15	20	24	19	14	14	10	21
not help own i	44	30	16	16	39	22	14	17	16	15	34	24	10	10	3	03	8	08	18	20	15	13	4	05	10	08	14	14	2	05
help own i	2	1	—	—	—	—	—	—	—	—	—	—	—	—	—	—	—	—	—	—	3	03	—	—	2	02	—	—	—	—
individual i	8	06	1	1	—	—	1	01	—	—	1	01	—	—	—	—	—	—	1	01	2	02	3	04	15	12	6	06	—	—
antagonism i	—	—	—	—	62	35	—	—	10	10	9	06	17	17	4	07	1	01	—	—	4	03	7	09	—	—	—	—	—	—
antagonism f	—	—	8	08	1	01	—	—	—	—	—	—	—	—	—	—	—	—	—	—	—	—	—	—	—	—	—	—	7	13
own i-conform i	25	17	—	—	41	23	15	18	37	35	30	21	22	22	17	31	24	24	27	30	47	39	12	17	24	19	20	20	7	13
open i-conform i	—	—	1	01	4	02	—	—	1	09	5	04	1	01	—	—	3	03	1	01	3	03	1	01	2	02	1	01	—	—
own i-antagonism i	3	02	—	—	32	18	—	—	10	10	2	01	16	16	4	07	—	—	—	—	3	03	8	10	10	13	6	06	—	—
open i-antagonism i	—	—	—	—	13	07	—	—	—	—	—	—	1	01	—	—	—	—	—	—	—	—	—	—	3	02	1	01	—	—

*On each level total is equal to double the figure.

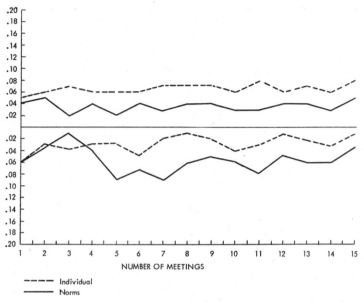

GRAPH 4–1.   Number of Meetings.

they too had their sessions where they blew their tops, but these were not very frequent.

An Example of the Board-Executive Relationships

So far, I have suggested that the board and the executives tended to have problems in terms of a low degree of openness (especially to feelings) experimenting, trust, and feelings of helping each other.

During the research project an interesting opportunity arose to examine in another manner the interpersonal relationships between the board and the executives. The opportunity came in the form of a meeting where the results from the interviews were to be presented to the executives and to the board.

If the analyses above are valid, then a high degree of resistance on the part of the subordinates can be expected in terms of discussing the results. The 18 executives should find the situation (1) a relief in that their true feelings were finally communicated and simultaneously (2) extremely uncomfortable because all the norms that existed inveighed against these problems being discussed openly with each other and with the board.

Also, if the diagnosis is valid, it can be predicted that none of the board should behave in a way that would facilitate the discussion of the results. The one board member who was most open might attempt to open up the discussion, but he should do it in such a way that he did not succeed (because an analysis of his scores shows he combines *openness* with *conformity* and *antagonism*).

An Analysis of the Group Dynamics during the Feedback Session

The feedback session was taped and the data below were taken from an analysis of the tape.

The writer presented each executive with a mimeographed report. The report contained the percentages reported for the answers to each question, as well as the verbatim remarks excerpted from the interviews that mirrored the statistical analysis. No interpretive or analytical remarks were included.

After the presentation was completed, the writer asked for reactions. The first executive to reply was an immediate subordinate of the board member who we have predicted will try to "unloosen" the meeting, even though he will not tend to do it very effectively.

EXECUTIVE 1: My initial reaction is that there are certain things that I violently disagree with and agree with here and I want to know much more (*silence*). And I should add that my disagreements are with the people around this table and not with the results as you report them.

EXECUTIVE 2: Are the comments supposed to back up the statistical breakdown?

RESEARCHER: Yes, they should at least not violate the breakdown.

EXECUTIVE 3: I get the feeling of contradictory answers. Things don't seem to fit well.

RESEARCHER: This is the same feeling that I have about the organization. The data are organized to illustrate this sense of. . . .

EXECUTIVE 4: I am impressed with the method here. I was candid, but now I find that you (*to the group*) were candid!

The discussion continued primarily on an intellectual level. The executives wanted to know how the illustrative quotations were selected. Also, time was spent pulling apart the wording of certain questions. Another discussion centered around the order of the questions.

The writer responded to the questions as fully as he could. So far, the group did not deal with the issues in the report. The writer had no intention of pushing them into such a discussion because he wanted to see if they would to it by themselves.

The discussion on technicalities continued for a half hour. The discussion finally "petered out" and silence ensued. The writer asked for any further comments. Another long silence. The writer then decided to make a short presentation organizing the data in terms of factors that facilitated and inhibited organizational effectiveness (as presented in the previous section). This presentation should serve to highlight the problem of the board's unilateralness, pressure, etc. If so, then it might provide a cue for discussion of these problems (although our hypothesis is that the executive will *not* be "seduced" by this attempt).

After the presentation was finished, three comments were made regarding how much the researcher was able to learn about the company "by his approach." After these comments, another long silence.

The writer then asked if anyone would agree with him that the silences and the sense of strain in the meeting were responses. The question was met by another silence. Finally, the board member that we predicted would move did. He said:

> I have never been in such a forced, close-mouthed meeting in all my 25 years. What is the matter with you? What's going on here?

As predicted, he did ask for more openness but did it in a punitive manner. Another silence ensued.

The writer then raised the following question. "Is the interpersonal competence of the 18 men as high as they imply it is when (in question 4) they state that they have few frictions within?" The strategy behind raising the question was based upon the assumption that one of the reasons the subordinates may have felt uncomfortable is that the report reprimanded their bosses. Perhaps they might prefer to "even things out" by admitting some of their own limitations. The difficulty with this strategy was that it ran up against the interdepartmental rivalries. The men did not feel free to talk about this problem with each other in front of the board. Another period of silence developed.

It was broken by the subordinate of the board member who we

had predicted would strive to create a degree of openness. He said:

> I can recognize me in the answer to your final question, "Do you think there is any value in continuing this program?" I answered, "I think so, I guess so, I hope so, but I am not sure." Isn't this kind of answer unusual in itself? Are all the groups that you talk to as cautious and uncertain as this one?
>
> RESEARCHER: No, they have not been as uncertain. But it may be that this group is able to be more open and admit its hesitation and ambivalence.

Someone said "I doubt it," and there was guarded laughter.

The brief sortie into the heart of one of the problem areas was abruptly terminated with a discussion of a side issue regarding one department. This discussion seemed strained and almost "dead." It was now over an hour after the presentation had ended. The writer decided that he had enough evidence that the group was not going to discuss the relevant issues. The next step was to see if they could be induced into such a discussion by the writer. According to the diagnosis, he should fail.

> RESEARCHER: Executive 1 inquired about the uncertainty and ambivalence. I believe that one of the causes for these feelings could be your fear of what would happen if you were in a laboratory with the board. (*Silence.*) Another possibility might be your understandable concern of whether or not all this would be worth it. Perhaps some feel that nothing can be changed anyway. (*Still more silence.*)

The same board member broke the silence by asking the writer:

> BOARD MEMBER: Let me ask you a question. You said that you found in the failure of verbal response an expression of an attitude?
>
> RESEARCHER: Yes.
>
> BOARD MEMBER: This is sort of like a hanging jury. Would you like to comment on that?

The researcher had now been manipulated into saying what he felt the group should have owned up to by themselves. One response could have been to state this feeling of manipulation. However, this would only coerce a discussion even more into the area that they were resisting. The researcher felt that it was not his responsibility to force them into such a discussion.[5] Also, it was now nearly two hours after the meeting had begun.

> RESEARCHER: Yes, I would say that if we listened to the tape, and if we erased your questions, Executive 1's questions and my comments, I believe that we would have a pretty dead group. This group does not at all mirror the sense of aliveness I experienced with each of you when we were alone in the interview situation.
>
> EXECUTIVE 5:   Well, it's hard to say anything more. I am waiting for someone to decide if we go further.
>
> RESEARCHER: This is helpful. I hadn't seen it that way. I saw it another way. How can you decide if you want to commit yourselves to a step if you don't explore it? As I see it, this is an excellent opportunity for you to decide if you wish to dig deeper into interpersonal and organizational problems.

After a relatively short silence:

> EXECUTIVE 7: I am fascinated by this material. I haven't fully digested it and what you have done is useful. I don't exactly know what we are talking about when we say to continue. It seems to me this project has gone (and I assumed it would continue to do so) much deeper than I expected. Now I would say that I am in favor of doing this, but I don't know what it is that we are considering.

The researcher responded that it was his hope that the group might use this hour to discuss some of the interpersonal problems noted in the report. Through this experience, they could decide better if they wanted to continue. Such a discussion would give them a living specimen of what might happen in a laboratory. He ended with the observation that two decisions were needed. One, should there be a phase of observation? Second, should they go through a laboratory?

> EXECUTIVE 8: The last time you were here, you said that communications in some organizations were frozen. Is that your conclusion about our communications?

Again the writer felt that he was being manipulated into answering for the group, but he felt the problem could not be fully discussed, so he said:

---

[5] This illustrates a point where research and consulting are different. As a consultant, I would have acted to be more genuine and would have mentioned my feelings of being manipulated into talking about what might be their responsibility.

RESEARCHER: I am beginning to feel that you want me to say the things that you feel are difficult to be said. Yes, I do believe your communications are frozen. Just as they are frozen here and now. How do you feel?

Executive 8 nodded his head and said nothing.

EXECUTIVE 5: Would your objective be, in any continuation of this program, to unfreeze the communications, or to redefine the organization, or don't you know?

RESEARCHER: My objective would be to help you create the conditions under which you can identify, for example, the extent to which the communications are frozen, whether the organization needs changing, etc. It would then be up to you to make a decision as to what you wish to do about these problems. You might wish to keep them frozen.

The questioning continued. The researcher found himself in the situation of answering questions that the group should be trying to tackle. However, by this time, he had concluded that if anything was to be discussed, it had to be through him.

EXECUTIVE 4: Do you think that this group is capable of learning and changing?

RESEARCHER: That is a very complex question. More important is what the group members feel about this. But to answer your question, I believe that the group has all the intellectual capacity. However, I wonder if it has the interpersonal competence.

Again Executive 1 hit at another key problem.

EXECUTIVE 1: I think this report is a big dose for the board to take. It seems to me that you have to have a pretty unfrozen top management to take this kind of situation. I feel frozen because it is the board's skeletons that have come out. This is why I feel it should be their decision whether they want to go further.[6]

Two points were important. This comment gave the board members an ideal opportunity to indicate how unfrozen they were and how committed they were to change. Also it was Executive 1's perception that only the top had been "indicted" with the report. The fact that the executives had also been indicted by their behavior in the meeting seemed to go unnoticed. However, this is understandable. In this situation, there is little doubt that the board was the crucial variable.

---

[6] There was some thought given to a laboratory-type program.

The same board member tried to continue to pry open the group. And again he did it in a semipunitive manner.

> BOARD MEMBER: There are many things that haven't been said here. I am sure that everyone is filled with things that they want to say. I have a feeling that this is one of the most uncandid meetings that I have sat in on in an awful long time. What's wrong with you?

No one responded. Another Board member then said:

> I can't see what harm would come from the program, and so why not try it?

The researcher asked that the commitment to the next stage *not* be on this basis. Such a commitment might help (unintentionally) to guarantee the failure of the program because it is a negative commitment.

Several executives then said that they would be delighted to vote for the project, but since it was top management that was being placed on the "hot seat," they could not feel free to vote.

This seemed, to the writer, an excellent moment for the board to ask if the people who were saying this meant to imply that they wanted to know where the board (especially the president) stood on the issue. Nothing was said.

Finally, the president said that he did not know how to respond. He couldn't figure out why the researcher was taking so much time. The problem was really simple. Did the men desire a next step? That's all there was to it.[7]

> EXECUTIVE 8: Hell, I think that we must proceed. I think each of us is a little surprised about some of the results. It seems to me that we are kidding ourselves to think that there is any point now in sweeping them under the rug.

Three other executives agreed that we should go on with the project. The Board member who had been active then said:

> BOARD MEMBER: Well that makes four of us now of this eloquent twenty-two. I am curious about the rest.

---

[7] Here is another example where the writer finds the researcher-consultant roles to be antagonistic. As a researcher, it was important to keep quiet and see how the members react. As a consultant, he would have raised the issue if the president was not feeling a sense of annoyance and mistrust of the writer. If handled effectively, it might have led others to talk about their sense of annoyance and mistrust of others.

PRESIDENT [and Board Member]:   I still can't figure out why all the delay and questions.

BOARD MEMBER: Chris has run into a most strange situation. We have talked to him at great length and with spontaneity when we are alone. When we get into a group we freeze up.

BOARD MEMBER: This meeting has been a laboratory of how our organization functions. In a sense you are reflecting the way that you want the organization to be managed. Some of you want to be told. A few want to participate in the decision. Some of you want to participate, but won't say in the group what you have said in the safety of a confidential interview. It is in this sense that a vote has occurred. Frankly, I won't trust a ballot.

A vote was taken. Eighteen for continuance and four against. To conclude, our hypotheses were not rejected. The group never talked about the emotional and interpersonal problems that they had identified in the interview situation.

Also, none of the board members were helpful in the group situation. The president "moved" the group in a direction in which it was by no means committed. The active board member tried at least four times to pry the discussion open, but he followed it with his typical reaction of punishing the group for not being open. A third board member, who disliked becoming emotional in meetings (but did when needled) tried to get everyone to agree on the ground that "no harm would come of it." The others kept quiet.

Further illustration is provided from the tape recording of a session held immediately after the feedback session. Only the board members and the researcher were present. The objective was to evaluate the feedback session.

The board was divided in its response. Half of the members agreed with the researcher's diagnosis, although they expressed a desire to see if something could not be done to help the organization prepare for a laboratory program.

The other half of the board agreed that the meeting was strained but it was their view that this was the responsibility of the researcher because he "handled the meeting incorrectly."

For example:

BOARD MEMBER: You were chairman of the meeting. I certainly would not have run it the way you did. I would have kept things moving. If I wanted people to talk, my God, I can think of a half a dozen ways to make them talk.

BOARD MEMBER: Yes, in fact, I was embarrassed during the meeting. Not for the men, but for you. It turned out more like a Quaker meeting.

BOARD MEMBER: I too was terribly embarrassed with the meeting. The group was saying, let's go home, and Chris wouldn't let them go home.

RESEARCHER: What did I do that prevented them from ending the meeting?

BOARD MEMBER: Well you refused to take control and end the meeting. You could have told them about the findings and then asked them to think about them and ended the meeting.

BOARD MEMBER [who agreed with the writer]: But, if he did that, he would not have learned what he did. We now have more evidence of what might happen if they and we were to go to a laboratory program.

BOARD MEMBER: I agree with you. I do not see how it could have been handled any other way if you keep in mind the objectives of the meeting.

RESEARCHER (to dissatisfied board members): The impression I get is that you wanted me to prevent the group from experiencing themselves as they really were. As I see it, they reported in their interviews a sense of dependence and helplessness in their relationship with the board. These came out during the meeting. Why do you wish to cover up? I guess I am beginning to wonder if you aren't evaluating the session more from your discomfort and less from what is good for the organization.

The session continued with those board members who were in agreement with the writer giving incident after incident to illustrate their (and the writer's) viewpoints. These included incidents of misunderstandings and frustrations involving the board members with one another or with their subordinates. Nine different examples were cited which led some executive to decrease his commitment, or his effort, or his risk taking, or his desire to cooperate, or his creativity. Apparently these incidents began to have their impact.

BOARD MEMBER [who was not in agreement with the writer]: Well, there is not much doubt that we have problems in the organization. Even if I don't agree with your way of running the meeting, maybe you're right. Maybe we have something to learn. That's why you're here.

BOARD MEMBER [also one who disagreed]: I don't know. I'm confused. (Turning to the writer.) All right, just exactly what do you propose to do about all these problems? Just exactly what are you going to do about this (*said with firmness and a sense of challenge*)?

RESEARCHER (*responding with similar feeling*): I am not going to do anything about this. It seems to me the question is what are *you* going to do about it. (*Laughter among all members.*)

BOARD MEMBER: Touché.

The discussion continued and primarily because of the evidence presented by the board members the board as a whole was ready to accept the possibility that the researcher was correct. Then the question arose, what next?

The researcher again reiterated his doubt that a laboratory program would work and be helpful.

BOARD MEMBER: But, you musn't forget this. We may abuse each other but this group is durable. We've been together for a long time.

RESEARCHER: This could be an Achilles heel or a strength. It could be that each of you needs such a situation.

BOARD MEMBER: You mean these could be neurotic needs?

RESEARCHER: Yes, they could be and if so, I doubt if the laboratory is the next step.

The board members asked if there wasn't something that could be done to begin to change the situation. The writer made two suggestions.

RESEARCHER: First, no matter what happens, I do agree with your concern that we ought not to leave the executives without sense of closure. At the very least, I could give them one or several feedback sessions about the data we obtained from analyzing their tapes.

We might also try this as far as the board is concerned. How about meeting and listening to a tape of a board meeting? Only this time we could listen to it with a view to learning about how we inhibit or facilitate each other's effectiveness during the meeting. But, I should like to emphasize that I do not know if this will work.

The board members agreed to the proposal, and a meeting was planned to be held in two or three weeks.

Summary of Results

As in the case of Organizations A and B, the top management of Organization C tended to hold the pyramidal values. Also they tended to behave during their board meetings in ways predicted by the theoretical framework. Finally, as in the case of the executive group of B, the board did not tend to be viewed as innovative and risk taking by the majority of its members or the majority of the immediate subordinates.

In this organization a new dimension was added to the diagnosis. The subordinates were also studied. They, too, held the same pyramidal values, and they tended to develop, in their relationships with their subordinates, the same deficiencies for which they criticized their superiors.

Finally, the feedback session in which the board and the immediate subordinates met to discuss their problems failed as predicted. This led the board members to request some help to improve their interpersonal relationships among themselves.

SUMMARY OF FINDINGS FROM ORGANIZATIONS A, B, AND C

About the Scheme of Categories

1. In three different organizations and in over 100 problem-solving and decision-making meetings, the system of categories was used to describe individual and group behavior with an encouragingly high degree of interobserver reliability and predictive validity.
2. In nearly 300 cases of executives, scientists, engineers, and technicians, it was found that the overwhelming majority held what I have called the pyramidal values.
3. Predictions were made about the frequency with which the behavioral categories of the model would be manifested in nearly 50 problem-solving and decision-making meetings. These predictions of rank order were confirmed in almost all the cases.
4. In all cases where the predictions were not confirmed, the group meetings involved issues that were threatening to the group. In all cases but one, the issues revolved around the adherence to one or more of the pyramidal values.

It seems therefore, that the a priori predictions extracted from the theory tend to hold in all meetings except those in which the subject under discussion is threatening to the group members. These subjects tended to classify themselves as dealing with the objectives of the organization, the competence of its members, and the processes of authority, reward and penalty, and control.

If these data are replicated, and they have been in case study groups and groups of university seminars, then the model may be valid for understanding and predicting the dynamics of many different kinds of group problem-solving situations.

In two cases the predictions were in opposition to the beliefs of the subjects, yet they were eventually confirmed. For example, in one case the predictions about the group's effectiveness derived from the quantitative pattern were opposite to the members' view of their group effectiveness. An analysis of the situation suggested that the researcher's predictions were correct, and the group members were (in many cases unknowingly) distorting reality. The validity of these findings was supported by the immediate subordinates of the top group studied.

In another case the top group disagreed with the researcher's prediction about that group's impact upon the subordinates. Subsequent research with the subordinates supported the researcher's predictions.

About Innovative Organizations

In all cases the consequences predicted as a result of the quantitative patterns were found to exist. In the first organization, (1) the superiors did not seem to be aware of relevant interpersonal problems; or (2) when they were aware of the problems, they were unable to solve them; or (3) they did so, in ways that they recognized tended to detract from the effectiveness of the problem-solving processes.

Moreover, data were obtained that indicated that the relatively low interpersonal competence of the members led to an overemphasis upon the need for autonomy, equipment, position, space, laboratory technicians, meetings, and communication. Although there was less supporting data, I suggested that the low interpersonal competence led to an increasing anxiety about superior-subordinate relationships, which was partially demonstrated in the poor relationships involved in report writing, discussions about research progress, and discussions of the ownership of patents.

In the second study, it was shown that the interpersonal competence of the top management group was also relatively low. Predictions were made from the quantitative scores as to how the members of the top group would evaluate (1) their group's effectiveness and (2) its impact upon their subordinates. In both cases the predictions of the researcher were in disagreement with the predictions of the top group. Subsequent research with the subordinates and the top group suggested that the researcher was correct. As to the former, the data did *not* support the top group members' perceptions that their group was cohesive, effective in decision making, and open and risk taking. As to the latter, it was found that the subordinates felt that they (and their units) were misunderstood, research was being undervalued, budgets were becoming too important while risk taking, innovation, and creativity were on the decrease.

As predicted, the subordinates never communicated to their superiors how they really felt, and the superiors were neither aware of a possible gap in communication nor did they tend to encourage openness and disagreement. Indeed, their behavior tended to create, in the eyes of the subordinates, a climate of conformity and slowly increasing organizational rigidity.

In the third study, the problem-solving and decision-making activities of the board were studied and analyzed blind for a period of seven months. On the basis of the quantitative pattern, predictions were made that the board members would *not* tend to view their meetings as engendering innovation, risk taking, and full discussion of disagreements. After some initial resistance, the board members agreed with the predictions and presented many case illustrations.

Predictions were then made of the board's probable impact upon the subordinates. As in the case of the previous study, the researcher and the executives disagreed on the probable impact. However, subsequent interviews with the subordinates supported the researcher's predictions.

A study of the subordinates' behavior when they were leading meetings indicated that they were behaving in ways that were similar to the ways their superiors behaved. In other words, they tended to behave in ways that were similar to those about which they objected in their superiors.

CHAPTER 5

The Change Program

Up to this point all the studies have focused on testing predictions about (1) the pattern of the categories that will be found if the individuals hold the pyramidal values, (2) the consequences of such a pattern upon perceived innovativeness and perceived risk taking, and (3) the degree to which individuals are effective in their problem-solving activities.

A next logical question is, can the pattern of the categories be altered? For example, if the pattern of *own i, concern i, conform i* is altered, are there any consequences upon perceived innovativeness, risk taking, and problem-solving effectiveness?[1]

Using the Theoretical Framework to Define the Objectives and Content of the Change Program

A theoretical framework that purports to explain interpersonal competence ought to be useful in providing specific leads as to the change activities that would be necessary to enhance interpersonal competence.

Change in the pattern of categories could be engineered to go in the direction of inhibiting or facilitating interpersonal competence. I personally doubt the probabilities of acquiring the cooperation of a busy and committed top management group to participate in a change program to inhibit their effectiveness. I also question the ethics involved in such an objective. If social science researchers

---

[1] See Chapter 1 for definition of problem-solving effectiveness.

ever considered harming individuals in the name of research, I believe such research would be doomed.

I make this obvious point, because so often work like that discussed in this book is described by researchers who prefer not to deal with problems involving values, as being conducted by individuals who are "selling" increased interpersonal competence. Although I value interpersonal competence, this value is not relevant (at this point). All I am doing is trying to alter the scores, and I know of no other feasible way.

However, since the change program is designed to enhance interpersonal competence and since such programs, if successful, may be of value in other action settings and in helping us to understand the nature of interpersonal competence, I should like to describe in some detail the thinking that influenced the planning of the change program. It is, I believe, an example of how research and action may be welded to the profit of both.

The objective of the change program was, therefore, to enhance the interpersonal competence of the board members of Organization C. Once the objective was defined, certain constraints emerged about the type of change activity that would be feasible. For example, since the frequency of the imbalance scores and the binds was relatively high, a laboratory program was considered dangerous. A more cognitive and less emotional educational program seemed appropriate as the first step. Also, the board, being enmeshed in many activities, could not find time within a six-month period to leave the organization for a week. Consequently, it was decided that a brief change program consisting of a series of one-day sessions would be defined.

Once the objective had been defined as enhancing interpersonal competence, it was possible to obtain some guideposts from the theoretical framework and the empirical research regarding the possible type of change program. For example, the change program should provide the board with as many opportunities as possible (1) to experience their own, and become aware of others', feelings; (2) to experiment and take risks, to help others to own, be open, and experiment. These are the categories in which the research showed the board to be deficient. Also, since the research showed that the imbalance scores were high, the change program should help the executives become more aware of their imbalance behavior and binds, and to decrease both of them.

From the knowledge gained during the research that the men were highly oriented toward the pyramidal values, certain further characteristics could be derived about the change program. Since the men were highly task-oriented, it seemed logical to expose the men to their behavior while they were trying to accomplish important tasks in which they were highly involved. One of the most important tasks of the board was to hold board meetings to resolve important organizational problems. Consequently, I decided that the executives' interest and involvement could be heightened by focusing on their behavior during the board meetings. This could be accomplished by asking the executives to listen to and diagnose the tape recordings of their board meetings.

Also, since the executives were highly task-oriented, they could resist the importance of expressing feelings by saying that they were hired "to get the job done" and not to explore feelings. If they took this stand, it would be difficult to deal with it rationally since its source is an emotional one. If they would unfreeze enough, they would realize that one of their biggest problems was that they were helping to develop an organization in which they and their subordinates would find it increasingly difficult "to get the job done." They might then realize that the consultant is very much in favor of effective problem solving. Unfortunately, this type of insight is rare during the early stages. Therefore, I have usually asked the executives, whenever they manifest this defensiveness, to continue their tape analyses. As the tape listening continues and the examples of misunderstanding, absence of hearing, distortion, etc., among the members increase, some members of the group may begin to realize that they are creating many barriers to "getting the job done" by their own interpersonal incompetence.

Also, from the research, it was learned that the men were highly oriented toward cognitive rationality, and they tended to suppress feelings and emotions. This suggested that one of the important lessons that must be gained during the change program is that feelings and emotions may have a very strong influence on cognitive rationality. It seemed important that the men learn that there exists a *rationality of feelings*. All relevant behavior, not only the intellective, had to become accessible, discussable, and self-controllable.

The knowledge that the executives tended to suppress feelings could be used to alert the researcher now turned consultant to this critical area as one where resistance would probably be shown by the executives. The consultant would, therefore, be especially alert to encourage the executives to express their feelings and to reward anyone who did so and, in the early stages, protect his right to express his feelings.

Some members, for example, may resist the expression of *some* feelings by stating that the consultant is suggesting that *all* feelings be expressed. If the clients were to observe the consultant, it would become apparent that he is not able to express all of his feelings (partially) because to do so could overwhelm the board members and (partially) because he is unable to do so. The consultant strives to express (in such a way) those feelings that could help him to be more effective and increase the probability of learning for all concerned.

The data obtained during the research also can help the consultant to realize that another crucial area of resistance will come from the fact that the executives believed that an effective leader is one who directs and controls others. Since they perceive the consultant as the expert, they naturally may expect him to direct and control. Since he will strive to do this minimally (hopefully, he will direct primarily only the more routine decisions), they may tend to become angry at him for not leading.

In doing so, the men would be not only expressing feelings, but they might be taking risks, because this would probably be the first time they have openly questioned their concept of authority. The consultant can help by encouraging the expression of these feelings without implying that the client's behavior is incorrect. As this is accepted, the men may be helped to explore the possibility that their presently held concept of authority could act to cover up their willingness to be dependent and to make others dependent. The logic would be:

1. Since their present values require that nonexperts or subordinates should be controlled by experts.
2. When they are the authority and the expert (in their everyday business life), they will expect their subordinates to be dependent upon them.

Exploring such feelings may tend to increase the members' feelings of dissonance. They may tend to try and reduce it by increasing their hostility toward the consultant. The consultant could then help them to consider that part of their hostility might be realistically aimed at themselves. All this provides further opportunity for challenge, *experimenting, helping others, trust,* and *concern* for feelings.

Another and somewhat more rational way to resist learning about the nature of authority is for the clients to assume that the consultant is against leadership. It is not too difficult for them to begin to infer that the consultant is implying by his behavior that he wishes the opposite to leadership, that is, no leadership. If they could decrease their emotionality enough to observe the consultant's behavior, they would note that the consultant is not implying this by his behavior. Actually he tends to direct and control in the more routine and programmed decisions, while he tends to focus on the members' developing self-enforced control for the more innovative experiences.

One further word about how the theoretical framework and the empirical results may be used to define the nature of the educational experience during the change program. In the analysis of all three cases, we saw how the relatively low interpersonal competence of the men tended to lead to few experiences of *psychological success,* to low feelings of *essentiality,* and to infrequent *confirmation.* In planning the change program, therefore, it is important that similar conditions are not repeated. It is important to provide as many opportunities as possible for psychological success, essentiality, and confirmation at the interpersonal and intellectual levels.

Psychological success requires that the members define, as much as possible, the educational experience that they will go through, including its operational goals, the means to achieving the goals, and the challenges to be overcome. Interpersonal essentiality requires that the members experience their behavior as being essential to their learning experience. This means that they need to expose their behavior and then examine it. Exploring their interpersonal behavior can lead to confirmation or discomfirmation. If the latter occurs, then the members will immediately be involved in a challenge situation to reduce their feelings of dissonance. This leads to Lewin's point that most education in values is a matter of re-education. Human beings have to unlearn or unfreeze the old before they can learn the new and subsequently internalize it.

At the outset, therefore, the consultant is faced with a difficult task. He must somehow create conditions for increased interpersonal competence with people who believe (up to this point) that these conditions actually inhibit growth and effectiveness. He must somehow help the members to see themselves as they really are, which usually produces high feelings of dissonance and accompanying guilt and hostility, and cope with these resultants in such a way that the group members will elect to move forward. He must somehow encourage the group members to express feelings (especially those of concern and help) which, up to this point, the men may have perceived as ineffective, inappropriate (and probably unmanly) yet to help the group constantly to keep in mind the importance of achieving a group task.

He must somehow strive to increase opportunity for psychological success, essentiality, and confirmation, but at the same time minimize long-range dependence upon him. It is important that the members define the amount of learning they wish to internalize and the pace at which they do so. To the extent that the consultant is successful he will tend to create the conditions where the members will see him as a caring, competent person who is decreasingly necessary.

A Cursory View of the Change Sessions

Before the results are presented of the change sessions, I thought that some of the clinically and action-oriented readers might like to have a more detailed description of what occurred during the change sessions. Therefore, specimens from each change session are presented below. Those readers who are interested primarily in seeing how the results fit the theory may turn ahead to page 163.

Session 1

The first session began with board member 3 stopping the tape and unexpectedly making a somewhat "deep" clinical inference about A's behavior without mentioning A directly. The consultant became concerned lest the members believe that the way they could help each other was to become amateur psychologists. One of the difficulties in intervening was that B's analysis was substantially valid. However, as we shall see, it made A defensive to the point that he contradicted himself and was unable to own up to his own feelings.

Note below that B responded to the consultant's "reprimand" by drawing upon information outside the group (or its history) which was difficult for the consultant to question. The response the consultant utilized was to do to B what B did to A and then explore with B the learning value that it had for him. Thus he told B that he might control people as much as he insisted A did, only in a different way. (Indeed, psychoanalytically speaking, B's analysis of A could be both true about A and an excellent example of projection.) B responded as defensively as A had, and he began to see how ineffective clinical inferences can be.

B: I would say there are certain people, generally fearful people, who protect themselves against their own fears by requiring absolute control of an environment. They are terribly afraid that things will get out of hand if they cannot control. It's not that they're afraid of the other people. They are really afraid of their own inability to control the environment. What I find in this is a manifestation not of A's concern that we are going to take up his time, but it is that even he himself may let it get out of control. Thus, for example, when complimented, and I can tell you this will always be the case, or when someone else is complimented, it is always important to A that the compliment be limited, or denied, or a footnote be put on it to make sure that it is an absolutely careful compliment, because otherwise you can't control the thing you've just lifted off the ground. I don't know whether I'm making myself clear.

Consultant: Can we check this? Did you see that comment as a compliment that B made?

A: Oh yes, oh yes, yes. But I think no fellow likes to just stand there and have somebody say something nice about him. I don't think that's unnatural. I think sometimes he compliments too much, but I probably err on the other side and don't compliment enough.

Consultant: And what's your reaction with B's analysis of you?

A: Well, I didn't understand the first part of it. The last part I understood and would not disagree with. I don't know what the first part was. I remember, but I didn't understand it.

Consultant: I think one of the problems we're going to get into in this next hour or so, is at what level do we make an analysis. I think B is saying that the reason A may be trying to keep something in his control is because of his own fears of his own incompetence as an administrator.

B: I wouldn't prescribe the fears. I said fears, and I didn't say anything about the business. I am talking about people or persons. I say the same thing will be manifest in an environment. Certain fearful people have to keep things in their control.

CONSULTANT: But are we talking about A now?

B: I am talking about A.

CONSULTANT: A, do you find this helpful? What's your reaction?

A: Well I don't know. That's the part I didn't understand. Let me explain something. I am very possibly uncomfortable with people and so are other people. I mean that's a matter of degree. Some are extroverts and some are not. Maybe that would be fear. I don't know. I never thought about whether it was or not. As far as being fearful about being able to do the job I've got, I don't think I'd fear that at all, because I've got a serious question in my mind whether I can do it. I'm not at all sure that I can, and I certainly hope we can find somebody better to do it. But if we find somebody better to do it, it doesn't bother me at all, any more than it bothers me because I can't play the piano or a whole lot of other things I can't do. There are some other things I can do, and if someone would say that I can't do something that I think I can do, I would argue with him, but I wouldn't argue about whether or not I could do a good job doing this. So I don't see how you get fear. And that gets a little deep for me. That's why I'm not sure I understand.

B: Let me say that objectively I have never, never been exposed to any human association involving more than two people in which there are as few compliments as there are here. The interesting thing to me, therefore, is that A has been saying that what I describe as few are extensive.

CONSULTANT: I guess the problem I'm having is that I happen to have some agreement with what you're saying, but I'm not sure, at this point, that's the most helpful kind of feedback to give each other. Because I think A's reaction might be if he's not saying it, "Look B, how can I trust your analysis? Are you an expert in this? You may be describing my feelings, but I don't have some of these feelings you describe, so I don't know what to do with the information I'm getting from you, other than to listen to it and say well it might be right, but it might not."

B: May I try to answer that? I have no doubt, or few doubts, that what I have said can be helpful. I made these comments in the context of having discussed with A a couple of times this week something which I have felt for a very long time: That A's conception of the effect of management of people or of operations tends to express itself primarily, sometimes exclusively, in two ways: criticism and control.

CONSULTANT: Now, could I ask you a question? How would you say your management differs from that?

B: My view of management is far less consistent. It may, therefore, have less virtue. But my view of management and the inconsistency flows from the contradictions in whether or not I am acting out my view. My view of management is stimulation rather than control.

CONSULTANT: Would you call this comment that you made to A, you know just now, an honest and sincere attempt to hopefully ask A to see something that might be helpful to him and therefore stimulate him?

B: I would call it that. Now there are other important questions. Those questions have to be answered to see whether or not there is even a possibility that this could be helpful: (1) What competence do I have in this area? (2) What reason do I have to believe that A would accept what I have to say? Let me say that on those scores I think A will tell you that he accepts my competence, and I have known that historically, not always, he will tend to accept the validity of my observations in this kind of direction. (Here the client falls back on the history of the relationship.)

CONSULTANT: Assume now, for the moment, that your comments are absolutely valid and he accepts them; from what I hear from him, I don't see what he can do with them. What seems to follow, is, in effect, maybe A ought to go through an analysis or something, because what can he do with the knowledge that whether he is conscious of it or not, he has a real need to control? Let's say it's true. If he then can't do anything with it, he's accepted information which is interesting, but of very little help to him right here in this particular meeting.

B: I'm working on the assumption that he, in fact, can, within limits, do something about it.

CONSULTANT: My problem is that I see. . . . I am now going to do to you what I am asking you not to do to him. I see your behavior—that bit of feedback—as controlling, and not stimulating because the criterion here of whether it stimulates one is whether the man can do something with it, not whether it is valid. One thing that occurs is that A might control people by either being negative or rushing things, but your control over people might be by being conceptually ahead of them, thinking conceptually deeper than they, and they can feel a sense of helplessness at the end, because not that it's wrong, but it's right, but you are operating at a level which they don't know what to do with.

B: I am in the worst position to determine whether or not that's so. My colleagues would have to.

CONSULTANT: Well, what's your reaction? It seems to me that my analysis wasn't too helpful.

The discussion continued with B defending his diagnosis of A by turning to the organizational context. He described A as a highly controlling executive. The other members agreed. One added that all of them behaved this way to some degree. Another agreed and called their behavior "stupid." The consultant, working on the hypothesis that evaluating their behavior as "stupid" will prevent further exploration of it, cautioned against such "evaluative" feedback. This led A to begin to expose his assumptions about the importance of control—behavior which he had just denied and which he continued to deny.

> CONSULTANT: I don't experience the stupidness, but I do experience how binding you are of each other. That is, each one does precisely that kind of thing that binds the other guy from being more of the kind of person he really wants to be, and I think does it unintentionally. A and B may have one way, C may have another, D may have another. One interesting topic may be, therefore, to what extent do we control each other quite unintentionally. You mentioned that this might be unimportant, but. . . .
>
> A: Well I think it's because I don't understand control. I agree with what B said all except the word control. I think if you control something, if you control a man properly, you would get production out of him.
>
> A (*later on*):   I can't tack it all under control because I don't think I want the control of people necessarily. I'd like very much for C to be successful; whether I help him or not I'd like very much for him to be successful. I don't think I have any desire to control him.

The consultant responded that as he listened to A's behavior on the tape he experienced it as controlling. A responded that if others experienced him that way, they were getting the wrong impression. The consultant added that one of the difficulties is that since this topic is not usually discussed, A will not tend to know if they are getting the wrong impression, nor will they know that their impression is "wrong." A responded by insisting that he did not wish to control others. The others questioned him. The consultant agreed that he may not wish to control, but maybe one way to decrease the controlling is to become more aware of it.

Executive C intervened in a way which led the others to talk about some of the ways in which the members were adapting to one another. He shifted the discussion from the personality level to the dynamics of the board. The consultant felt this might be useful since A had shown signs of resistance to owning up to his strong desires to control.

C: Well, aren't you saying that in most of the discussions that we have, nobody really encourages the other person to express or get his point of view across. For instance, all of the pleasant discussions, sometimes we have some wonderful, pleasant discussions. Usually those are when the two people are in complete agreement with each other. But, when they're not, there is little tendency of trying to pause and mentally say maybe this fellow is right.

CONSULTANT: I experience very little of that, at least on the tapes.

C: We have a lot of very strong convictions about what we feel is right. We use all kinds of methods to convince others, and if the other fellow is a little stronger than we are, we finally shut up.

B: What is "we?" I don't agree with what you said and I don't think you do. And D, I observe, is shaking his head no.

CONSULTANT: What is it that you heard him say?

B: I heard him say that we have very strong convictions. That is the one thing that by and large is not true: that there is a set of strong convictions and there may be intermittent strong resistance to the convictions, but there is not a set of counterbalancing convictions which are assorted.

D: I agree completely.

B: I would agree that I have not significantly changed my convictions. I've done something worse than change my convictions. I've not expressed them. That didn't use to be the case.

C: Well, I am assuming that there are changes that have taken place and so forth, but I still say, B, you have certain specific feelings about these things and most of them are relatively the same, 75 percent the same as they were 20 years ago.

B: Well, my actions are not the same as they were 20 years ago, and some of my decisions are in violation of my convictions, and I do not fight for my convictions. Now that's not a 100 percent rule, but a great difference has occurred in that I yield on the convictions. Now I may privately have them, and they may come out with a sense of frustration, precisely because I know that I'm really not advancing the convictions. But I do know that one of the things that makes me uncomfortable is that I'm not acting by the convictions to the extent that I would have 15 years ago.

A: Well, don't we always have to sometimes do something that is against our convictions and isn't that all right to do once you have expressed yourself and argued and made every effort to get two people to agree, but then eventually something has to happen. You got to go ahead and do something, and you can't always agree with what has to be done. In any organization with a lot of people, you can't always have agreement. Every one of us probably at some time or other has to give in and say, "Well, I don't see it that way but if I can't convince you and it's two against one or something, then go ahead and do it."[2]

The consultant continued by asking the group to explore the impact of A's last statement. The members concluded that A's impact was to tell them that they shouldn't express their negative feelings.

The conversation ended, and the group listened to a few more feet of the tape. With the next episode the group focused on how they dealt with each other when they suspected each other's motives. C said that when he mistrusted a statement from, let us say D, he asked D questions ostensibly to understand his "point." Actually, he would be probing the motives behind the point. D then remarked that he could always sense this "lawyering" when it occurred. All the members agreed that this strategy was common, although now they realized that none was aware of how well the others saw through it.

The next episode on the tape brought up an interesting problem of awareness of feelings. The board members experienced A (on the tape) as being irritated. B remarked that he experienced A as being irritated. A denied it. D came to A's defense by asking, "Of course he was irritated; shouldn't he have been when he heard those results?" The consultant responded, "I am not saying that he shouldn't feel irritated. I am suggesting that he should be aware of his irritation and its probable impact upon others."

A responded that it may be a good thing that he is unaware of his irritation. C pointed out that whether A is or is not irritated and is or is not aware of his irritation, he, C, will act toward A *as if* A were irritated. Others agreed. This became an important lesson. Feelings may be denied or not owned up to, but they can still have an important impact upon others. Moreover, since A is unable to be aware of them or unwilling to own up to them, the others will *not* tend to discuss their impact.

This led to a discussion of how much openness was useful in business. Some board members felt openness was not useful. Important data were developed that illustrated the consultant's hypothesis

---

[2] These last paragraphs provide added evidence of the lack of innovativeness diagnosed earlier, as well as some insights into the causes of this phenomenon.

that some of the board members were not ready for a laboratory program.

D: Well, if the others in the group were strangers, it would be fine. But if it were people around here, I think it might or might not work out. There's a lot of problems that you don't want everybody to listen to necessarily. And I wouldn't think they would want everybody else to listen to them. And I would be much more critical of them with just them there than I could possibly be if there were a table full of people.

CONSULTANT: If they felt it would be O.K. to discuss it with the others, how would you then feel?

D: Well, I think what we're talking about here, I think we could discuss. I think it is an illustration that would be helpful to everybody. But I do think there are questions that you couldn't discuss that way.

CONSULTANT: I think if we ever do have one of these sessions, we ought to get sort of an agenda of these questions and decide ahead of time whether this agenda is going to be sacrosanct, because what if a man got quite upset and leaned forward and said, "All right, D, damn it, you brought this up, now let me tell you," and he suddenly started talking about one of the items on the list. Then I think we would harm him and his relationship with you.

A: Well then, with a whole lot of other people around, I wouldn't want to express myself.

CONSULTANT: O.K., that's important, because if you wouldn't, then I think it would be frustrating to them. Say you're in a T group now, and we're talking about. . . .

A: You mentioned I was irritated about something C was doing. I would ask questions of C with C that I wouldn't ask if there were a group of other people.

CONSULTANT: But if we're talking about the way to control each other, and C said, "Well, A, I'll tell you the feeling I have is you control me by asking me questions, and let me give you a 'for instance.' The other day we were talking about Miss Susie Q and you wanted her fired, but you didn't say so. You kept asking me a million questions trying to get me to the point where I had no alternative but to fire her." Now would this be a subject you'd just as soon not discuss with other people?

A: I have an idea we'd feel our way on that, you know, and every now and then we'd skirt around something, which would be all right. If it got too sensitive, I'd just skip it and pick an example that isn't so sensitive to illustrate your point.

CONSULTANT: C, D, B, what would be your reactions?

B: It is my judgment that if you have that kind of a meeting, you almost cannot have an index, a prohibitive list, you almost cannot, and that, in fact, to some extent you're getting into what would be imprudent areas, and there's no question there would be some that would be imprudent. But getting into them and having executive candor facing them would, without any reference to the merit of the situation, would be itself one of the most reassuring things that could happen in this place.

C: It all depends on what happens. If you are discussing a subject, for example, and trying to pursue it, fine, but if you then try to use other methods to shut this person up and somebody else got into it, somebody else might feel strong enough to put their two cents in, and then if we shut them up, which we would, by jumping to one of their weaknesses, they'd clam up and we'd have trouble. And we tend to do that a lot of times.

CONSULTANT: And my own feeling would be that if you had a list of subjects that you didn't publish obviously, but it was apparent to the people when they arrived, then that would be a confirmation to them that this organization is the kind of place that their worst fears said it was, and then I think a week of this would harm your organization more than help it. On the other hand, I also think you have a right, everyone has a right to say, "I'm sorry, I don't feel that I want to discuss that subject." But, we must keep in mind there's a cost to saying that.

E: No, I don't think so, B. My viewpoint is, of course, entirely different from your viewpoint. I am interested more in organizational structure than, as we called it one time, the style of management as distinguished from management capabilities. Style, I don't much care. There are so many different ways to get to the same result. I have had various bosses in my career—lovely fellows and complete s.o.b.'s, I can't say that I particularly liked one more than another.

B: Are you saying you didn't like any of them?

E: No. I've always felt that I've been extremely fortunate. But you get a nationally known s.o.b. like they had at Organization X, he was a highly stimulating and charming guy really. All you had to do was do your work. So I am saying, I don't care how you do it, what your style is.

C: Then you really had no feeling, even though you, more than most, are organization line minded and propriety minded and you did say several times, "Look, you know you do this too often and people are going to look for other jobs." But what I hear you say when you say that is, "Look, do that to me other than infrequently and I'm not going to take it." Now was I wrong in hearing that?

E: That's very interesting. I meant something a little different. What I was saying is, each guy has got an area of his own and if he gets invaded by somebody, well, he will move away from part of his pasture to another part.

C: That's what I heard. That's exactly what I heard.

A: You begin to think of quitting and getting another job.

B: The way he moves from his pasture will depend on the individual. There are different ways of quitting. One way of quitting is to leave and go somewhere else. Another way of quitting is you don't do that anymore, that part of the pasture, you've quit it. You're still on the payroll, but you've quit it. We may have a fair amount of that.

CONSULTANT: It might be better if they'd quit and leave rather than quit and stay.

E: You have a different feeling towards that part of the thing. It's yours, but if something goes wrong with it, you don't think about it.

The next discussion again dealt with messages that the "sender" never sent but most of the "receivers" received. This led one of the board members to say that he felt he had been used as a scapegoat a number of times. True, he may control people, but he did not believe it was as much as some suggested. Two of the board members agreed that he might be a scapegoat, but they insisted that he was partially responsible for this impact. They cited several incidents.

The next discussion dealt with an episode where A had reprimanded C during the meeting. C said he felt slapped down and added:

C: Oh, obviously, he said we were not going to have this nonsense, and I felt that it was said specifically to me, and I wanted to see if I couldn't tie it down to me.

A: Well, I still think just the way it sounded there that it was nonsense, and hearing it right now, I was ashamed to think here are these grown men talking like a bunch of kids. It's certainly a waste of time, and I still think it's nonsense, and not that we don't have to do it, but we can do it and get back to work.

D: Isn't it more than a waste of time? Isn't it positively negative?

A: You might have to do it, but you sure don't want to have to do it forever. Unless it's remedial, is that the word? Unless it's going to do some good, you better stop it and get on a different track.

D: What I was saying. A waste of time, well, that's only time. That isn't that serious. I am really asking the consultant, is this helpful?

CONSULTANT: Could we go back a moment now to the tape when A said I think this is a waste of time. As an officer of the company it seems to me that he has a right to make a judgment about something that is going on. So, so far you'd agree.

D: What I'm trying to say. I don't care about the time. I'm saying the feelings.

CONSULTANT: I hear you. I want to make a point, but I don't know how to make it without sticking very close to the behavior. Would you agree that A has a right to say what he feels: namely, that this is a waste of time? That the discussion that C and he had was a waste of time, and that it was nonsense?

D: Sure.

CONSULTANT: Now, if the next step is that now C had some feelings, and if I hear you correctly, if C expresses these feelings, as he did, an abrasion is caused. And I agree with you, but where I think I have difficulty is your assumption that if he doesn't express them, there wouldn't be any abrasion.

D: No, I was trying to say if we hadn't had the machine there to give you a tape, this whole interplay would never have occurred, and it might well have been better if it hadn't.

CONSULTANT: I have gone through a stack of tapes, and these kinds of abrasions occur frequently. I don't think they're acting. I think it's quite spontaneous. I think D's point is very important. He feels all this is dangerous I think, yes it can hurt, but I don't know any way of overcoming some of these problems without going through some of this hurt. The other side of it is that all you're now experiencing in this situation is something that C or Mr. X or Mr. Y experiences everyday except now we're talking about it.

A: It's all right to talk about it, provided that is the proper medicine to correct it. Not if we're just talking about it just for the fun of talking or. . . .

CONSULTANT: The question, if this session is going to be remedial or not, is whether I have some magic. It is whether in this case, E and C and D and B want to learn something from it.

The interchange again brought out the members sincere doubts about the validity of the session. Although the consultant could not agree with him, he did attempt to support his right to disagree. Then A added:

A: It's good to listen back to realize how bad we really are, because we don't realize it. When I say nonsense, I'm not thinking it's nonsense what C's doing, I'm saying the whole operation is an unhappy situation.

B: You specified what you meant by we're not going to have this nonsense, and C asked you, "Am I to understand that I wasn't supposed to speak?" What do you mean by nonsense?

A: I mean we're not going to have these differences as to what actually occurred. Well, what do you think I meant by that?

B: It's a very clear statement. I'm not going to permit us to differ as to past facts, which means I am not going to permit myself to be challenged on which version of the past is correct. Whether you meant this or not. . . .

A: If I said it that way, I may have said it, but I don't even know what I meant myself because I could get no meaning out of the words.

CONSULTANT: Well, we asked C, and C said he did feel slapped down. Now are you saying that . . .

A: I'm saying C misread what I said, or to put it in a more diplomatic way, I didn't make myself clear.

B: An old refrain of A's most frequent in recent years, has always been that people don't understand me. That isn't what I meant.

CONSULTANT: At this point if I listen to you and B, I feel that B thinks he's found something on which he can sort of pin you, and I do have the feeling I wish there was another way of making this point than the way B's making it.

Session 2

During the first change session the members worked hard at various subjects and produced much data. At the end of the session a request was made for some conceptualization of the process. One member said to the consultant, "I know you are concerned that speeches could be taking us away from work, but I for one would like to have a conceptual map of where we are heading." The consultant replied that he had resisted giving talks because the group had not "worked" and it had not, as yet, generated data about itself. Now that it had done so, he too felt that a short talk could help to provide a framework with which to begin to understand—although he emphasized that the intellectual level of understanding could not be substituted for the interpersonal. Both were needed for learning to take place.

A short talk was given by the consultant on the development of the self, the defense of the self, requirements for self-awareness, esteem, psychological success, and competence.

D, one of the members who believed in control, remarked that in his opinion leaders were born not made. B and C disagreed, while A seemed to be undecided. B asked if the consultant would outline some reasons why people lose their sense of internal commitment and give up. The consultant responded that internal commitment tended to decrease as control from without, as a sense of psychological failure, and as pressures to conform increased.

A apparently perceived the reply as a condemnation of all controls and polarized the discussion by the use of an extreme example.

> A: Well, suppose this bottom guy wanted to handle the accounting by pounds, sterling, pence, and suppose D insisted that he wanted the decimal system and this fellow is a very smart boy and you want him to operate on his own without the controls. Yet, he feels that he wants to operate on that system. Now D's got a job. First, he pretty well has to be on a decimal system. So he has the job of trying to sell that guy on the decimal system.
>
> CONSULTANT: There's something in your illustration that at least I don't want to go along with and that is I cannot conceive of a person with a lot of psychological success wanting to do that. You're taking a cantankerous person, and cantankerous people are defensive people.
>
> A: He came from England. He might have a good reason. We operate in some English areas, and he might have some really plausible reasons for it.
>
> CONSULTANT: But if he is this kind of person he will get into a relationship with D where he can explore the pros and cons and if he has a high sense of psychological success, if what I said before is true, he will be the most open guy to learn. Now if it turns out he is right, now that's another issue, but you're saying what if he really was wrong. My feeling is that it's the man who has a lot of success who can give.

Here is an example of where the consultant missed an important opportunity (an error which he repeated several times during the session and was unable to correct until the third session) to focus on his feelings that the issue had become polarized. Instead he defended his theoretical notions in a way in which he helped to enhance the polarization.

B then gave some examples of the negative impact of tight management controls which implied that A was incorrect. A responded defensively again, but his response was rich with the

problems and frustrations he was experiencing. Also the interchange illuminates D's lack of trust in others' competence.

A: Yes, they do, but we have something that works right now.
John Doe wants to change the compensation plan in X division.
Well he might have a very good reason for it. I am not questioning
it. Let's assume he does. Yet we have change after change after
change in compensation plans, they just seem to come marching out
one every month or two. There is undoubtedly a certain amount
of logic in each one of them. Yet, the whole thing just doesn't make
any sense at all. Now that gives us the job. We can tell him no soap
and here's a plan you can use, or else we can go through a long
laborious method of trying to educate him on: first, you can't spend
the same dollar twice; and second, he's got to get some feeling for
the economics of the operation, and it isn't us deciding how many
dollars he can have. After all, he's the one who creates the dollars,
we don't. He's the guy that goes out and brings the dollars in. All
we want to do is hang on to a few of them. And I think it's a long
process by which, either because of poor management or poor personnel below management, we've not done a good job of explaining
it up to now.

Now speaking of challenge, I am speaking of the challenge to see
if it's conceivable for John Doe and I to get together and both agree
on the same plan. The thing we have so often done in the past on
compensations is that we follow a certain plan, and there's no agreement on it. And that could be a reason why, as you say, they blame
management for being arbitrary. Well, maybe management is. Yet,
management isn't entirely wrong either. And if they blame the
financial side of the operation, maybe it's because it's the painful
duty of the financial side to show them, look, you can't spend a
dollar twice.

D: After all this, apparently there are two of you telling him,
leave this one be. It's all set. Why did he spend this time writing
you a memo on it?

C: Well now, we agreed that there should probably be some
changes.

D: Well, in other words, you are saying it's open for grabs.
Every new sales manager can write his own compensation plan.

B: No, no.

A: Now you're being unreasonable, D, because look, John Doe
can say this. There's been no change in X division for three or four
years, and he can give good evidence that a change is needed. Now
if that is the case, he shouldn't be penalized for the fact that we have
had so many different compensation plans.

D: Theoretically, I agree. Practically, I'm not moved. I'm not
moved because he obviously doesn't know about it. He's a babe in

the woods here, and he's going to tear his pants and make an ass of himself before he's done with it.

The consultant asked D how he would feel about permitting John Doe to explore different ways of doing something that has already been done well. He replied, "It would be quite devastating." C disagreed and felt it would be a good idea. The consultant asked the group to explore if the two differences in viewpoint did not occur because C and D hold different assumptions about John Doe's competence.

The polarization continued with D again insisting that a decrease of control meant an absence of control and guidance: "Are we stopped from any guidance at all for these guys?" The discussion continued with C and the consultant trying to show that a decrease in control did not necessarily mean the absence of control. D then said, "I don't think we are as far apart as we seem to be." The consultant inferred from the tone of voice that D said this to prevent further exploration of the basic issue. Apparently B felt the same way. He said:

> B: Now that's what A has said, and that's what you have now said, and that's what I want to challenge. And it also seems to me that I am also challenging the wisdom in a real sense of continuing with this whole effort, because there are certain premises it seems to me that really are being tested. The consultant says that he has found evidence through his process that key people working for you express one way or another a number of undesirable things. I don't know what they are, but they express them. You do things a certain way. A has just said, "Well I know the way D has done them and that is just the way the consultant is talking." Now if that's so, then the feedback is wrong or this whole premise is wrong. I for one don't have much patience sticking with it. If the premise is right, then I don't understand, on the one hand, accepting the premise and, on the other hand, accepting the notion that the way we've been functioning is the way that's right.
>
> D: Now you've got the advantage over me in that I don't know what the phenomena are.
>
> B: I don't know any more than you do. I only heard what the consultant said.

D insisted that controlling and telling people what to do would not reduce their internal commitment for work. He ended, "I just don't believe it, because it wouldn't decrease mine."

This comment helped the consultant to point out that D was the least participative, and by his own evaluation, least contributive member of the board. The consultant also recalled that D had agreed with several other members that he (D) had become apathetic in certain areas because of the fact that others were controlling him. "You are the best example in this group of a person who has been affected by 'overcontrol,' " said the consultant. "May I ask you," the consultant continued, "why do you attend these meetings?"

D responded, "That's a good question. I've never been asked that before." He continued his reply by bringing up the concept of "propriety" again. This time, however, it led to a discussion in which D began to open up about his feelings of frustration and bewilderment. B added that he, too, was bewildered, but it was not about the concept of management. He was bewildered with A's apparent inconsistency.

D: Oh, if you want me to try to answer it, there are a great many reasons. First of all, it would be a question of propriety. If B wants to talk at great length about his technical problems, I can't particularly contribute and I think it would be entirely inappropriate to wander into that. If B and A have long and serialized continuous dialogues on this and that and the other thing, I think it is inappropriate for me to get into that. And the same thing with sales. I feel that the sphere that I have is relatively more limited and less important than those of other members of the group.

CONSULTANT: Then why do you even come? Are you saying you feel little responsibility for the effectiveness of the group?

D: Well, I don't know. I never even thought of that.

C: D has said many times to me that why keep talking about something that isn't going to happen, that isn't going to change. And I say this is an intelligent approach if it's there. I mean you talk about something for ten years, whatever the subject is, and it's always the same, sooner or later an intelligent man stops, because it's an excuse for conversation. You get tired of the damn conversation.

B: I would like to ask D, therefore, since he would put it that way, why did he not give that reason as the reason for not participating more rather than a question of propriety. Because I believe that it's not unlikely that outside of this room your answer would tend to be more readily say, well, there's no sense, you're not going to change anything. Whereas here that isn't the answer you gave.

D: This is a new question for me, and you have a perfectly valid point. I got to digest this. It all sounds a little unreal to me. I cannot come to grips with the question of how any manager gets anything done. I would not want to be the kind of manager that gets the good score according to this new scheme.

CONSULTANT: And I am not saying you must be. I've been trying to say that that's your decision.

D: Neither do I concede that it's more ineffective than the "good score."

B: Let me say, incidentally, I do want to say this. I hope you [A] will listen to this tape today, because for a reason that I cannot understand, especially since you're again behind having this meeting, you have stepped on me every single time I've made a comment. Listen to the tape and you'll see that the sentences were not quite finished. In any event, to complete the sentence. If you're right and there's a good chance you are, I don't have much patience in continuing with a premise which is wrong. But if the premise is right, then I cannot accept your assessment. Now A just finished saying, but I do. Now I want to know what you were about to say.

A: I think that there is more than one way to skin a cat, and I think especially in the type of work that D does, that tends to fit his particular method of operating better than the other way. If I were in D's position, I might try to operate somewhat the same way that D operates.

B: Why is D in this room? Why is D in this room of all places? Why do you have him in this session of meetings which must at a very minimum throw him off track in his normal. . . .

A: I don't think we have to be so pure that we can't dare have somebody in the room that operates a little differently than we do. I think it's very healthy if he disagrees, that he's in this room and expresses himself just as he did a few minutes ago. I think that's very important that he does that. We should all hear it.

The discussion continued with B making the point that he was concerned because A and D did not truly believe in such values as "openness," and "internal commitment," and therefore he questioned why they should have this particular program with the consultant. This brought up the question again of the motivations for the program. The consultant again stated that it would harm the organization to have a laboratory program that emphasized one set of values and to have the subordinates who attended find that two or three of their superiors have no interest in considering them. It would be best to be open about what the management philosophy would be and not have a program ostensibly designed to develop mutual participation in the development of a new philosophy of management when this was not desired.

In an attempt to understand some of the causes of the polarization in the discussion, the consultant openly analyzed some of his behavior. He wondered if A and D were not feeling that he was trying to convince them that they must be more open. He also wondered if they had the feeling that the consultant was trying to argue them out of their views or perhaps even trying to "trip them up."

A responded that he did not experience this at all. He was not worried about someone trying to trip him up. He continued, "Hell, that happens to me all the time and if I'm wrong I want to know it." The consultant inferred from the tone of A's voice that he was not owning up to his feelings. D said that he had felt the consultant was "selling" sometimes and not other times.

B then began to wonder about his own behavior. He explored the possibility that in talking about D's resistance to openness with feelings, might not he have been partially projecting on to D what he felt was more true for A (and then he added) "or perhaps for myself."

D responded that he felt that he was learning something and that B should not worry about him.

C then asked how would it be possible to increase the rate of learning. He revealed that B and C had decided to bring to each other's attention any helpful comments that they could make about a meeting that both attended either as participants or formal leaders.

The consultant agreed that such analysis could help to speed up learning. He also recommended that the board members experiment with stopping their task activity periodically and examining the group processes to see how effectively they feel they are operating as individuals and as groups.

B then expressed some feelings that he had about D. B was concerned whether D had been hurt during the session. He turned to the consultant and asked how could such a message be sent effectively. The consultant suggested that B and he might explore a few possibilities, then B could try it out on D and then obtain some feedback to see how D responded. B developed several different messages. With his own examination, he was able to develop finally a message that described his feelings about D but did not make any evaluation about D nor did it require D to respond. The interchange gave the group an opportunity to experience one of the first specimens of nonevaluative feedback, which, as we have suggested earlier, will tend to decrease the probability that the receiver will become defensive.

B remarked how difficult it was to give nonevaluative feedback spontaneously, and yet how easy it was if one stopped to think about it. C agreed and said that this organization was full of highly evaluative feedback, and much of the time it was based upon criteria that were either unclear or seemed to be inconsistent to the subordinate.

C then said he was becoming more and more aware that he really knew very few of the subordinates well enough to know what they were really thinking about it. For example:

> C: I'll tell you at least my evaluation of how those fellows feel. I don't think any of us know. I don't think D knows how F feels. I don't think you know how J feels and I don't think I do. I happen to get the kind of playback from these various fellows that give me a reason that I don't know whether they're feeding to me, the other guy, or doing what to who. I don't think today, with the climate we have here, that we can in any way know what these guys honest to God feel.

The meeting ended with D remarking that he was beginning to understand more clearly what B, C, and the consultant were trying to say but that he was by no means in agreement. The consultant added that perhaps the learning to focus upon in this meeting was how to create a problem-solving process in this group where he and the others could truly explore such knotty issues without the condemnation, antagonism, polarization, and misunderstanding that keep occurring.

Session 3

The meeting began with the consultant asking to explore some of his problems of effectiveness. He noted that he had listened to the tape and at the time found himself "selling" his views. He felt that such behavior on his part would not be very helpful, and asked the group if they experienced him doing so and if they did to let him know if he did it again.

Also, in an attempt to decrease the predisposition for polarization, he tried to emphasize that the objective of these sessions was *not* to get the men to accept a new philosophy of management.

Rather, the objective was to help them increase their capacity to explore with their subordinates the kind of management philosophy and practice that they wished to develop.

D said that the most important problem was to get the chairman to accept the new values and "everything else would be fine." I don't think all this has one chance in a thousand," he said, "if the chairman doesn't really and truly go along with it."

The chairman responded that he was willing to go along with the new approach. He pointed out that he was the most fervent supporter of the program. He also noted that small but significant changes had occurred in recent formal meetings. "It seems to me this spells real progress."

The consultant asked D if the chairman's statement was adequately reassuring. D replied, "I doubt if his interest will last six months. This has happened before. You (to the chairman) become involved in some new ideas, but it soon wears off."

The chairman again reiterated his deep interest. It seemed to the consultant that he was not being believed. "Perhaps," said the consultant, "we could give the chairman some idea of what kind of behavioral change we would like to show if we are to trust his commitment?"

A asked that the chairman's behavior be more consistent with his philosophy. C said that he wished that the chairman would not "back off" when he was making a point and C looked as if he was upset or under stress. "I know that you do this to help me, but it is not very helpful. I may feel good that night, but we have to face the problem later on. I don't think you should try to be pleasant or worry about my morale."

B turned the subject to a list of objectives or goals toward which the group could work. They were:

More profit.
Enjoy what I'm doing.
What I'm doing is valued.
My person is valued.
We better understand each other.
"Signals" change less often.
I'm more involved in the "signals."
We are now growing or improving.
I know, believe, and trust "what's going on."
"They" want to listen to me—and do.

He listed them on the blackboard. They were easily accepted. However, the members realistically faced the fact that although these goals were laudatory, little has been said as to how to achieve them.

D again emphasized that he would find it difficult to make a move toward these goals "without the chairman being first." The chairman then noted that he seemed to be a problem for all of them. He announced that he had been doing some serious thinking about this and had come to a tentative conclusion. If the diagnosis suggested that he indeed was "the" big problem then he would be willing to step down. "I owe it to the organization."

B reacted by rejecting this as a "threat." C said he felt that the chairman was "hurt." It was not realistic to assume that the problems would be solved by the departure of the chairman.

The consultant remarked that he wondered about the predisposition of the board members to insist that the chairman simply could not consider leaving. "Perhaps we are concerned about him. Also it may be that if we accept his solution as a principle, then it may be a threat to us."

D became somewhat anxious about the chairman's suggestion and began to back down from his original position that the chairman "be first." This infuriated B who accused D of always backing down when his behavior seemed to displease the chairman.

B's comment upset C, and he made a remark to the effect that at least he (C) did not permit others to take over some of his prerogatives. A heated discussion ensued. B and C insisted that whenever this occurred it was because the chairman "was built that way," and he wanted to "cut in and get into the act." B added that the chairman probably has invaded D's area several times.

The chairman insisted that he had not invaded D's area for the last two years. He added with some open indignation that the primary reason that he entered into B's and C's area was that "someone had to take a hold of things and move the ball forward." He insisted that he no longer desired to meddle in other people's areas. He has realized that this was not an effective way to run a business.

The discussion raised the question of how effective were the performances of A and B. The latter became upset over the implication that he was perceived by A as not performing adequately.

He felt that he was overworked and understaffed. If they really wanted him to take full control over all the areas, then he needed much more help.

The meeting ended with B apparently feeling hurt. He left the meeting with a sober look on his face. D was worried that B had become "too upset." The others felt that "B would snap out of this." The consultant, verbalizing a feeling of unfinished business, suggested that whenever it is possible, the change meetings should be planned on a day when the executives could remain a while longer if it were necessary (as all felt it was at the end of the session). They all agreed.

D ended the meeting by saying, "I am amazed at what we tell each other and yet no one blows up. All of us seem to be able to take much more of this than I ever expected."

Session 4

A began the change session by asking it if was not time for a progress report from the consultant. "How are we doing on your scores?" he asked the consultant. "My scoring system," replied the consultant, "does not give out grades, but the pattern suggests that I'd better be careful lest I make you dependent upon me. I must say, I wonder, too. How do you feel you are doing?"

"But," continues A, "isn't that why you're here? Shouldn't you be telling us how well we're doing?" "Perhaps," replied the consultant, "but as I see my job it is to help this group increase its competence with a decreasing need for me."

"Well, I think we are better off," said C. "I know that I have experienced fewer communication blocks. I also think I'm causing fewer blocks for us. I'm encouraged."

"That worries me," continues B, "that word 'encouraged.' We keep using that word around here when we are trying to bolster each other."

"Well, I don't mean it that way," replied C, "I honestly see changes in A and D's behavior."

"Especially in D's behavior," added B.

"I'm not sure," commented D, "yes, I know I speak my mind more freely now. But, I still wonder, for instance, would you say what happened to you last week (during the change session) was good?" (B had been upset.)

"By all means," replied B. "It was my responsibility that I became upset. However, I learned a lot."

"I'm satisfied," continued D, "that there has been more openness and even some trust. But I am not sure why. I know that I have made a conscious effort to be more open. I am still not sure, however, that it is always a good thing."

"Is there a way to use the group to find out?" asked the consultant.

"Would it make any difference to you to know that I have seen your new openness and trust and I find it most helpful?" asked and commented B. "I agree with that," said C.

"This is important for me to know," replied D.

The discussion then turned to what change if any had occurred in A. B challenged A's idea of change but did so in a hostile manner. The consultant intervened to ask B to look at his hostility.

"I see your point," said B "instead of talking about A let me talk about myself. I know that I have strong feelings about these meetings. Why not recognize them? They're operating in me. Now A says he has no feelings. Frankly, I do not believe that. I *do* believe however, that he believes that he has no feelings. But this is the frustrating thing."

The consultant inquired how C and D perceived A. Both replied that they saw A as being a very sensitive person who had to hide his feelings. The consultant then added that he, too, experienced A as being full of feelings during moments when A had denied he has had any feelings on the matter. He also pointed out that the apparent (from the consultant's view) not owning up to his feelings stimulated the consultant to withhold any very serious feedback. The consultant feared that if A were hurt by the consultant's feedback, he would probably never say so.

"So," said A with some irritation, "what am I to do about it? Can I help my unconscious? Honestly, I do not feel the things others do."

"I am sorry that helped to irritate you," replied the consultant. "As far as I am aware, my motive was not to require you to change, but to let you know some of the difficulties that I have with you."

A discussion then developed on the importance of being aware of feelings. Each member cited an example where he felt that he had been blind in the past. B then added, "I think that I have learned one very important new thing. For years I have been critical of A. He always told me that he welcomed it. For years I believed him. Now I am beginning to realize that I really hurt him, and he did not welcome it."

A replied, "Well, that may be true, but I have found your criticism helpful. And what's more, the organization has benefited." (Yet A had said at a meeting four months before that he felt B was too intellectually critical of others.)

What is hostility and does it help the organization, quite naturally became the next topic of discussion. And D felt that little "clobbering" of people took place in the group. B and C felt just the opposite. "For years," said C, "we've been clobbering each other. Why hell, we have had several sessions at various times to solve this, and we never have so far."

"What's wrong with clobbering?" asked A. He then added a statement about B which B felt was an attack. (The consultant made the same inference.) B became quite defensive and responded with antagonism.

The consultant intervened and asked the group to examine this situation in order to obtain a living picture of the impact of "clobbering" on B. The group developed some excellent insights into how B defended himself from A (and perhaps from others) by becoming extremely academic in content and pedantic in manner.

A then implied that he was not holding back. He was simply waiting for someone to ask him a question. "Ask me anything," he said. "I'll let you know the answer."

"But," commented the consultant, "that places me in a bind. If I ask all these questions of you, it is I who has to take many of the risks. If the questions, for example, are not valid, then the individual can blame the other and not explore his self."

"I'll try," added A, with a smile, "but it is not easy."

Next a discussion was held of the need for new and more efficient financial statements. A detailed analysis was made of the inconsistencies of top management behavior regarding the use of financial statements. B and C felt that A was a major cause of the inconsistencies. A, in turn, replied that B and C were more inconsistent, but it was more difficult to diagnose their inconsistency. B and C denied this.

B then returned to the financial controls. C suggested that the way the statements were handled by top management implied to the people below that the top did not fully trust the bottom.

"But, if we are inconsistent," stated A, "let's write it down—so that we know when and where we are inconsistent. Once we have pinpointed it, then we can change it."

"I doubt this," replied D. "We have said this before and we never have been able to do anything about the inconsistencies."

The meeting was coming to a close, and the discussion was turned back to how the group could be made more effective. The consultant made a suggestion. He noted that C and D had said that A and B frequently "get into each other's hair." "What do you do when this happens?" asked the consultant of C and D. They both replied that they had learned that the best they could do (in the past) was to stay out of it "and let them go at it until they are tired." The consultant asked if they could not take a more active role. Perhaps they could help A and B to examine their process.

During this discussion B pointed out that he was tired of being the one to expose his feelings and behavior. "I have decided I want to cut down. I feel a sense of self-disadvantage in this group because others are not exposing their feelings as much."

"It may not be a disadvantage," replied D. "Every time you express your feelings strongly, it blocks me." B said that he had not realized this before, and he would keep this in mind for future meetings.

Session 5

A opened the session by saying that he had done some homework. He felt that the consultant wanted the board members to take as much responsibility as possible for their growth and that is why he was circulating a document. The document contained his analysis of the report presented by the writer of the diagnosis of the top 18 executives. He tried to note where he agreed and disagreed with the writer. He said, "I'm surprised to say, I might add, that out of 39 points, I only disagreed on 11, and six of these comments were all in one area. So the disagreement is even less. The reason I made this analysis is to help me see if I have noted any changes and to get your reactions. You may disagree completely with me. That's fine. Let's kick it around."

The members looked at the report quickly, and C commented that he, too, had an agenda item. He would like to discuss whether anyone thought anything had changed so far outside the group. He realized that they all felt changes were beginning to occur within the group. The other members seemed to agree that this was a good place to begin.

A: All right, so I would say that, well, I don't know this from actually talking to the various people about how they feel, but I just have a superficial feeling that it's a whole lot better. In the department A, in a way, it's more upset now than it was before, but on the other hand, I think it's the type of upset that's healthy, and I think that there would be less criticism from other places in production, just because a whole lot of things are being done, and they're not being done haphazardly, they're being done constructively.

That's pretty much the way I see it. After all, and I'm conscious of the fact that I tend to be optimistic about all of this, but none the less, I find myself optimistic now, not only in what we have done, but in the fact that each week and each month we are still going in the right direction. Now I'd be interested in any disagreement in those areas.

D: I wouldn't disagree with the analysis. I don't know about the other group, because I'm much removed from it. I agree with what you said about the field.

E: I wouldn't disagree, no I wouldn't disagree at all. What is going through my mind as you were talking, I think from where I sit the important thing is, have we got the new product, have we got the new direction for the company, is the whole organization going somewhere.

Consultant: I would like to ask, I'm not sure that I understand, what would be the answer to the second question that you asked, Are we going some place, do we have the product?

E: It would seem to me that would come from the directors, that's the key issue; the other is important, I don't mean to say it isn't, but you can hardly mention it in the same breath as the—

B: And what would be the answer from your point of view?

E: I really don't know, I would have to ask B and C. My feeling is, not yet.

Consultant: So you're saying, if your interpersonal relationships are getting better, at least this has not been translated to do what you're worried about?

E: It wouldn't be, the time isn't enough.

A: That was my feeling; I agree with you. In my opinion, things are being done, some in department A and some in department B, some of which you wouldn't be too familiar with yet, and maybe I'm too optimistic. I can't help but be optimistic. In other words, I don't think we're going to get anywhere without doing these things, and we are doing things now that may not be successful, but at least we're not going to be successful unless we do them.

E: I don't think the personal relationships we talk about are necessarily better than those which are quieter. I think people are spending much more time trying to get the job done. Maybe when we've gotten out of the woods we can take another look at interpersonal relationships.

C: If that's the case, you wouldn't need any of this stuff. If a guy's busy doing his job, he'll say, I'm not mad at anybody, and I don't have time to get mad at anybody right now. I'd say that the sense I feel, it isn't one of people having tested the new atmosphere; I don't think anybody's testing it by saying anything or doing anything that would test how well the interpersonal relationships are; it's only my opinion. Well, I think that's an important point; I think that now a larger percentage of people have their eyes on the ball and are working hard than there's been for a long time.

Up to this point B had not said anything. D looked at him and asked him to comment. A remarked that he, too, wished that B would contribute to the meeting, but that he (A) was not going to prod B to do so. B remained silent. It was interesting to note that (to the writer's knowledge) this was the first time that a quiet member was not forced to speak. No one seemed overtly upset.

A stated that although he was very much in favor of a laboratory (he was its most ardent supporter), he felt that the organization was busy working on some crucial problems (e.g., new products and more efficiency) and that he would not want to do anything to decrease the "steam" with which people seem to be working.

The consultant agreed and added:

> CONSULTANT: I think the best index of the effectiveness of an organization is that it is at work in a meaningful way, accomplishing something important. That's the best kind of feedback you can get. I gather from A and from C that D's description of the situation is that all is moving forward. If this is relatively accurate, I just don't think we ought to monkey with it and add any new input.

At this point B decided to comment. He felt that although some progress had been made (especially within the board) he did not think that the picture of change presented by the others was valid in his area.

B: Let me, at this point, venture a guess. There are other areas where you'll get some difference, but in the areas of criticisms of common day activities, I would be surprised if there would be a profound change. I think it's also important to recognize that there is a real disparity between that we might feel we have a right to expect and what is occurring. In a number of places the changes in programs are an improvement and that should be an inspiration. Well, the fact is, and the fact on this level, I'm now guessing that for a number of people this has not been inspiration, it has been positively threatening. There is a group of people who have surmised that several of the programs are coming to an end, and they do not see jobs for themselves.

This view was discussed thoroughly and all agreed that the degree of change varied enormously. They also developed several courses of action to try to decrease some of the threat mentioned by B. To summarize, they seemed to agree that the organization was hard at work in such key issues as new products and that a laboratory program would get in the executives' way. The writer agreed. He added that, however, someday he would like to feed back to the top 18 executives an analysis of the tapes that they had sent to Yale to be scored. Everyone agreed that a feedback was necessary. A suggested that during the feedback the consultant might wish to explore with the executives whether they wanted to go further. The others agreed, and E made the suggestion (which was accepted) that the board not be present during that meeting.

D, who had initially fought the entire program, led the group through a discussion to make certain that the consultant was not thinking of "pulling out" or canceling a future laboratory program with the top executives. "I can see the sense to this stuff now, and I don't want to see this program stopped."

The consultant stated that he was not suggesting an abandonment of the program. He was simply agreeing with a postponement.

B again reminded the group that major changes had been made in structure, personnel, and programs. Many people, he continued, had become fearful of these changes. They were wondering if their department or if they would be next. He asked why they were not being told about the plans, even though they were not completely jelled.

A: Don't you think they probably know or should know?

B: Yes, they do, but they know it inspirationally. It doesn't matter too much in terms of degree, but what I'm trying to say is, I'm not ready to tell them. One of the reasons I'm not ready to tell them is because I have the feeling that there isn't quite the precision in this room that might be. I have the feeling that as we reached the question, we fudged a little about the conclusion ourselves.

A: Well, if I had heard by the grapevine that we're going to discontinue two or three of the programs, I would a whole lot rather have B say that we're going to upgrade this and upgrade that and discontinue these two areas than that we're still not quite sure what we're going to do about it. We're going to take more talent and more effort to get done what we've done, but most of the talent is right here already.

The discussion concluded with a meeting being scheduled so that the board could develop the precision then lacking in the plans but needed so that the upper level of management could be apprised of the situation.

A then remarked that one of the values he found in the meetings was that they helped the board think through more clearly some of the implications of, and problems associated with, the changes.

A: Well, we've got a lot of very ticklish things to do in the next three of four months. It would seem to me that these meetings might be a safety valve, or they might be a little oil that keeps the machine going better than otherwise. And I can't be more specific than that, but it just seems like it might.

CONSULTANT: This is a question that's very important to me, and I would like to have few more minutes' discussion about it. I gather from A he feels that at least it provides some assist for him. I would be interested in what others think about this. I also want to give you my view of it, too.

D: I'd be in favor of it. In fact I wonder why did he let a month go by and didn't have another session sooner?

B reminded the group that the reason the meeting was delayed was simply because of the vacation schedules. D again emphasized the importance of these meetings to him and then added that he felt that this meeting was less involving for him. The consultant agreed. He thought it might be that the group was consolidating its progress and would then move forward.

D: Don't you sense that these meetings should have more continuity than they've had? Don't you sense that we're sort of starting all over again? We had a lot of fun in the last meeting, and yet we're not saying much.

CONSULTANT: Maybe we're cleaning up outside problems and then we'll get back to this group.

D: Maybe time has to pass to let things happen. But at the same time you've got to have several meetings in a row.

CONSULTANT (*to B who had been quiet*):   I'd be interested in your views on whether to continue or not.

B: I would say it's worthwhile. With about that much emphasis. Just as I said, I have no reason to feel that we have made dramatic progress. I think by and large, as a group, the group has gained fewer insights in my view of what should be expected from any group of roughly this intelligence. I think this executive group has difficulties, but that it has achieved, certainly not unimportant but not terribly important, pieces of health. It hasn't added up to a significant growth towards health. I would say that talking now of the group individually, it's my guess that only one person here has fundamentally been effective, and that's D.

E: You started with more enthusiasm than you've got now.

B: No, I started with a greater sense of institutional urgency and real ambivalence. The ambivalence is gone. I was concerned with the danger of this process as well as its potential good. I'm not concerned with the danger of this process any more.

A: You mentioned this as an ineffective group, and—you're the first to come up with medicine. Do you have any other type of remedy?

B: That's a very intelligent question; a question I will give a great deal of thought to. I may place too great an emphasis upon age. I think I'm not. But if all of us in this room were ten years younger than we are now, I would recommend intensive psychotherapy for four out of the five people in this room. And I'd exclude D.

A: I was wondering which one you'd—

B: I'd exclude D. This kind of industrial "group therapy" is good any old time in life.

CONSULTANT: But it might well be a palliative.

B: Well, that's one of the reasons why as I said, I didn't anticipate dramatic results, with a palliative kind of effect. I've seen it as part of the scene when something consequential comes up; when something consequential doesn't come up, it shows its attractive head. But the real test should be the other way around. How durable this is in abrasion and under—

A: Well, I think its acting as a palliative is a good thing. If you get operated on, you're having a shock, they add a saline solution in you to help you over a difficult period, and we're going to be going through a lot of pretty difficult things here, and this kind of meeting might do the same thing.

The discussion turned to certain critical issues about benefits and retirement plans. At one point A behaved toward B in a way that would have created a bind. A told B that if he could do simple arithmetic, he would not have come up with the figures that he proposed. The consultant interrupted to ask the group (and especially A and B) to take a look at a bind, as it was being born. A, as we will see, quickly agreed that he was creating a bind and added that he actually misunderstood B and was not being very helpful.

CONSULTANT: If I can interrupt, I think that if you continue you're going to get into one of your famous binds. If we can just go back and listen to the tape, I think what happened was B was trying to describe the situation at which he was shocked. I got the feeling that maybe you (A) were a little upset because B was implying that the present sum ought to be increased, and I too got the impact that B did, namely, how stupid can you be.

A: Not only that, I got way off track because B brought it up for an entirely different purpose, and made that point which is an important point and ties in with what was the purpose and that was what we were talking about, not the pension plan.

This led to a discussion about why binds existed in the group and how the members could overcome them. Because of the importance of this subject to some other crucial questions, it is discussed separately in the next section.

A lull occurred in the discussion. The consultant decided this might be a good opportunity to explore a difficulty he experienced with C. He felt that C tended to hold back his feelings, especially those that were aggressive and hostile. The consultant felt that it would be of great help if C would become more open about his feelings. He reasoned that if C suppressed his feelings and if the consultant implied that this does not lead to increased competence, then C might, at times, be irked at the consultant, and later (if change occurred) with the other members. If he could free himself to express these feelings, he then might be able to experiment to see what happens when he levels.

The consultant began the discussion by indicating the problem as described above. Then he gave an example of what he experienced as C holding back his feelings during the meeting.

C agreed that the consultant liked to express his feelings more openly than he did.

> C: I admit that friction is the uncomfortableness, but I have a different style to avoid this. I admit I could have said, why in the hell don't we talk about this group, we're dodging the subject, etc. I don't approach things that way. I don't talk in those terms.

> CONSULTANT: Yes, and I'm not suggesting that you should, for to do that would be to reject you for the person you are. I am suggesting that the issue of bringing this group right back to itself is an important one. From my point of view I found your interventions very helpful. It also could have been that you could have then taken a next step by saying, "I'd like to tell you some of the feelings that I have about this group."

> D: I won't argue with you on your conclusions, particularly, say, in the last six months. I can agree now. I guess it depends on the way you say it. Maybe there's a form of not making a fellow face it himself and get him to say I'm wrong and so forth. I think as long as you bring up the subject, then you should not go further because it might upset someone, then where are you?

> CONSULTANT: I think what it does to some is it makes it difficult for them to attack the idea, and they go around other ways of getting the point across. I think that burns you up more, because I think you'd prefer to have them be more open.

> C: Yes, but my whole feeling is that people do jobs in different ways. The fact that we haven't been successful, I can't prove my way yet. All I can prove is, get the job done, and if I want to run my method of doing it and being very successful, it is so far, I am not sure it pays to give a lecture on my opinions.

> CONSULTANT: I sense somehow that I have gotten myself into the position of being viewed as condemning you.

> C: I don't think you should feel that way. I'm condemning it myself in this area.

D then mentioned that he, too, does not express his feelings openly, when he sees that the disagreement is a big one. In the past, he has kept his views to himself and has planned long-range strategies to "educate" the other person. He also admitted that when someone completely misunderstands him, he feels as if he is in a "win-lose" situation, where the other fellow or he will have to come out on top.

A and B agreed that they had similar feelings, and B added that under such win-lose conditions he finds that he tends to see issues much more black and white than they really are and that he is less predisposed to listen to the other. E agreed, and added that he notices he is aware when he polarizes the issues and becomes perturbed about himself for doing it.

This led the group to explore the problem of how to give nonevaluative descriptive feedback to people, especially when one disagrees with the other.

CONSULTANT: Let me try it another way. What if I said, "A, there is something I'd like to tell you. I don't really know how to understand your openness to criticism. Sometimes I experience you as a person who is open so that you can feel free to hit me and others twice as hard. When I have those feelings, I also tend not to trust your openness. I should like to explore this issue."

D: But yours is the more hostile.

CONSULTANT: That, I think, is the interesting issue. Why is my view more hostile?

D: Here's what you said, I don't trust you.

CONSULTANT: Yes.

D: That's what you said, I don't trust you.

CONSULTANT: But that's the truth. I said nothing about A, I referred to myself. These are the feelings that I have; this is not an imputation of A.

D: Incidentally, let me say that on one level I do trust his desire to receive criticism. And I may be right and I may be wrong, but I see it dynamically related to the need to criticize. But if I say the latter, then I'm really analyzing it. Then I'm really setting myself up as a real psychiatric authority opening up the dynamics of his behavior.

B: Let me try once more. If I tell A what he is, then I think I'm acting as if I am an authority. If I tell A what he is doing to me, then all I am describing are my feelings about A's impact on me. A could then say, that's your view. That's not mine. But if I say A, you're overanxious, I'm not telling him anything about me, I'm telling him about himself. I think it's just the opposite.

D: Well, fundamentally I've got to concede the principle. I have only two defenses: (1) I am the directive kind, and (2) I am of course in better control of the situation if I play up my analytic skills. I am aware of it.

CHAPTER 6

Evaluation of the Change Program

The Level of Change Being Developed

PREVIOUSLY, it has been pointed out that the board members create binds for each other resulting, at times, in organizational policies and practices that create binds for the top operating personnel. (The interview data suggested that the lower-level managerial employees also experienced these binds.) The board's internal binds were related to such factors as imbalance behavior, antagonisms, conformity-producing behavior, etc.

One difficulty with such an analysis is that it is not adequate to produce insights as to how to change the binds. We need to know more about the processes that compose these binds. Asking *why* do the executives create these binds, one opens up a Pandora's box of many possible levels of analysis. The explanation could range from one that is close to the surface to one that is highly analytical (clinically speaking). Each level is probably important. The crucial criteria to help select the proper level of diagnosis are the purpose and the methods available for change (or permissible) in the situation.

Recalling the definition of competence, we may state that competence will tend to increase as the board members (1) are aware of the binds that they cause for each other (2) and are helped to decrease these binds in such a way that the members will continue to reduce their binds after the consultant has left.

The process of change selected in this case is the one that focuses as closely as possible upon surface behavior. The choice is made primarily to experiment and to see how valuable such a level of understanding can be in helping to bring about changes. This means that the analysis should focus as closely as possible on the relatively conscious (and, at most, preconscious factors) as well as on group factors. One might characterize the process as therapy in "width" rather than in depth.

This relatively surface emphasis is not chosen because of some hostility to the more clinical methods. These are deemed as important change processes. Indeed, later on the writer will argue that they could be used with profit in this case. We are interested to ascertain how much change can be made in human binds in a relatively short time and with minimal use of clinical concepts. In other words, the focus herein is to experiment with the feasability of change methods that require the subject to become aware of that behavior which his colleagues, the consultant, or he can describe without resorting to clinical concepts (that will take him away from behavior he can "see"; behavior in the here and now; behavior in his immediate intuitive awareness).

Perhaps an example can help to clarify these admittedly fuzzy distinctions. Let us describe some of the binds, utilizing as few evaluations and clinical concepts as possible. For the sake of illustration, a frequently observed bind between A and B is selected.

1.0.   A can be observed frequently antagonizing B by saying something to B that is perceived by B as "needling": for example, questioning his competence. "Look here," said A to B, "anyone who can do simple arithmetic would realize that. . . ."
1.1.   B responds by fighting. B's way of fighting back is to utilize his extremely high capacity to verbalize and intellectualize. B's favorite tactic is to show A where he missed five important points and where his logic is faulty.
1.2.   A becomes increasingly upset as the "barrage of logic" finds its mark. He tends to counteract by:[1]
1.21.   Remaining silent but by manifesting a sense of being flustered and becoming red-faced, and/or
1.22.   Insisting that his logic *is* sound even though he doesn't express it in "highfalutin language" as does B.
1.3.   B pushes harder (presumably to make A admit he is wrong)

---

[1] We will discuss some reasons why A becomes upset in a moment. At this point we are trying to remain as closely as possible on the descriptive level.

by continuing his "barrage of logic" or implying that A cannot see his errors because he is upset.

1.31.   If B continues the "barrage of logic," A responds by continued 1.21 behavior (silence and/or condemning intellectual behavior).

1.32.   If B then tries to show A that he (A) is upset, A responds by insisting that he is not; for example, "The point you are making is so simple, why anyone can see it. Why should I be upset?"

1.4.   B responds by pushing harder as described in 1.1 (more fighting through intellectualizing).

1.5.   A eventually reaches his breaking point, and he too begins to shout and fight.

1.6.   At this point, C, D, and E may be observed withdrawing until A and B wear each other out.

Once A and B place the bind into orbit, it becomes repetitive and channeled. It acts to distort reality for A and B, and to make them less effective in terms of understanding and cooperating with each other.

These are the kinds of behavior patterns that Kubie[2] has identified as being the basis for neurotic relationships and that Kroeber[3] had shown will not tend to help the individuals cope with problems competently.

Kroeber also points out that this kind of defensive behavior involves, and is tied up with, relatively "deeper" factors of which the actors are usually not aware. This leads to another level of explanation of the bind above which could also be valid. (Although no clinical study was made of either A or B, some data were obtained during the course of observation that illustrated the plausibility of the relevance of deeper clinical factors.)

There are some data to suggest that B may have strong unconscious dependency needs which lead him to fight authority. His fight reaction might be ascribed to his being counterdependent.

A, on the other hand, has provided evidence that he wished that he were more articulate, logical, analytical, and verbally facile. He has tended to become defensive when someone points up his limitations in this area. One might speculate that A is attracted to B

---

[2] Lawrence S. Kubie, *The Neurotic Distortion of the Creative Process* (Lawrence, Kansas; University of Kansas, 1958).

[3] Theodore C. Kroeber, "Coping Functions of the Ego Mechanisms," in Robert W. White (ed.), *A Study of Lives* (New York: Atherton Press, 1963), pp. 183–85.

partially because of his anxieties about his own lack of articulateness and logical ability.

A also constantly denies feelings. Such denial might be related to a mistrust of his own competence to deal with feelings. If so, this could help to explain why one of his reactions to B is to deny his own feelings of being upset. B, on the other hand, would remain in this binding relationship because of his needs to fight and to win.

One might also speculate further that winning from an individual who admits he is not as competent in verbal argumentation as he wishes will not tend to provide B with much sense of success (because A would not be a real challenge). Such victories are hollow and can lead B eventually to feel hostile toward himself for "getting tied up with such an intellectually inferior guy"; but B will project these feelings by focusing upon, and becoming antagonistic toward, A for his "obvious intellectual limitations." A, also being a projector of his feelings, may attempt to protect himself from his own aggression toward himself (for not being intellectually superior) by becoming hostile toward B for his "constant intellectualizing." Such latent hostile feelings could provide part of the motivation for the imbalance behavior they manifest toward each other.

Both levels of description of the binds just presented may be valid. Change on either level would bring different results. The deeper level would presumably help A and B to become aware of the probable psychological causes of their behavior. But, in order to do so, psychotherapy of some kind would probably be needed.

There is a question whether understanding at this level is necessary for the effective functioning of the executives within the organization. Without data one can only guess. In the writer's opinion, B's intellectual capacity and A's administrative realism may well complement each other and offer the organization two sets of skills that would be hard to find in one individual in such large amounts.

If some of the rigid, compelling, blinding aspects of these binds could be reduced, then organizational effectiveness might be increased without the necessity for long and costly psychotherapy. This is the strategy that has been utilized in this study. It seems to have some small measure of success. Thus A and B, listening to their binds became more aware of them. Next, by realizing that each created binds to protect himself and that neither desired to hurt the other, the animosity toward each other was reduced somewhat and the willingness to identify future binds (when they occurred) tended to increase. We have seen a few examples where A and B have succeeded in identifying several binds after they have occurred. The reader may recall that in the fifth change session, A stated that he would have stopped the bind he created for B if the consultant had not done so. B responded that this was encouraging to hear and that he hoped he could do the same when he created one. In one case (not observed but reported by A), A and B began to identify their bind as it was being created and then stopped it before it went into their compulsive orbit.

Another source for change was A's and B's deep sense of responsibility for the organization's effectiveness. This is what Charlotte Buhler has called people's "constructive intent."[4] In the writer's experience, it is motivation of this type that probably "coerced" A and B to see themselves differently. Even though it was somewhat of a painful process, they were willing to experience the pain because they believed the change would help the organization.

Finally, success in decreasing the imbalance behavior seemed to have been another factor in motivating further learning and change. Some data have already been presented to show quantitatively that the imbalance has been reduced. This reduction, the Board members have reported, has helped them realize that binds *can* be corrected.

It would be interesting to speculate how lasting the changes could be with this less clinical approach. The writer wonders if this more cognitive-oriented therapy can actually have the potential of psychotherapy. As one of the board members stated, "I feel some of us have made some changes, but how many of these fall apart under pressure and stress?" But, one might ask, isn't this somewhat true of changes developed through psychotherapy?

Another important dimension that should not be overlooked is that the other members of the board have also participated in the change process. As a result, they have decreased the degree to which they withdraw when a bind occurs between A and B. They, too, are now more hopeful of being able to help stop the bind

---

[4] Charlotte Buhler, *Values in Psychotherapy* (New York: Free Press of Glencoe, 1962), pp. 36–39.

before it becomes too deep. Thus A and B are supported in their attempts to change.

Moreover, C, D, and E are involved in their own binds with one another and with A and B. Thus C has learned to adapt to fighting by withdrawal and refusal to deal openly with negative feelings. This withdrawal is accompanied by a "remarkable skill" (to quote A) "to keep people happy and contented. Everybody loves him and we need him for that."

Such a comment again illustrates the relationship between the interpersonal binds and organizational effectiveness. Thus it may be that the organization needs C because as a "nice, warm executive," he may help to counteract the more aggressive and pressure-oriented behavior of A and B. However, a clinician would probably argue that "overloving," "overfriendly" people like C can cause other types of problems. For example, their subordinates may tend not to communicate negative feelings to them lest they be hurt.

In this case, not only are the subordinates somewhat hesitant, but so are the board members. They reported that there were a number of times that they wished C were more aggressive and forceful, but they hesitated to state this too forcefully lest it disrupt their working relationship. In the eyes of the board members, C was needed as an "organizational smoother."

Interestingly, the board members began to reduce their fear of hurting C during the change sessions. During these sessions, there were moments when C was on the receiving end of some strongly emotional and somewhat negative feedback. In one case, the feedback was so strong that the other members became concerned when he left the room hurriedly. Actually, C left simply because he had another appointment (which he had announced at the beginning of the meeting). The other board members saw that C weathered the feedback quite effectively. Indeed, it became clear that C's major concern was that he began to see more clearly that others perceived him as being weaker than he perceived himself to be!

To summarize, the change process that we have been describing has as one of its objectives the identification and reduction of binds through the help, initially of the consultant, and later of the board members. Although the changes are not as deep as those that may be obtained from psychotherapy, we are encouraged to believe that they can lead to some increased individual and organizational effectiveness. This, in turn, may provide an emotional uplift to executives who feel a deep sense of commitment to, and responsibility for, the organization.

Although the change process lacks in giving the individual clinical insights into the causes of his behavior (so that he can hopefully become more self-corrective sooner and in different situations), it has the advantage of drawing upon the support for change available to each member from his fellow board members. This may mean that the changes developed may tend to be more specific to the situation (although learning may eventually generalize somewhat to other situations if the board members continue to help one another).

Some Difficulties Encountered during the Change Sessions

Even a cursory reading of the anectodal material illustrates the often-made assertion that reality is far more complex than practice and practice, in turn, tends to be ahead of theory. Looking back upon the change sessions, at least four problems were encountered that I had much difficulty in trying to resolve. Indeed, I doubt if I succeeded, even partially, in any of the four problem areas.

Many and Multilevel Episodes

The reader may recall that the first step was for each person to hear himself and the group in a way that was, for him, new and different. It was hoped that this would lead each executive to take a new look at (1) the unintended messages that he was communicating to the others, (2) the actual and unintended impact he was having upon the others, (3) the reaction others had toward him, and (4) how all these factors influenced the group dynamics that lead to the kind of quantitative patterns plus their concomitant "states" (mistrust, lack of creativity) that have already been described.

The process of learning from the tapes involved (1) listening to one's self and others, (2) "stopping" the episode in question for as long as necessary to explore all the issues that each individual felt were important, which would (3) shift the activity from "listening and talking about the tapes" to the activity (4) of listening and talking to each other as they tried to help each other understand the behavior on the tapes.

Thus, every episode on the tape that was examined immediately formed another episode of a "here and now" quality: namely, talking about what one was trying to learn from the tape. The richness of an episode and how it can lead to other episodes can be attested by the following examples. The first change session lasted 3½ hours yet only 6 minutes of a tape had been played. In the second session which lasted 4½ hours, the tape was played for a total of 12 minutes.

Another type of episode also developed during the discussion. It was related to the organizational context in which the board worked. For example, A listened to the tape and realized that he, in a given episode, blocked B. The tape was stopped, and he asked B how he felt about the episode. B told him he felt blocked. A responded, "This may sound odd to you, but until now, I never realized that I did that to you." B responded, "That's hard to believe because you do this to me all the time." A replied (with surprise) "Really? Can you give me a few examples?" B gave several "organizational examples" with others adding a few more. This moved A to talk about those "organizational situations" to justify his behavior.

Preventing Learning by Generating Too Many Episodes

The fact that a change session usually contained, at least, three different levels of episodes rich with learning potential, and all inducing a high degree of involvement, complicated the problem of learning. Any one episode was rich enough to focus upon. With three levels it was possible for the members to jump from one level to another without working through any single problem, thereby delaying a systematic understanding of their problems. Indeed, it was possible that the indiscriminate or compulsive creation of episodes could become an indication of the defensiveness of the members. Each might feel it necessary to defend his behavior by drawing upon episodes from the "organizational context." It was also possible that the proliferation of episodes could be an (unconscious) strategy to prevent growth.

One of the difficulties experienced by the writer was to ascertain when he should intervene to stop the further creation of episodes and to help group members "work" on those already generated. It was especially difficult to "cut off" the episodes related to the organizational context because therein lay what in the minds of the board were the "real" problems. Moreover, the writer frequently became personally involved by the richness of the data that each episode provided about the organization. His research interests "seduced" him into listening and at times encouraged the men to add more data. This was especially obvious when the episode "confirmed" a research hunch held by the writer. The need to have my views confirmed sometimes got in the way of my being helpful.

The Relatively Low Interpersonal Competence of the Board

Complicating the picture further were the dynamics of the *group* already described. When the members began to discuss the episodes, the group *process* was full of *conformity, antagonism,* and *mistrust* which led to the already described defensiveness and lack of innovativeness which were serious blocks to learning. Initially, therefore, the group tended to develop a milieu which did not facilitate learning in a session designed for them to learn.

Whenever the consultant felt he could intervene to get the members to look at what they were doing to each other, he did so. But this turned out to be much more difficult than was initially expected. Many times I had to "break into" the men's discussion of organizational problems because the milieu that was being developed did not help anyone to listen, much less learn. However, the very act of intervening tended to place the writer in the situation of creating *conformity* and *antagonism.* The consultant found himself, at times, "helping" by using the same behavior that he was asking the board members to reexamine.

The Limitations of the Consultant

This leads to the final complicating factor: namely, the writer as the consultant. The consultant perceived himself as being somewhat competent in helping people in the personality, interpersonal level as well as on the organizational level. These competences (granting for the moment that they existed) became a problem for two reasons. First, the consultant did not have an adequate theory of change to help him decide when to intervene and at what level. Second, since he perceived himself as being competent, he tended to intervene whenever he heard something which sounded "exciting," and, from his view, "loaded with learning potential."

As the writer listened to the tapes and analyzed his own behavior, he concluded that, at the outset, his interventions seemed random. The interventions tended to be situationally caused and in response to some comment by a board member. Consequently, the interventions were, in some way, "controlled" by the members. One could ask, who was guiding whom!

Another difficulty caused by the consultant was his predisposition to make "clinical inferences" about members' behavior. An analysis of the tapes suggested two results of these interventions. At best they were "accepted" by the board members as "interesting hypotheses." ("You may be right, but I don't see myself that way.") At worst, the board members felt either "stopped" and thus dependent upon the consultant or called upon to defend themselves with long speeches about how little the consultant really knew about them (which was true).

The second problem with the clinical interventions was that they tended to be made by the consultant when he was confirming to himself an hypothesis held about a board member *or* when he felt frustrated and ineffective in helping the members. Little learning developed under the first condition, because the hypothesis was his, not the board members'. Moreover, it was based on a complicated clinical theory which was unknown to the client, and thus he could not make much sense from it.

Little learning also developed under the second condition. Indeed, if the analysis is correct, the consultant probably created some anxieties in the clients. Imagine how the client must feel if he begins to realize that the consultant will defend himself by "giving" the client the "clinical medicine" when the consultant is being defensive. Is this medicine or is it a smoke screen? If it is the former (the client may continue), I can't give it to my people. If it is the latter, is this the kind of help that I need?[5]

A Quantitative Analysis of the Change Sessions

Each change session was scored in order to see what changes, if any, took place during the change sessions. The results are presented in Table 6–1. They are also presented in Graph 6–1 on page 173.

---

[5] This does *not* necessarily argue against the more clinical interventions done by a competent therapist under different conditions, such as longer group psychotherapy sessions where these problems might be worked through.

The first conclusion is that, in line with the expectations, the scores became worse before they became better. This was expected because openness and feelings had been pent up and unexpressed: (1) the expression of feelings due to the low interpersonal compe-

TABLE 6–1

Change Sessions
(Without Consultant)

	1 $n = 132*$		2 $n = 139$		3 $n = 139$		4 $n = 142$		5 $n = 143$	
	n	%	n	%	n	%	n	%	n	%
own i	88	66	82	361	100	71	86	61	111	63
own f	2	02	8	06	1	01	5	04	1	01
concern i	51	39	48	34	52	37	93	65	104	70
concern f	2	02	5	04	1	01	4	03	—	—
conform i	32	24	26	18	41	29	10	07	17	11
conform f	—	—	—	—	1	01	—	—	—	—
open i	26	20	31	22	23	16	28	20	23	16
open f	—	—	1	01	—	—	—	—	—	—
antagonism i	44	33	42	29	43	30	26	18	2	01
antagonism f	—	—	2	01	—	—	1	01	—	—
not help own i	12	09	9	06	12	08	2	02	5	04
not help own f	—	—	—	—	—	—	—	—	—	—
experiment i	1	01	4	03	1	01	—	—	—	—
experiment f	—	—	1	01	—	—	2	02	—	—
trust i	1	01	3	02	2	02	—	—	—	—
trust f	—	—	2	02	—	—	2	02	—	—
help own i	1	01	1	01	—	—	2	02	8	06
help own f	—	—	1	01	—	—	—	—	15	10
individuality i	5	04	7	05	1	01	10	07	—	—
individuality f	—	—	—	—	—	—	—	—	—	—
not open i	—	—	1	01	—	—	—	—	—	—
not open f	—	—	—	—	—	—	—	—	—	—
not own i	—	—	—	—	1	01	—	—	—	—
not own f	—	—	—	—	—	—	—	—	—	—
mistrust i	—	—	—	—	2	02	—	—	—	—
own i–conform i	11	08	8	06	21	15	9	06	15	10
open i–conform i	—	—	—	—	—	—	—	—	—	—
own i–antagonism i	14	10	20	14	23	16	21	14	4	03
open i–antagonism i	10	07	7	05	13	09	1	01	—	—

* Each number should be doubled because two levels are included. Each level has its own percentages.

tence tended to be awkward, and (2) the initial expression of hostility and aggression toward the consultant, and later one another, tended to increase the minus behavior (e.g., *antagonism* and *not helping others*).

The second conclusion is that the imbalance behavior did decrease as expected. This was expected, in spite of the predicted initial difficulty, because if the change sessions were helpful, the hostility would become more open and less indirect, thereby decreasing the imbalance scores.

Comparing the last two sessions with the first three, we note that *concern* and *individuality* increased in the last two sessions. The difference is statistically significant at the 0.004 level.[6] *Conform i* and *antagonism i* decreased. This is statistically significant at the 0.001 level. *Not helping others to own* also decreased, and the decrease is significant at 0.0001 level.

Turning to the imbalance scores, they too decreased as expected. The decrease from the first three sessions to the last two sessions is statistically significant (0.0139).[7]

The Impact of the Change Sessions on the Regular Board Meetings

The next question is, do the changes in behavior developed during the change sessions seem to carry over to the board meetings? One way to answer this question is to compare the board's behavior during the board meetings *before* the change sessions with those during the board meetings *after* the change sessions. If changes are found, they may not be connected causally with the change sessions. The change sessions were but one of many influences that must have constantly impinged upon the executives. Causal connection would require a control situation, which was not possible.

However, I believe that it is reasonable to assume that the change sessions were a powerful influence. This inference is supported by the fact that the theory predicts the kind of change processes that were observed. Also, the board had been observed for nearly a year before the change program, and no change in behavior was noted. One could argue that since the external environment did not change during and after the change sessions, the probability is low that factors emanating from the environment caused the changes. As we shall see, this argument is unanimously supported by the

---

[6] X^2 test, *concern i* and *individuality i* are combined since they are not independent of each other.

[7] Quinn McNemar, *Psychological Statistics* (New York: John Wiley & Sons, Inc., 1955), p. 60.

board members. They attribute the changes ("good" and "bad") to the change sessions.

Another word of caution is that I am *not* trying, at this point, to evaluate the effectiveness of the board as a result of the changes in behavior. All that I am trying to establish is, did the behavioral changes noted in the last two sessions of the change sessions transfer to the regular board meetings?

Seven board meetings were analyzed after the change sessions. The first five were held within 6 months after the change sessions (about one each month). Session 6 was about 8 months, session 7 was 12 months, and session 8 was 14 months later. The results are in Table 6–2.

If we compare the results of these sessions with the results of the before-change board meetings, we note:

1. *Concern i* scores have replaced *conform i* scores in the number two positions. In the last three sessions, *concern i* became the most frequent behavior.
2. *Open* i scores have increased to the point that they almost equal the *conform i* scores (in sessions 1 and 2) and go beyond them in sessions 3, 4, 5, and 6.
3. The *helping others* scores increase, and the *not helping others* scores and the *antagonism* scores decrease.
4. Imbalance scores also show a significant decrease.
5. Finally, although some feelings are reported, they are few in number.

One possibility is that the change sessions drained off the feelings. Another is that the board members have "decided" to hold their feelings until the change sessions where they can be discussed. Still another is that the board members decided to withhold feelings from board meetings.

The changes have been charted in Graph 6–1 and Graph 6–2. The first shows the competence scores on the individuals and norm plus and minus for each level. The second graph depicts the change in the imbalance scores.

It should be noted that the first two trends also hold for session 6. However, as it can be seen, the imbalance and antagonism scores increased somewhat. A content analysis of the taped session showed that the subject was the same as the one discussed during session 1 (after the change sessions). The decision that was explored was a

TABLE 6-2
Board Meetings After Change

	1* (n = 175†)		2 (n = 175)		3 (n = 175)		4 (n = 175)		5 (n = 175)		6 (n = 170)		7 (n = 175)		8 (n = 100)	
	n	%	n	%	n	%	n	%	n	%	n	%	n	%	n	%
own i	117	67	133	76	113	64	123	70	110	63	98	58	100	57	69	69
conform i	49	28	34	19	16	09	19	11	14	08	11	07	21	12	16	16
concern i	99	56	114	65	138	79	138	79	123	70	112	66	116	66	44	44
open i	35	20	22	12	46	26	36	21	44	27	37	22	47	27	18	18
individuality i	4	02	3	01	27	15	11	06	20	11	32	19	27	15	31	31
antagonism i	22	12	18	10	2	01	—		—		5	03	7	04	—	
n.h. own i	20	11	11	07	7	04	4	02	6	05	6	04	4	02	4	04
n. own i	4	02	7	04	18	10	14	08	9	06	16	09	15	09	1	01
h. others exp. i	—		—		—		—		—		—		—		—	
own f	—		7	04	3	02	5	03	10	07	9	05	5	03	4	04
open f	—		—		—		—		—		—		4	02	—	
concern f	—		7	04	1	005	4	03	9	06	2	01	2	01	1	01
individuality f	—		—		—		—		—		9	05	2	01	3	03
experiment i	—		—		—		—		—		—		—		4	04
experiment f	—		—		—		—		—		1	006	—		—	
trust f	—		—		—		—		—		1	006	—		5	05
own i-conform i	31	17	23	13	8	05	5	03	7	04	6	04	17	09	10	10
own i-antagonism i	20	11	—		2	01	2	01	—		—		3	02	—	
open i-conform i	2	01	14	08	—		—		—		4	02	—		—	
open i-antagonism i	—		—		—		—		—		1	001	—		—	

* Sessions 1 through 5 were held about one month apart. Session 6 was taped about eight months after the end of the last change session. Session 7 was taped about one year after the last change session.

† There are two levels represented. The total is double the number shown.

most difficult one. It involved the possible termination of some products and the possible development of other ones (some of which were considered highly controversial).

The discussion during both of the sessions was animated. However, in session 6 several things occurred that did not occur in session 1. Although A tried to withold his antagonistic feelings, he apparently realized that he was too emotionally involved to carry the discussion alone. He backed off, and unlike in previous sessions, someone else who was less upset continued the questioning. His

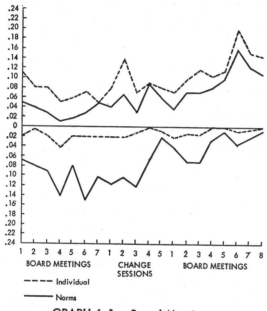

GRAPH 6–1.   Board Meetings.

lower defensiveness led to the "other side" becoming less defensive. Moreover, C, who (the reader may recall) was described previously as passive, took the initiative to bring the problem out into the open (hence the experiment-trust score). This helped both sides to level, yet with less emotionality. This, in turn, seemed to decrease the initial defensiveness and to emphasize openness. These inferences are illustrated by the quantitative scores. In session 6, the *open i* scores were higher, whereas *antagonism i, own i–conform i,* and *open i–conform i* were lower. This suggests that the board may now be more able to discuss difficult subjects with greater openness and less defensiveness. This conclusion is extremely tentative since one might conjecture that the group had learned to deal with the subject more effectively as a result of the first discussion. This possibility does not seem too probable to the writer since the board members had considered the second session to be the one where the final decision was to be made. Thus, one might hypothesize that the second session potentially was the more threatening of the two.

Sessions 6 and 7 represent measurements made 12 and 14 months after the change sessions. The plus scores decreased in session 7 but

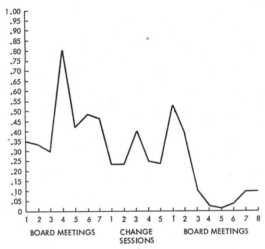

GRAPH 6–2.   Percentage of Imbalance Scores, Board Meetings.

leveled off in session 8. The minus scores continued to decrease and seem to be approaching zero. Turning to the imbalance scores, they increased in session 7 and leveled off in session 8.

These scores do suggest that the changes, by and large, still exist but that the degree seems to vary with every session. Exactly what is the magnitude of the variance could only be ascertained by longitudinal studies. However, it seems that the leveling off that we describe may not be a trend. It may be that the next session could be much worse or better.

One other interesting point can be made by examining the categories in Table 6–2. The highest number of *experimenting i* and *trust f* scores recorded came in session 8. The reason that this fact did not pull up the averages to the level of session 7 is that in the latter session there was a more *helping other* behavior (which by our system is assigned a higher potency score).

In order to test the statistical significance of these changes, I compared the scores of board meetings 6 and 7 *before* the change sessions with the scores in board meetings 6 and 7 *after* the change sessions. The changes in level I scores noted above were significant at the 0.001 level (X^2 test). The changes in the level II scores were significant at the 0.01 level. The decrease in the imbalance scores was significant at the 0.001 level.

A comparison was also made between board sessions 6 and 7 *before* the change sessions with the scores of board meeting 8 *after* the change program. This board meeting, you may recall, occurred 14 months after the change program ended. The changes in the level I scores were all in the desired direction, and the change was significant at the 0.001 level. The changes in the level II scores were also in the desired direction and statistically significant at the 0.001 level. Finally, the imbalance scores decreased, and the change was significant at the 0.01 level.

Validity and Interobserver Reliability Studies

Before closing this discussion, one further point needs to be considered. Since the writer scored the change sessions and the board meetings after the change sessions, the results are subject to a bias. The writer may be so involved in the success of the project that he tended to see more change in both types of sessions than actually occurred.

In order to check this possibility, one change session (session 3) and one board meeting (meeting 2) were selected. A sample of the meeting was scored independently by a researcher who (1) had not participated in the study, (2) was unfamiliar with the results just cited above, and (3) did not know whether he was scoring a before- or after-change session. In addition, the writer scored the same sample as another interobserver reliability check.

In Table 6–3 we note that there is a close agreement in the recheck of the tape of the change session. The difference in sample sizes may be due to the fact that a slightly different length of the tape was used and/or that the observers scored some units differently. The agreement in the board-meeting tape (Table 6–4) is

TABLE 6-3

COMPARING ORIGINAL CHANGE SESSION 3
SCORES WITH LATER VALIDITY CHECK*

	Original $n = 139$ (On Each Level)		Validity Check $n = 137$ (On Each Level)	
	n	%	n	%
own i................	100	70	99	70
own f................	1	01	1	01
concern i............	52	36	53	36
concern f............	1	01	1	01
conform i............	41	29	42	30
conform f............	1	01	1	01
open i...............	23	16	24	17
antagonism i..........	43	29	42	30
n.h. own i............	12	08	12	08
experiment i..........	1	01	1	01
trust i...............	2	01	2	01
individual i...........	1	01	1	01
not own i............	1	01	1	01
mistrust i............	2	01	2	01
own i–conform i......	21	15	24	17
own i–antagonism i.....	23	16	22	16
open i–antagonism i....	13	09	12	09

* There is a discrepancy of two units. It could have been caused by the scorers scoring differently, or it could be that the tape was not begun precisely at the point where it had been started for the original scoring.

TABLE 6-4

COMPARING ORIGINAL BOARD MEETING 2
SCORES WITH LATER VALIDITY CHECK

	Original $n = 175$		Validity Check $n = 175$	
	n	%	n	%
own i..............	133	76	132	76
conform i..........	34	19	35	19
concern i..........	114	65	113	65
open i.............	22	12	23	12
individual i........	3	01	3	01
antagonism i.......	18	10	18	10
n.h. own i.........	11	07	11	07
h.o. own i.........	7	04	7	04
own f.............	7	04	7	04
concern f..........	7	04	7	04
own i–conform i.....	23	13	22	12
own i–antagonism i..	14	08	15	09

even more encouraging. This is understandable since the board meetings tend to be much easier to score because of the lower number of categories that are usually involved. These data suggest that if any distortions are operating, they were not found by an independent scorer, nor by the writer when he rescored the tapes.

TABLE 6–5

COMPARISON OF SCORING BY SAME OBSERVER
AT TWO DIFFERENT TIMES
(Expressed in Percent)

	T_1	T
own i	76	75
open i	12	15
help others to own	05	03
not helping others to own	05	07
individuality i	13	10
concern i	57	51
conform i	27	33
antagonism i	05	05

Another type of reliability check became unexpectedly available. The writer had scored a particular session and forgot it. About two weeks later he scored it again using a smaller sample. When this was discovered, the two work sheets were given to another individ-

TABLE 6–6

INTEROBSERVER RELIABILITY CHECK

Type of Session	Number of Units	Total Agree-ment	% Agree-ment	Total Disagree-ment	% Disagree-ment	A Influ-ences B	B Influ-ences A	Total Final Agree-ment	% Final Agree-ment
Board meeting	350	330	94	20	06	12	8	349	99
Change sessions	274	242	88	32	12	14	16	274	100

ual who was told to total them up. The sheets were not identified as being the same session. The results are presented in Table 6–5.

Finally it was deemed useful to have one more interobserver reliability check for each of the sessions. The data show that the agreement is encouragingly high.

The Board Members' Perceptions of the Influence of Increased Interpersonal Competence on the Board's Effectiveness

The primary research purpose for altering the scores was to see if it could be done. The reader who may be interested in the applied aspects of the research may wonder what difference, if any, did the new level of interpersonal competence have upon the effectiveness of the board.

It is very difficult to obtain valid data on the productivity of a group such as the board. It is even more difficult to obtain data that are relatively objective. It is almost impossible to obtain objective data that can be clearly and unambiguously related to the program. The reasons are, first, the output of the board is rarely of the nature that can be measured in quantitative terms. Second, in a field situation, there are so many factors that can confound the results that it is difficult to develop unambiguous cause and effect relationships.

To make matters more difficult, I desired data that were relatively independent of the variables used in the study and hopefully publically verifiable. The latter criterion became almost a barrier to the study for two reasons. First, the board hardly ever communicated many of its important deliberations to others outside of the board. Second, since the study ended before the next level of officer was involved in the change process, it became difficult to use these men to supply information on change.

Nevertheless, I attempted to collect all the data that seemed relevant. Before they are presented, a word about what I hoped to find.

Following the theory presented in Chapter 1, it would be my hypothesis that as the plus scores overcome the minus scores and as the imbalance scores are reduced, the competence of the board should increase. Competence has been defined as (1) increasing awareness of problems, (2) solving them in such a way that they remain solved, and (3) solving them without deteriorating the problem-solving process. Since it has been shown that the plus scores have increased and the minus and imbalance scores have decreased, there should exist evidence that any one (or all three) of the indices of competence has been increased. (The exact amount of increase would require much more understanding of how the

different changes in scores influence each of the indices of competence.) For example, do the board members report that they have
become aware of problems that they did not realize existed or that
they did not perceive accurately? Do they report that they are now
able to solve problems that before they believed were unsolvable?
Finally, have the activities that admittedly deteriorated the
problem-solving processes decreased?

Some readers may note that in a field situation it is not possible to
relate causally the changes that may be found to the program.
Although I agree with the position, I do believe it is helpful to
present data (if they are available) to show that the board members
causally relate the results with the program. But even if this were
not the case, one might speculate by what logic may it be assumed
that suddenly, after 30 years, and precisely at this time of the
change sessions, certain forces influenced the board members to
change in such a way that they are unaware of them?

Become Aware of Problems

As far as the writer was able to ascertain, the board members,
before the change sessions, were not unaware of any major *organizational* problems that were within their range of possible awareness. They seemed to have identified the organizationally caused
problems. Their major difficulties lay in the other two criteria,
namely in solving them and doing so without deteriorating the
problem-solving processes.

Turning to small-group problems, the situation was different.
The board members were not aware that the values they held about
effective human relationships were a major cause of such unintended consequences as the lack of openness, risk taking, and innovation. They also were unaware of the binds that were created by
the internal dynamics of their group. Finally, each member tended
to be unaware of his actual impact upon others as well as of the
degree of interpersonal strength of the others.

I believe it is fair to state that data were presented in the description of the feedback sessions and the change program to show that
the board members were helped to become aware of the small-
group and interpersonal dynamics of which they had been unaware. If this is valid, then the next step is to see if the board

members perceive that they have begun to solve problems that previously had been diagnosed by them as relatively unsolvable or difficult to solve.

Solving the Unsolvable

The reader may recall that the more important unsolvable problems mentioned by the board members were:

A. *Organizational Problems*

1. The increasing inability of the board members to help less competent executives and professional employees to increase their effectiveness and, if this was not possible, the board members' inability to ask them to leave.
2. The inability of the board and other relevant officers to develop new products that had a high potential for economic success.
3. The increasing number of occasions when the board had been promised a particular achievement by a specific time, but the result was a failure.
4. The increasing number of pronouncements that were made of "new" and "existing" products which did not materialize.
5. Inability of the board to obtain the necessary information to assign responsibility for failure.

B. *Internal Board Problems*

6. The difficulty to discuss and to explore risky and different issues.
7. The "binds" people experienced which tended to cause them to withdraw from the discussions and to lower their feelings of responsibility for the difficulties of the organization.
8. The level of innovativeness of the groups seemed to be lower than the members believed it should be.

What effect, if any, did the increase in competence have upon any of the solutions of these problems?

1. Several inadequate executives (at various levels of the organization) have been finally terminated. It is interesting to note that the board members were by no means certain that the fault lay primarily with the individuals being dismissed. They reasoned, for example, that the environment in which the employees had been placed had not been helpful. However, the men were terminated because the board, not the executives in question, seemed to be able to develop solutions that would meet the new standard of excellence.

2. A new product line was developed which the trial sales tests proved successful beyond expectation. Moreover, other products were actively being explored. This is not to imply however, that the board believed that all the new products that were desired were developed.

3. The number of unfulfilled promises and missed deadlines by managerial personnel have been reduced but not eliminated. The board reported that they were encouraged. Several members believed that they have not developed a clear schedule with which to eliminate waste and unnecessary and unprofitable programs.

4. New financial and other control procedures were developed to diagnose points of failure.

5. Evidence has been presented to suggest that C and D have been helped to become more open and active during the board meetings. For example, we have suggested that both men played a crucial role in the relative effectiveness of session 6 over session 1. Also, A and B have helped each other to begin to curb the binds that they create for each other. The situation is by no means completely resolved, but progress is being made.

There is no evidence available that the board members have helped officers and other nonboard members to become more effective. Nor is this necessarily to be expected. As we have pointed out, increased competence between two groups has to be earned. Since the board has not attempted to work with the next level below, it is difficult to develop increased competence. They do, however, create such learning opportunities as soon as they believe they are competent enough to truly learn from the officers and to encourage them to learn.

Without Reducing the Effectiveness of the Problem-Solving Process

If we may judge from the interview comments of the board members and from our observations, the problem-solving processes were enhanced. The members reported greater freedom to say what they believed, greater willingness to think out loud; increased understanding of each others' position; thereby reducing meeting time and increasing commitment. These reports were supported, the reader may recall by the quantitative scores. For example the *conformity i, not helping others i,* and *antagonism i* scores have decreased, whereas the *concern i, individuality i, helping others,* and *openness scores have increased. Again, it must be emphasized that the board members and the writer did not* believe the board had reached a maximum possible effectiveness. The most that can be said, at this point, is that some progress had been made and still more seemed to be indicated.

Some Evaluations Made One Year After

About one year after the program ended A asked the board if it would consider continuing the change programs (I had advised against this because I felt the organization was busy remodeling itself). The discussion was taped and excerpts are presented below.

As can be seen, there is a range of opinions regarding continuing the program as well as about the impact it had had upon the organization. The excerpts are presented without much comment, because I will make a detailed analysis in the next section. The only point that I should like to make now is that B reports that the board members do not feel free to disagree with A as much as they used to. Nevertheless, it is a fact that the board turned down A's suggestion to continue, and about two months later, during the interviews, the members felt that part of the reaction was an attempt to convince A not to continue the sessions for a period of time.

> A: My feeling is, as I have said, that we have just opened this thing up, and I for one feel that we have benefited a great deal from it. I think I have improved; maybe I am merely reflecting the fact that you have improved. But at least I think there has been improvement in our relationship. I also see signs of not as good a relationship in other places as there might be.
>
> I think on the whole we are much better off today than we were a year ago. I think there is a whole lot less friction today than there was a year ago, but there's still enough of it.
>
> Now we have a much clearer organization setup; if we were to sit down here and name the people, we would probably all name exactly the same people. I don't think there is much question about who should be included and who should not be included; we've got a pretty clean organization.
>
> B: You're talking now about asking the consultant about going on with this week's session?
>
> A: It would be very nice to have the consultant if he can do it;

then we should see how we can do it without him, but it'd be better with him.

B: But that's the step, as I understand it, that should be taken at this stage. Is that right?

A: Well, I would certainly favor doing something. I don't know what. I'm not making a specific recommendation; I just don't like to let go of it.

C: What do you think?

D: I'm not as optimistic as A. I wonder if anybody here agrees with me that maybe we haven't made as much progress as we think. I've personally enjoyed these experiences, and I'd like to see them continued.

A: Would you like to venture to say why I think we have made progress and why I might be fooled?

D: Well, I think maybe you are in the worst position to evaluate progress because if the worst possible thing that can happen is for people to no longer fight and struggle, but to say, yes sir, you might call that progress. That might be the worst thing that could happen, and I sort of sense some degree of resignation—I don't think it's progress. I don't know. I might be all alone in this. What do you think?

C: On one level it is progress. Whether it is institutional progress and whether it produces commensurate institutional benefits is a debatable question. It may in fact do so. I think what A was reflecting, we'd eventually guess why he thinks we'd made progress. I think it's very clear that there is in our meetings and in individual contact less heat, less overt friction, petulance, tension, than certainly was consistently the case. Do you agree?

D: Yes, I think so.

C: It made us a great deal more aware of the extent and nature of the friction and clearly has made all of us intent on having less fight. There's some benefit to it; but there are some drawbacks.

A: Well, if you and D are right, I would say for that reason we need more of the program.

B: I don't think it follows either. What you've got though is a sudden shift in management philosophy. In other words it is more in your [A's] hands now. Don't you agree to that?

C: This I agree to one hundred percent.

B: Is it possible though, that it's a fact that you may do it less often than you did before? But being aware of this at the time that you do it, actually effects more change?

C: It's possible. Yes, it's possible. In other words, I feel that, well, what —— says, someone might feel you could either say that you've resigned, or that you may be more careful when you start to effect change. You should take a look at yourself a little more carefully—now, I'm speaking about me—and don't react to every-thing, but weigh it and try to be perhaps effective. Now you could say to yourself, well, I must be getting more resigned, or you could say at least when you've taken action, at least you're aware it's the best you can do at that time. I would agree with A that if we abandon this activity, we would lose it very quickly. Wouldn't you?

B: But you see, I'm not saying that. Nor would I reach that conclusion—in fact, I have great difficulty understanding both you and A at this point, with your feeling that we have left something incomplete. I feel that we left something complete and can now take arbitrary action to take any step beyond it.

A: Would you agree with that, C?

B: I think we've shaken down into our new pattern and that's our pattern; and we'll stay there until something else moves us.

C: Maybe you've got something. I think as a measure of this, you'll find it very hard and artificial, at least in the beginning, to start up something now. However, I think we're quite different than we used to be. I suspect our discussions are a little more open; certainly, they are from my standpoint. I will say things that I wouldn't have dreamed of saying before, because I thought they weren't helpful. Now I appreciate that not saying them was wrong in that I probably misunderstood the situation. I have changed significantly. That to me is one of the clear results for me.

A: But don't you think that in most of our meetings a couple years ago, half or all of us would leave the meetings frustrated? And I don't think we're leaving this meeting frustrated. I don't think each one of us leaves with a whole lot of things that we didn't get that we thought we should. I think we covered quite a bit of ground and we didn't get everything done, but we made steps to get it done. I don't know of any special disagreements on anything.

C: Something very odd has happened. Our meetings—

B: Our relationships are worse?

C: No. I won't say our relationships are worse. Our relation-ships are different, but our meetings—

A: Well, you're saying what——was saying: I believe that our other relationships are worse.

C: No, No. I think that's an exaggeration. I don't think they're worse.

A: Well, if they're worse they're going over my head.

C: No. They are not worse, but they are different, in that quite consciously I'm sure as hell I'm not rising to every bit of bait that I find dangling in front of me.

D: And I'm not sure that the stimulation that these prior re-lations used to generate aren't myths.

B: On the other hand, at least I've observed that C now is not diverted from something he wants to get across. Before I used to see him rise to the bait, and 25 minutes later we didn't accomplish the business purpose that he really intended to start. I think that's a plus, for what we're trying to accomplish now. I do miss some of the other, but you pay a price for it and I think maybe the end result is worth it.

A: Now, one of the things that we got from the consultant was the reaction to this from the key executives. We were shocked to hear some of the things that they told him. Do you think that would be just as bad if they did the same thing again?

C: That wouldn't change very much.

A: You think not?

C: No, that wouldn't change very much. Again let me say— well, I don't think it would change much. Incidently, one change that has taken place is that there was such a shake-up in those key executives that if nothing had been done, you'd get tremendous changes through change in their status, in their power, their presence.

A: If you don't think there's a change, that's a very good reason for going ahead with—

C: I say there is some change, but I don't expect the radical results I think you do. I'm really trying to give you a balanced picture.

Some Evaluations Taken 14 Months After

About 14 months after the change program ended, I interviewed four of the board members to obtain their final perception of the impact of the change program.

As one can readily see, the board members still felt that the change program had been of help to each of them. All but one stated that the program was of help to the company. The one who questioned the value to the company did it on the grounds that the board members had become "too open." He gave an example of what he defined as "too open." It was when B explored spontaneously and openly that perhaps he had made the wrong decision years ago in joining the organization. As the reader will see, all the other members felt positively about B's being able to explore this issue. Indeed, as we shall see, D began to wonder also about why he evaluated such behavior as bad for the company.

In Table 6–7 the results are summarized from the interviews.

An analysis of the major themes presented during the final interviews by individuals suggest that:

A feels most clearly that the program was very helpful for the organization. The major personal learnings that he reported concerned (1) the binds in which he became involved, (2) the degree to which he inhibited others and was misunderstood by others, (3) the degree to which others were dependent upon him, (4) the degree to which he permitted this, indeed may have needed this, and therefore, (5) the degree to which he might protect others from making decisions and taking on responsibility.

C is the next most certain person regarding the positive impact of the program upon the organization. As he describes it, "We are more open and yet I volunteer less. I say more clearly what I

TABLE 6–7

PERCEIVED IMPACT OF CHANGE PROGRAM ONE YEAR LATER

$n = 4$

I. Positive Impact:
1. More open; more frank; 3
   Openness tends to be skin-surfaced at times 1
2. Less hostile 4
3. Less binds 4
4. Problem solving is more effective (e.g., people do not stray; stick to subject) 3
5. Decreased occurrence of pentup feelings and frustration at the end of meeting 4
II. Overall Evaluation. The organization is now:
1. More effective 2
2. Slightly more effective 1
3. About the same or slightly worse 1
III. Impact on the Next Level:
1. Hard to judge, but if anything plus 3
2. None 1

believe and do not hedge as much. On the other hand, I am less apt to tell someone else what's wrong with his operation or with the company as a whole. I've become much more humble about how accurately I understand things."

B is close to C in his belief that the program has been of help to the company. As to personal learnings, he reports the same as the first three mentioned by A.

Moreover, B now wonders if he had not made the wrong decision many years ago in joining the company. Although he enjoys exploring this issue, he is also hard at work developing what he hopes will be the finest new products the company has ever marketed. He is attempting this with one third of the staff that he used to have reporting to him.

Finally, he is finding it satisfying to be able to decrease the kind of compulsive commitment that he had which partially caused him to be the most active member of the entire group.

D believes that this withdrawal of B is not good. A, B, and C do not agree. All agree that it has been a major reason why D has participated more. D still wishes he did not participate as much. He longs for the day when B would become his, "articulate old self again." He freely admits that this indicates his dependence upon B but believes it is rationally based, since B is the most articulate Board member. B, probably recalling D's comment at the beginning of the change program that he enjoyed B's "art," now responds to D's request for more participation with a smile and, "I will if you will."

The members also report limits to the changes: B feels A is really trying but wonders about depth of change. "A's behavior has been remarkable. He tried hard as hell. I discount this because I do not believe it will last. I am beginning to believe that it is necessary for him to whittle down others in order to mask his own insecurity."

C wonders if it isn't a good thing for people to be patted on the back, even when they do not deserve it. "If you tell people they're better than they really are, it'll make them feel good. Maybe they'll work harder. I know it sounds foolish, but I miss the old pats on the back. If you tell people, even in a sensitive way, that they are not performing well, they become demotivated . . . maybe the problem is to help them discover this, but I honestly don't know how to do it."

To summarize, the majority of the members reported that the experience was a very meaningful one. They felt that there was more openness, less binds, less frustration. Interestingly enough, three men thought (a year later) that they had had more than five sessions.

The experience also helped them to become more aware of their limitations as a board and to begin to explore who they would need to bring into the board to strengthen it.

One man felt that the experience was not very good for the company because people began to question their own motives as well as whether or not they had made a correct decision. He seemed unclear about this because he also admitted that this very questioning has led to the point where some major changes might be considered that could help the company. He also concluded that he was not too comfortable with his new role of being more active and longed for the days when he could sit back and let the more articulate members "battle things out." He admitted, however, that the change was definitely good for him and he hoped, for the company.

One final point. I was frankly surprised to see how alive and active the learning from the change sessions continued to be during the 14-month period. There were many discussions among the board members examining and re-examining what they felt were the results. Moreover, individuals were still experimenting with new kinds of behavior. Thus, although it was not my initial intent to develop a change process, it may be that the type of process described may be worth further exploration by those interested in organizational change.

CHAPTER 7

Organization, Interpersonal Competence, and Innovation

In DESCRIBING the results up to this point, I have remained close to the data obtained. Now, I should like to go much beyond the data and develop a model of how interpersonal competence and innovation may be related. I plan to develop the thesis that the degree of interpersonal competence observed in these studies is low enough to be a major cause of the deterioration of innovation in organization.

The thesis is presented in the form of a theoretical model that was evolved from the three studies plus a review of the literature. Consequently, this is *not* a fully tested model. At the moment all one can say is that it is a guide for further research.

The model conceives of an organization as having inputs, an internal system that transforms the inputs into activities that eventually leads to outputs, plus feedback loops to maintain the system's steady state.

Intellectual Competence Is High Relative to Interpersonal Competence

In both the research organizations, the researchers were above average in class standing and in recognition by fellow researchers. For example, in Organization B, 79 percent of the new researchers at B.S. level, 83 percent at the M.S. level, and 58 percent at the Ph.D. level were in the top 20 percent of their class. During the period of the study, nearly 35 percent of the incoming researchers with B.S. and M.S. degrees were first in their class. Although formal records were not available in Organization B, the technical competence was high, partially because it was a new laboratory and had attracted attention in the field as a laboratory that had all the advantages of a young dynamic organization. As a result, aided with excellent salaries and close to a first-rate university, the laboratory attracted first-rate industrial researchers.

Measuring interpersonal competence is extremely difficult. There are no validated methods and no norms to be used to compare groups or individuals. Consequently, all I can do is infer from the data already collected that the interpersonal competence was relatively low.

First, the reader may recall that the respondents didn't seem to be aware of the discrepancy between the values they expressed and the values that they reported they (would) use in their relationships with others. For example, almost all the researchers spoke vividly, enthusiastically, and with deep conviction, about the importance of such factors as openness, risk taking, internal commitment, individuality, and concern for the truth. Time after time, I was admonished about the importance of trusting the creative people and leaving them alone in their work. Autonomy and self-determination were values constantly coming up in the interviews.

A rather simple sentence completion questionnaire was administered to the subjects to ascertain their values about effective interpersonal relationships. The values of the subjects were inferred from the answers they gave to complete the sentence. They were asked, for example:

To Describe ($n = 250$)	*They Tended to Reply* ($n = 250$)
1. How an effective leader behaves in a problem-solving meeting.	1. He directs, controls, leads and inspires men (about 80%).
2. How an effective member of a group behaves.	2. He is rational, objective and well versed on the topic (about 90%).
3. The most serious blocks to effective meetings are. . . .	3. Emotional disagreement, subjective reactions, defensiveness, inability to listen (about 90%).

4. The best thing to do when a disagreement involves personal feelings and/or erupts into open hostile feelings. . . .

4. Do not deal with the problem openly; use humor, get them carefully back to the facts, ask them to be rational, remind them to be "mature" and keep personalities out of discussion, and adjourn meeting (about 85%).

5. How is trust shown in meetings?

5. By realizing emotional limits of others and not violating them. Courtesy, diplomacy, disagreement without generating hostility (about 80%).

The findings suggest that there may be an incongruence between what researchers say they value and how they behave. For example, they tend to value directive leadership in getting a group to accomplish a task. They prefer a leader who inspires. This could lead the subordinate to become dependent upon the leader. Their openness and risk taking seem to be limited to those discussions and problems where emotions and interpersonal relationships are not involved. How many crucial problems exist in organizations in which people do not have some emotional investment? They speak of self-determination but, how is this possible under directive leadership? How can risk taking be encouraged if emotionally toned issues are not to be discussed openly?

Another finding was that many of the researchers reported that they were not very competent in dealing with emotions and interpersonal relations difficulties. For example, in one of the organizations nearly 45 percent of the senior researchers rated themselves as "low" in ability to deal with conflict and 55 percent as "moderate" or "average." None rated himself as above average. "I never did like conflict," "I become easily embarrassed by emotions," are illustrative of the comments made by the researchers in describing themselves. Of those who felt feelings were handled effectively in the department, the majority had a different meaning of effectiveness from that the writer held. For example:

WRITER: How are issues loaded with conflict handled in this department?
RESPONDENT: I'd say very well.
WRITER: Could you add a little more?

RESPONDENT: They don't discuss it too publicly, and the decisions are made without people realizing that a decision is being made, and once a decision has been made and goes into effect, there is very little to talk about. Very few men have resigned, except to take better positions.

By the way, these researchers, as a group, did *not* differ significantly in the values they expressed about effective interpersonal relationships from managers that I have studied. These findings are in agreement with those of Tagiuri, who reports that scientists and managers do not differ significantly on values as measured by the Allport, Vernon (later revised with) Lindzey test. (The values were theoretical, economic, aesthetic, social, political, and religious.) Interestingly, when Tagiuri asked each group to predict how the other would answer, the replies fell into the expected stereotypes.[1]

Finally and most importantly, the observations of the behavior of the executives provided evidence of low interpersonal competence. In all these cases, the overwhelming majority of the subjects behaved in such a way to permit us to conclude:

1. There was a high degree of owning up to ideas and of expressing opinions. However, it was not shown that the amount varied among members. In all cases, the superiors tended to speak much more than the subordinates.
2. The most frequently supported norm was *concern* for ideas. The second most important norm was *conformity* to ideas. The third most important norm, whose frequency was less than half of the *conformity i*, was *individuality i*.
3. Openness to ideas from others was high when:
   a) A subordinate wanted to learn the view of the superior.
   b) A superior wished to "show up" a subordinate. The superior asked questions in order to show the subordinate the incorrectness of his thinking.
4. *Antagonism i* was relatively low in all the sessions except the first. All but one unit of these were made by a supervisor who, according to the reports in the interviews, was the most competitive individual in the laboratory.
5. *Not helping others* was slightly more frequent than *helping others*

[1] Renato Tagiuri, "Value Orientations and the Relationships of Managers and Scientists," *Research Management* (in press). These findings are in contrast to those of Barnes, who finds a difference of values between scientists in "open" and "closed" systems. See Louis B. Barnes, *Organizational Systems and Engineering Groups* (Boston: Harvard Graduate School of Business Administration, 1960).

because of the interruptions that tended to occur among participants during the meetings.

6. Behavior that was hardly ever observed:
   a) The expression of positive or negative feelings.
   b) Risk taking.
   c) Trust.
   d) Mistrust.
   e) Overtly refusing to give one's point of view or overtly refusing to listen to someone else's point of view.

Moreover, in Organization A, the subjects seemed unaware of several crucial interpersonal problems between the superiors and engineers. Also, they were unable to resolve a major rivalry that they believed was affecting the administration of the laboratory as well as its technical output. In Organization B, if our analysis was valid, the executive committee was unaware of its own major interpersonal and group problems, of the perceptions their subordinates had of the executive group, and of their feelings that the organization's innovativeness was low. In Organization C, we found the board unaware of the impact it was having on the subordinates, unable to make its own deliberations effective, and unable to resolve some major interpersonal and organizational problems.

The Predisposition toward Interpersonal Incompetence

If these studies are validated in other organizations, then I would tend to hypothesize that researchers (engineers or physical scientists) tend to be predisposed, relatively speaking, toward interpersonal *incompetence*. In making this assertion, I hope that it is clear that I am not questioning the integrity of these people. Indeed, most of them aspire to be interpersonally competent. They desire a world where they could be granted autonomy and be helped to actualize the self. Nor does their degree of interpersonal incompetence differ significantly from that of other managers studied (although the researchers' interpersonal competence scores tend to be slightly lower). However, the researcher may differ from the manager in that as long as he remains a first-rate researcher, he will tend to experience enough sense of success and accomplishment at his work that he will not tend to find it necessary to explore his interpersonal competence. A line manager, on the other hand, usually finds that he is coerced into exploring his interpersonal competence because of his need to work through people.

I also should like to point out that the values the scientists hold of (1) emphasis on getting the job done, (2) emphasizing rationality and de-emphasizing emotionality, and (3) control and direction, are part of the heart fabric of the scientific method. Great stress is placed upon the scientist's training to develop clear-cut research objectives and to work on them with commitment, to be rational and minimize the subjective and emotional, and to conduct experiments where the individual is in control (as much as possible) of the relevant factors (and the irrelevant ones in that he is able to show he has excluded their influence).

To put this another way, I would agree with Bennis[2] and Morton[3] that the values of administration can be congruent with the scientific method. However, I am suggesting that if we take a look at the *behavior* of the researchers toward each other, they may not tend to create such administrative processes.

Some Consequences of Low Interpersonal Competence

The next step is to predict what may happen if researchers do have a relatively low interpersonal competence. Or, to put it another way, *if* the participants in a research organization tend to manifest relatively low interpersonal competence, what consequences would it have upon the problem-solving effectiveness and the *perceived*[4] innovativeness and risk taking of the organization?

From Birth to the End of the Honeymoon Period

The early years of a research organization is usually marked with frenzied activity on the part of the research supervisors to build a plant, hire competent people at all levels, develop effective teams, define problems, and begin to produce as quickly as possible. Top corporate management is usually cooperative and patient. It is usually willing to provide the funds it promised and wait until the research organization has its shakedown cruise. Laboratory A was precisely at that point. It was young enough to have been left alone

---

[2] Warren Bennis, "Toward a Truly Scientific Management," *General Systems Yearbook* (Ann Arbor: University of Michigan, December, 1962).

[3] Jack A. Morton, "From Research to Technology," *International Science and Technology* May, 1964, pp. 82–92.

[4] I emphasize "perceived" because I have been unable to find any relatively well-accepted criteria to establish "objectively" the innovativeness of the organization.

by corporate management. Also, it was able to produce results during the early stage (although the top research people admitted some were on the easier problems). The laboratory had just begun to feel the impact of the relatively low interpersonal competence of the professional members (at all levels) upon its internal effectiveness.

The impact of this low interpersonal competence was not overwhelming during those early years (I hypothesize) because pressures were off, people were usually working on their own projects (since top management was leaving them alone and trying to build up the organization). In other words, it was possible during this period to be left alone: not to be coerced to work with others to do a study not in line with one's interests and not to be arbitrarily moved from one project to another. Under these conditions the reader may recall that I found:

I. *The effectiveness of the technical activities of the organization is perceived as high:*
   1. The employees reported a high degree of satisfaction with the technical activities of the enterprise. For example, they reported a high degree of challenge, risk taking, and feelings of essentiality and commitment in relation to the technical activities of their work.
   2. As a result there was a relatively:
      a) Low absenteeism and turnover.
      b) High positive evaluation of the organization by participants at all levels.
      c) Low desire to have one's job changed or to alter or add to existing policies.
      d) High satisfaction with wages.
      e) Few employees who felt that the organization was not facing up to its problems in the future.

The results related to the interpersonal activities of the laboratory did not present as positive a picture as the technical side.

II. *The effectiveness of the interpersonal activities of the organization:*
   1. According to the observations that were made of the supervisors' behavior, they tended to behave in such a way as to emphasize (*a*) *concern* for ideas and (*b*) *conformity* to their ideas.
   2. *Openness* to ideas was not very high, and it was found primarily when a subordinate was trying to learn a superior's view.

3. Helping others, risk taking, trust, mistrust and not helping others were rarely observed.
4. The expression of feelings was suppressed (many times unknowingly).
5. The interpersonal competence at all levels was relatively low. As a result (*a*) the superiors tended not to be aware of the problems unearthed by the research that they conducted with their subordinates; (*b*) when they were aware of them, they are not able to solve them; and (*c*) most of the problem-solving strategies that they used tended to make the situation increasingly worse.
6. There was a trend acting against cohesive interpersonal relationships among the participants at all levels.
7. Some consequences of the above were:
    a) An increasing inability to solve interpersonal problems that could greatly influence the effectiveness of the laboratory. For example, the strong rivalry among certain supervisors between and within the departments.
    b) An increasing feeling on the part of the subordinates that they were not essential (as far as the human side of the organization was concerned).
    c) Decreasing experience of interpersonal relationships that build feelings of psychological success and internal commitment to the organization.
    d) Increasing emphasis on effective leadership as being a leader who leaves people alone.
    e) Increasing overemphasis upon space, desks, files, technical assistance, equipment, prizes, etc.

The Beginning of Organizational Rigidity and Problem-Solving Ineffectiveness[5]

As I mentioned before, one of the most important variables in the research organizational culture is, I hypothesize, the discrepancy between the values and policies of the top which encourage openness and risk taking and their *behavior* which, as we saw, tended to do the opposite.

Under these conditions subordinates learned to play it safe and take their cues from the behavior of the executives. Since the subordinates sensed a gap or incongruence between the top people's behavior and their stated values and policies, they tended to infer

---

[5] The reader is again reminded that this is a model which attempts to relate interpersonal factors to ineffectiveness. We are assuming, for the moment, that the individuals are technically competent.

that it would embarrass them if they (subordinates) pointed out what seemed to them to be a discrepancy. Given the values against exploring interpersonal and emotional subjects, the subordinates did not want to cause anyone any embarrassment. Thus the values of the system tended to inhibit open communication about their feelings.

Once the subordinates decided to follow the strategy above, they too, were behaving in an incongruent manner. In order to avoid embarrassing anyone, they were not being open. But, if they hid the information they felt might make others uncomfortable, perhaps others were doing the same to them? Perhaps what they heard in meetings was not how people truly felt about difficult issues? Perhaps their subordinates were doing the same thing to them?

Worse yet, maybe the superiors were also behaving similarly. As we saw in the case above, the top people did not tend to believe that they should be open about issues that would embarrass individuals. The subordinates might therefore wonder, did the superior really mean what he said or was he being overprotective. If the latter, why did he need to be overprotective?

It is not long before such a culture can produce a predisposition of mistrust. People will mistrust each other's behavior but not necessarily their motives. That is, they will not tend to feel that information is being withheld because of some sinister insincere motive. They will tend to assume that if information is being withheld it is because the individual is uncomfortable in being open or that the individual feels that the recipient cannot take the negative information.

From an organizational point of view, this perception can lead to further difficulties. If the superior, for example, could be certain that his subordinates were withholding information because of some insincere motive, he might tend to feel more justified in violating the norms and become more open.

As these conditions continue, the members could find themselves in a world where "leaving people alone" or "not receiving negative feedback" meant all is well *or* there is deep trouble. It is difficult for individuals to operate effectively when the same behavior can imply trust or mistrust and when it is against the accepted norms to openly inquire about its meaning.

Since open questioning is frowned upon, the individual may

attempt indirect questioning to discover the information that he needs. Or, he may, like a detective, look for cues, especially those the other tends not to be aware he is transmitting (because, being spontaneous, they might be more easily trusted). Under these conditions, the subordinate could easily overexaggerate the importance of, or unknowingly distort the meaning of, what he is hearing. If he sits by, asking or making what he believes is a discreet comment, the superior (who also is looking for cues) may begin to wonder what the subordinate is really thinking and doing. If the superior also attempts to cope with the situation discreetly, he may say things that give the subordinate incorrect cues. It is not long before a situation exists in which people are no longer able to differentiate valid from invalid information.

To make the situation even more complicated, many of the research administrators reported that when they heard subordinates say something that they did not like, they would tend to withhold examination of the subordinate until some later date after they had conducted some "discreet" questioning and after they had figured out an indirect way to ask the subordinate what he truly meant. In one case, the upper levels tended to make decisions about the loyalty and commitment of individuals partially on the basis of the number of upsetting things they said. The result was that some of these men were not promoted.

The subordinates soon may learn that the safest thing to do is to strive not to say anything that will upset anyone (especially those in power). Holding such a strategy may lead the individual to prevent much negative information from reaching the top. This, in turn, may have an impact upon the subordinate's effectiveness. For example, he may pass up to the top some negative information and ask for a decision. Time passes with no reply. When he asks why he has not heard, the reply may be, "You just don't go to the top and ask them these questions directly. You have to find the right moment and raise the issue carefully with the appropriate top people when they are alone. All this takes time." The subordinate may protest the time required. The answer is usually, "Well you want a positive answer, don't you?" The subordinate soon learns from this type of statement (1) that his superior has a relatively closed relationship with the upper levels on difficult issues; (2) that "diplomatic" behavior tends to lead to success; and (3) that he better behave in the manner suggested if he is to succeed.

To summarize: Top management's incongruence between stated values and policies about innovation, initiative, and risk taking and its behavior, given the degree of interpersonal incompetence of the researchers, tends to lead to a decreasing openness, risk taking, and trust. Stability, mistrust, and "survival conformity" (to quote one individual) tend to increase. Since the causes of these problems are not openly discussed, the situation is one that will tend to breed even more mistrust, conformity, and playing it safe.

Increasing Management Dissatisfaction and Impatience

In many research laboratories, there comes a time when top line management begins to feel that the laboratory is not as efficient as it ought to be. The initial cues for this, I believe, are not necessarily lack of technical accomplishments. As mentioned before, management at the outset is willing to be patient and give the laboratory a chance to grow and develop. Moreover, many research directors strive to solve a few problems early, because they are aware of the value of solving some problems as soon as possible in order to develop a positive image in the eyes of the rest of the corporation.

I believe that one of the major cues of organizational ineffectiveness comes from management's recognition that the laboratory has its own internal management problems. In a culture such as was described above, it will not be long before miscommunication occurs, before incorrect information is sent to the top, before the research director expresses some concern about whether his people are giving him all the information he needs. Sensing some administrative inefficiencies, the corporate management may feel that administrative issues are something that they know about (and researchers presumably do not) and that, therefore, they ought to intervene and help.

Equally, if not more important, I believe, is the feedback the top management may receive from the other divisions in the corporation who are the "customers" of the laboratory. These are the people whom the laboratory tries to help. But, from the operating people's view, it may be that the researcher causes difficulties in the interpersonal and technical area. In the interpersonal area, our observations lead me to doubt if all the fault lies with the researchers. Indeed, there are data available to show that the customers are plagued with the same degree of interpersonal incompetence as are the researchers. But more important is that the line divisions probably have problems of their own in maintaining a positive image with corporate management. Consequently, they may find it difficult to admit that researchers have solved problems for them. And in cases where help is indisputable, the customers have been known to charge that researchers really only solved the problems in small sample sizes. They have further charged that the researchers showed little appreciation for the complexity involved when their recommendations had to be put into a real production situation.

I believe, therefore, a good portion of the resistance of the customer may be based upon his sense of organizational survival. He cannot admit that he needs too much help. Moreover, it is to his benefit to show that any new design conceived by the researchers could never be put into production if it were not for the skill of the line people.

> 1. Our customers have people whose primary job is to evaluate research efforts. These people have to come up with a negative evaluation once in a while. What else can they do? Obviously they can't say that they're wholly in favor of everything that is going on, otherwise what would be the point of their job.
> 2. Many times I think that they don't understand what's going on and they're shortsighted.

Feelings such as these irritate the researcher. But, as we have seen, neither he nor the customer tends to be competent to deal with feelings—especially negative ones. The magnitude of the problem may be illustrated by one laboratory where 83 percent of the engineers and 75 percent of the research managers reported a lack of cooperation and trust between research and plant people. They placed the fault largely on the plant people. For example:

> 1. The biggest problem, I think, is that the man at the plant feels that he will look foolish in the eyes of his boss if something new comes out that he hadn't thought of. Also, many people at the plants are afraid to change anything. If they upset things, then somebody will get on their ass. Also, there are people who try to create a sense of completeness in their plant by implying that everything that's

being done in their plant is perfect, and this leads to a feeling of nothing's good that isn't invented in the plant.

As research costs increase, corporate expectations remain unfulfilled, research output in terms of usable new ideas decreases (because the more difficult problems are being tackled), and the top management may turn to an evaluation of the research organization. Usually, corporate management turns to the line or customer divisions and asks for their evaluation. In many cases the line divisions may have been waiting just for such an opportunity. They have probably been charged for the research in their budget, yet they may have had little to say about its content. Many of them may be disappointed in the research laboratory, probably because their expectations were unrealistic. They were not exposed to the top corporate deliberations where expert scientists cautioned the top to be patient and not to expect too much. Moreover, the line executives may feel a sense of hostility because, in their eyes, researchers are not pressured as are the line organizations.

It is not surprising to learn that the management's evaluation of the research does not tend to be particularly positive. Nor is it surprising that line management usually recommends that the laboratory work more on what it believes it can sell and produce. Also it may ask for more control over research schedules to be able to get technical problems solved more quickly.

Increasing Management Controls and Pressure

Top management may react by developing new budgets for the research organization. It may even separate research in terms of that which the line divisions will pay for on a pro rata basis and research that is done to solve a specific line division's problems and for which, therefore, the expenses can be billed to that organization. Once a billable budget is established, the pressures are enormous to increase it and to decrease the more exploratory research budget. The more the billable budget becomes predominant, the less influence the researchers will have over the research activities. Moreover, a line organization can begin to alter the degree of urgency it applies to its requests. This can create problems for the research organization. It may be coerced to pull people off from one project and put them on another. In many cases, this may occur when the researcher feels he is just beginning to understand the problem and a solution may be in sight. His desire to complete a study is increasingly frustrated. As one senior researcher put it:

> 1. I think the biggest problem that is facing all of us is the financing of our projects. Quite often I feel that we get arbitrary decisions, that the division shall stay at a certain level of effort and sort of arbitrarily lop off problems to get at this particular level; and sometimes things get done on an arbitrary basis rather than each problem being evaluated and those problems that they are really not going to work on being thrown out.

This arbitrary assignment of projects to the point where the researcher's competence is not really taken into account is upsetting to the researcher. He, we may recall, lives in a world in which he is not at all clear as to how his superiors and peers feel about him. He is in a world where interpersonal uncertainty and mistrust can be relatively high and thus where every cue is important in understanding his position.

If he suddenly is moved on the grounds that a line division is applying pressure, he may interpret this behavior as meaning that the company is no longer interested in utilizing him in the competent manner that it faithfully promised when it hired him. Moreover, being moved from project to project prevents him from gaining a sense of completion of anything. His need for confirmation as a competent researcher is frustrated.

The impact on the central mission of research may also be negative. As the movement of people continues, the depth in technical competence is depleted. It is not long before, as one senior researcher said, "We have too many people who know a little bit about a lot of things." In Organization C, for example, 80 percent of those interviewed felt that the constant movement might be helpful to an individual's career, but it raised havoc with the quality and speed of research.[6] Some illustrative comments are:

> 1. This constant shuffling of projects around tends to make a guy who really wants to do something worthwhile throw up his hands and start so-called playing a game. His job becomes strictly eight to five. Any other real interest is beaten out of him with his obvious

---

[6] I believe that these findings can be viewed as consonant to Barnes's. He reported that engineers liked being moved around because it added variety to their work. In Barnes's study, these engineers were in an open system. This one is a closed system. "Shuffling" people around in a closed system would, I believe, be extremely frustrating (Barnes, *op. cit.*).

lack of importance as witnessed by the way these whole things have changed. Also, you get the impression that the main purpose of our division and our company is to create managers. By and large, technical matters are definitely secondary in this company.

2. If I could change something it would be this terrific amount of rotational assignment business. From my point of view this has a dreadful effect on our ability to accomplish something. Continuity of work and building up of skill and knowledge are being shattered. We are constantly undertaking something, abandoning it, and doing it over again, and I suspect if you look at this over a period of years, you would find that we have attempted to do the very same thing in cycles, time after time after time. We've always lost a lot of our effort this way, with brand-new personnel, building up our knowledge to a certain point and then scuttling it and then going off on something else. It hurts morale, too, because the men don't have a sense of accomplishment.

3. If I were to put myself on the receiving end of this, I would tend to favor this, because I feel it would give you a broader understanding of the overall company operations and therefore, better prepare me for advancement. I think I would be more inclined to view this as being in a more favorable position to advance on the administrative ladder. But I don't think it does research much good.

There is little that the researcher can do. He may not react aggressively—at least not too much so. The culture does not encourage it—nor may he feel particularly comfortable in being aggressive. The researchers may complain to themselves or to one or two friends but in our three cases most tended to suppress their feelings. If they suppress their feelings frequently enough, they may tend to dislike themselves for "taking it" without a fight. In order to resolve these negative feelings, they may either leave the organization or rationalize that other situations would be as bad. They may also encourage others to leave ("Boy, if I could pick up and go, I would."). If they succeed in inducing others to leave, it is probably those who can find jobs elsewhere. These tend to be the more competent researchers. Researchers who dislike themselves for remaining behind may feel especially good when the best men leave, because they can now feel (probably unconsciously) that they have helped to punish the top. They can also feel more secure when they have less competition.

Another possible reaction is to interpret management's need to pressure as a lack of trust in the research group and as a sign that it really wants second-class research. Again, the first-class researcher will tend to leave such a situation. The researcher who has decided to remain can live with his frustrations by reducing his level of aspiration as to the quality of research that he will perform. The more he reduces his level of aspiration, the more he becomes a second-class scientist and the more he provides management with a self-fulfilling prophecy (i.e., the researchers must be controlled if they are going to be productive).

As the situation continues, the researcher may attempt to adapt by placing greater emphasis upon the need for technicians, secretarial help, space, equipment, and meetings within the organization as well as with outside consultants, etc. Indeed, he may emphasize these items as a way to confirm that top management believes that he is important. (If they spend all this money on me, I must be important.) However, as budgets are cut, these are the very items that will be cut first. Thus the symbols that the researcher has used to infer that he is needed may now be slowly but significantly reduced. This will tend to increase his feelings of rejection and further reinforce the adaptive processes described above (lowering aspiration, withdrawal).

The researcher may also attempt to rationalize his position by saying that he should remain because the financial rewards are high. Once this occurs, the potency that he placed upon the intrinsic satisfactions of being a researcher may be decreased and the potency of money may be increased. As one unhappy senior scientist put it:

> Well, as far as I'm concerned my future is at an end. Senior technical advisors seem to be largely a matter of convenience rather than a functional part of the organization. So as far as I am concerned, actually the only thing they can give me is money and that's all.

But, a researcher is faced with a ceiling as to how much money he can earn. If he is to go beyond this ceiling, he must become an administrator. Thus, another force arises to take him away from research. This force is adaptive in the sense that the researcher may realize he is becoming less effective in research and it may be best to leave this activity. The choice of going into administration may partially help to overcome his own guilt feelings for no longer being the researcher that he felt he could be.

In a few organizations management has responded to complaints of the researchers by developing the technical ladder. The basic idea is to give a researcher the opportunity to obtain much higher financial renumeration and greater control over his research world. Data have been obtained that question the extent that the technical ladder does resolve the issues or the extent to which the financial issues are the basic ones for the researcher.

In one organization, for example, the technical ladder became, at best, a reward for being a competent scientist that took the best men away from the everyday pressures of the organization. In other words, it helped symbolize that good men were taken away from the very pressures that management had created to make research more effective.

Another problem with the technical ladder in this organization was that in taking the best men away from the administrative activities of the laboratory, it reduced the probability that first-class researchers would influence the administrative processes. This was precisely what the organization needed. The result was that the less effective researchers became the ones to obtain the power positions. Since it is the administrative ladder that selected those who joined the technical ladder, the organization ended up having the top researchers selected by men who were not top researchers or who once were top but decided to adapt to the pressures by lowering their level of aspiration in research.

Some examples of comments made about the technical ladder were:

1. Let me tell you what you hear by the grapevine. I think the feeling is that the man who is on the technical ladder is only half a man, so to speak. And the guy who makes it administratively, not only has it made technically but has also made it administratively. And you will find that we people who are on the technical ladder have a real desire to think and act like administrators whenever the opportunity presents itself.

2. In our department I think there is something left to be desired. We changed, and quite frankly, it has not worked like the way it was announced by the top management several years ago. The people thought, for example, that they could operate pretty independently; this has given us some real administrative problems, and not until recently have we been able to make the thing manageable; we have had to crack the whip on this.

RESEARCHER: Can you give me an idea what you had to do? On the surface it doesn't sound like much, but, for example, we have taken away some of the administrative authority that these people have had in approving work without issuing reports. We have more control in determining the course of action of these people. Of course, what this has resulted in is basically that these people now feel that they are reporting to section heads who are younger people than they are.

3. I think the people who go up the technical ladder are not at all convinced that this is as rewarding as going up the administrative ladder. When you get right down to it, on the technical ladder you don't really have, shall we say the title that you can point to, and the status that the administrative people have. Also, I think there have been quite a number of people appointed to the technical ladder who weren't really competent.

4. Sometimes I wonder if a technical ladder isn't an organizational sham to keep the older people happy.

With increasing management control and the tightening up of budgets, there is an increase in reports to keep everyone informed of the status of projects or to request money for new projects. In both cases the forces exist to make such reports become more sales pieces than accurate descriptions of research activity. Initially, this is resisted by the researcher. However, he tends to run into a stone wall in the form of his supervisor, who knows that if he is to remain visible in a positive way, reports must be written to please those above.

As pressure and anxiety increase, the superiors, at any level, may begin to protect themselves by editing reports in a very detailed manner. They want to make certain that they are not placed in a possibly embarrassing situation. Sending only the "good" news to the top becomes standard operating procedure. For example:

1. There is a problem which is in some way not the fault of the top. There is a tremendous urge to carry only good news, to be ashamed of the bad news. And this is a tremendous waste. Again let me emphasize I don't think it is the fault of the top. I think this is a problem of middle management. I would rate the top very high on willingness to listen to this, but I think our middle management isn't about to say anything. So to put this another way, I would say that the top is too sheltered, much too sheltered.

Another high-level research administrator said:

My own feeling, at the moment, and I don't know whether you will quote it or not, but it doesn't matter, my feeling here is that I think that I would be most hesitant to give the research director a lousy performance report. I think I would not have the same degree of openness, wouldn't have the same feeling of openness that my problem was going to be accepted and let's say, well received with understanding. I would feel I really researched the hell out of that thing before I presented it to him.

The detailed scrutiny results in the people at the lower levels spending more time rewriting reports as well as learning to write further reports in the way the superior will be pleased. In six different cases, I observed that the process of rewriting was so long that the technical material was outdated by the time it got to the customers. Again, due to the lack of interpersonal competence, these emotionally toned issues were not discussed, and the result was more problems. For example, in one of the laboratories 75 percent of the research supervisors stated that there might be a "few" problems with reports, but these were primarily caused by the inability of researchers to write clearly.

The researchers held a different viewpoint. They believed that the problem with report writing was in the superior's inability to handle the situation competently. For example, 75 percent of the researchers indicated their views in comments like: "My ideas get massacred"; "no matter how you write, they'll rewrite it"; "my reports get emasculated." Thus:

1. No matter how you write a report and how many times you write it and what you say, it's rewritten and rewritten and rewritten. So you learn to write a report, hand it in, and become like a machine, keep making the changes.
2. Well, the reports get cut up six times or so. They're very word-conscious around here. Anything that leaves the laboratory, they're afraid it might be misconstrued on the outside. They don't have any confidence in the engineer to report properly without being misconstrued. The joke of it all is that most of the reports are probably not read.

Along with a greater emphasis upon reports is an increased attempt to evaluate projects. The majority of researchers and research administrators reported that they knew of no program that had been developed that evaluated accurately the effectiveness with which research was accomplished or predicted the probable payoff of research. For example:

1. So you find people scurrying around and trying to come up with project analysis sheets. Productivity of research men,

are they really productive, how to measure productivity from research and so on, are the major questions. I think the simple fact of the matter is we haven't progressed far enough along these lines to know really how to access productivity. We don't know how to make a really good project analysis sheet, so that I think in many cases all we have succeeded in doing is to stifle research. For the good research projects which can't really be analyzed, people are going to be forced to come up with project analysis sheets; unless they are big liars, they just can't justify them, so I think this has been a very stifling thing.

2. So this is why I feel so strongly about this project analysis sheet business. These things are awfully hard to put down on paper when you are just starting to conceive something or even to define it. I defy anybody to come up with a meaningful analysis sheet, because if you knew all these answers, it is not research.

3. One thing that has been getting worse and worse is the justification for everything. What happens is that the higher-level people spend so much time justifying to each other that they don't have time to get the work done right.

Given all the problems outlined above, it is difficult to see how an accurate evaluative mechanism can be developed without including as parameters such factors as the degree of risk taking, rigidity, lack of openness, fear, anxiety, etc., in a unit. Yet, these are emotionally toned factors and are rarely discussed, much less acknowledged in writing.

Another kind of evaluation that became increasingly frequent in the older laboratory, but which was hardly reported in the younger one, was "witch-hunts." A witch-hunt was a rather symbolic label given to a postmortem evaluation of a research project that did not succeed. The orders came down from above to find out the causes of the failure. Although stress usually was placed on not pinpointing individuals, the subordinates did not take chances on being identified with a research failure. As will be pointed out, most researchers and administrators agreed that success in the laboratory was partially a function of being associated with a successful research project. One research manager described the witch-hunts as follows:

1. When a project fails, and it may take years to know that it has, we have a witch-hunt and ask, "Who did this, why and when?" We say that we don't identify people, but it can't be helped. In my experience most of the research projects are so complicated that it is difficult to place the blame on any one individual unit. What really

is frustrating is the number of cases where failure could have been prevented if people felt free to communicate nasty news to the top.

As budgets tighten, pressures increase, assignments to work become (from the researcher's point of view) more random, evaluative procedures increase, the researcher is forced either to give up and permit himself to be pushed and pulled as the pressures go, or to retreat into his own work and insulate himself from others. As we have shown, this strategy is not accepted by line corporate management that keeps emphasizing "being on the team."

Research groups can also try to protect themselves by becoming more insular. The research director, if he is to be respected by his subordinates, will tend to spend much of his time keeping pressures away from his unit and protecting it from raids and negative evaluations. What I am suggesting is that the very repetitive compulsive activities that bind individuals and groups so tightly that they do not feel they can change this situation actually creates a psychological gulf among units. In an organization increasingly tied up by organizational defensive activities, the director is almost forced to defend his group and compete against the outside world.

In this connection over 84 percent of the researchers in Organization B spoke of competition among units. "We almost enjoy learning that someone else is in trouble," said one research manager. Another described the situation as follows: "There are an awful lot of rocks that go over fences before things get crystallized."

The more the research manager becomes defensive, the less cooperative and the more insular he will become. This may disturb the top management which wants research directors who have a "total" point of view. But, there is little the research director can do about it.

However, the more insular each group becomes, the less it will be ready to cooperate when the time comes for joint effort with other groups. Moreover, the increased insularity increases the probability that two or more groups could be working on similar or mutually related projects without knowing it. In some cases, I found that researchers had known about the projects but did not meet to compare notes. As one research manager put it:

> Maybe I can put it in more concrete terms. The men working on project X may accidentally make an observation which could be

very useful to a man working in another building on project Y, and yet this information is never conveyed, and the man working on the project X is not really interested and doesn't know there are problems in which these skills could be useful. I think it is made very difficult by the fact that we have a split location.

In these cases, I observed a rather strong sense of rivalry with the accompanying feeling that anything the other groups did could not be as good as the work of their own unit. Such attitudes, on the part of individuals or groups, are defensive and may indicate much about the lack of inner confidence of the individual or the lack of internal security of the group.

As these pressures increase, researchers may adapt by becoming overoptimistic in setting schedules. They become overoptimistic in order to obtain the scarce resources and to keep their group's image with the top as untarnished as possible. This is not to say that overoptimistic schedules are not due partially to the nature of research. Clearly, it is difficult to predict ahead of time exactly what one will discover when research is conducted. My point is that this problem is accentuated by the administrative culture of the laboratory. For example:

1. I think overoptimism is something generated in an organization. By and large you have to do a powerful selling job to really get things in motion around here. I would say most of the optimism is not necessarily poor judgment, but the researcher is trying to figure out the way he can get what he needs to get.

2. Yes, I do think that they are overoptimistic and I think they overrate the importance of their problems.

RESEARCHER: What do you think causes this?

I think it is partly due to the fact that in order to get company interest and company backing, you have to be optimistic and enthusiastic.

3. Yes, I think there is [overoptimism]. I think we normally, on our development, set a timetable which is sooner than we think we can get it done because it represents a money saving to get it done as quickly as possible. If you set a timetable and really anticipate all the problems, you're not going to get anybody to approve the project. You also set up a short timetable in order to keep the pressure on and to keep them moving to try to meet these deadlines, even though it might take extra action to do it.

4. Yes, I think people are optimistic. The problem is that there's a feeling, I believe, that the top welcomes an optimistic forecast,

and they get what they ask for, and I think they are afraid of pessimistic forecasts; they are afraid of trouble; they don't like to make any waves."

The increasing default on schedules, interdepartmental lack of cooperation, insularity, researcher turnover, and the decreasing involvement may well make top corporate management more anxious, if not angry. If top management becomes simply more anxious, it may increase the pressures which, if this view is correct, will only set off further pressures in the same direction.

If the top corporate managers become angry, they may indeed change the management of the research organization. Under these conditions their need for change may be so great that they may bring in an outsider as the research director or promote someone within who promises to make a clean sweep. In either case, the impact on those at the lower levels will tend to be that top management does not trust or respect them (which is true, and the researchers are partially the cause for this) and that to succeed now in administration one must become a hatchet man for the top, which may result in everyone becoming more anxious and cautious. For example:

> 1. I think the biggest problem that prevents me from being as effective as I'd like to be, are the frequent reorganizations. I get going and start a project. My job is really to originate the project; I do that, and I think we have been quite successful. About the time that I feel I've got everybody really working, the project moves somewhere else. You're out of it despite the fact that you might have the background and everything. There seems to be, in our organization, for some really obscure reason, a real reluctance to acknowledge even conversationally the work of other people. I don't know what it stems from, whether it is an element of competition or what it is, but curiously enough, the people who will generally do this, have no reluctance at all about citing the literature.

The new research director may also become more cautious in the projects he approves. In order to please the top line executives who appointed him, the research director may work primarily on the less risky and less innovative projects. The researchers at all levels may take their cues from this, and begin to think less innovatively and take fewer risks. They may decrease further their commitment to generate new ideas. "If the customers are going to run this laboratory, fine, let them think up the new ideas." Such an attitude may provide the customers with proof that "These fellows are not innovative" and serve to decrease their confidence in the researchers and to encourage them to apply further pressure to control the research.

The new research director realizes that if he decides to make any major shifts or raise basic issues, he may upset the top corporate executives who, up to this point, do not tend to be open on difficult issues. The research director may therefore resort to individual meetings with the top corporate managers in order to "feel them out" or "sell them" on the new ideas that he wants to put into action.

This results in the main business being done by individual contact. The executive committee no longer operates as a dynamic forum for the exploration of issues where each individual speaks out. Rather, the members may soon learn that the real decision making goes on during the private meetings. The executive committee meets, as one executive put it, "To pour holy water over the decision already made."

In cases where the new research director does ask for serious debate on his new ideas, few members of the executive committee will say anything controversial. Most will raise some issues about the working of the plan but hold their reservations to themselves. For example, the reader may recall the organization in which the top executive group was asked by the new research director to give its views about a new structure he had developed. Most accepted it "enthusiastically" during the executive committee meetings, spending all the time questioning minor aspects such as the wording. However, subsequent interviewing uncovered the fact that many of the members had serious reservations about the new structure.

The final impact that may be hypothesized is that eventually the men who go to the top are individuals who do not upset, interpersonally speaking, the top executive group. This, in the long run, may lead to the development of managers in the image of the superiors. In some cases, this can lead to important problems. In the case above, for example, the men who are willing to be, or to act as if they want to be, dependent and submissive to the top will tend to be rewarded. This may be perceived by the subordinates as another sign that the organization is anti-innovation and risk taking, which in turn, will tend to reinforce such adaptive activities as withdrawal, lowering of level of aspiration, and increasing energy put into the defense of oneself or one's unit.

As the upper levels of research management become populated with individuals who are more comfortable with the relatively more passive and dependent roles, two important consequences tend to occur. First, they tend to promote those who are not interpersonally threatening to them. If our analysis is valid, this means the top may become populated with research executives who minimize risk taking and openness but who can be articulate in "selling" (the management's view) and who are skillful at playing "organizational politics." For example, in all organizations the majority of the members reported that in addition to technical competence, "selling," "being articulate," "knowing the right people," "being lucky by being on a project that paid off," were very important qualities for success. In the oldest of the research organizations, technical competence became secondary to administrative skill. Thus:

1. Since I've been on both sides of the fence, I can say it is a lot easier to progress from the administrative end. If you want to succeed, you have to have a reasonably good rating in ability to communicate, to persuade people and not to get in trouble with them. I don't think their record would indicate that they [those who got ahead] have been outstanding in either technical or administrative work.

On the technical side I would say that to be technically competent and to produce a project that really succeeds, that's how you get rewarded.

2. Initially there is no question in my mind but what a real good technical job is what counts. Another thing is a man is going to really have to understand his objective and to be able to present the findings in a lucid way, so that people will understand him.

3. I think that the one feeling most people have is that administrators can get by, and be promoted, as long as they don't make mistakes, and they don't make mistakes by not making decisions.

4. I think the fellow that gets ahead the most is the fellow who can aggressively push something without appearing to be either pushing or to be that aggressive, or appear to get emotional.

5. He must be highly technically competent, as everybody who gets promoted is. He must be aggressive, with a degree of smoothness, so he doesn't irritate too many people. And there is a mold which you see a lot of people falling into. He's got to conform.

But the organization, under the conditions above, may need executives who are willing to take risks and are quite open in their dealings with conflict. Some research organizations may resolve this problem by finding one very aggressive and directive research director who, in effect, will be asked to pull the organization out of the "rut." If he moves aggressively, he will threaten personally many of the people on top. If he moves cautiously, he may displease the corporate management which is probably expecting him to make changes.

One long-range move may be to place new emphasis upon developing research administrators who are more aggressive. Indeed, highly authoritarian, directive leaders would be necessary in such a defensive system, although once in power, they will tend to compound the difficulties. This may mean dipping down into the organization to select the bright young men who may not have as yet become involved in the "organizational brainwashing" processes. Although this may help to hasten the career of some researchers, it raises difficulties in research schedules. Good men are picked out of teams conducting research to become administrators. In two of the organizations studied, the researchers acknowledged the value of this "shuffling" of good men, but complained about its negative impact upon research. For example, over 85 percent of the researchers in Organization B expressed views illustrated by these comments:

1. I think the moving of people, the frequent moving of people as we do, harms the organization. Many times it takes months to educate your superior on what you are doing; when you finally educate him he's moved and you have to begin all over again.

And at times I have felt that these people are aware that they are not going to be at a particular area for too long a period. The best way that they can continue their climb upstairs is not to upset the apple cart. Consequently, they tend to emphasize the work that is minimally risky and could get them into the least number of difficulties.

2. People change so frequently that you can hardly get acquainted with them. I feel in many instances that I have a hard time understanding why certain administrator people are in charge of certain groups. The last boss that I had didn't know anything about my work and in order for me to communicate with him, I had to start right from the beginning.

3. If I were to put myself on the receiving end of this, I would

tend to favor this, because I feel it would give you a broader understanding of the overall company operations and therefore better prepare me for advancement. But I don't think it does research much good.

Another problem that arises from management developing leadership that is uncomfortable with conflict is that such management will tend to find it difficult to be open and forthright about their evaluations of their subordinates. At the moment when the subordinates are probably most anxious about their status (since so many of the traditional cues are gone), they are faced with a superior who will tend to create even a greater degree of uncertainty. In all three organizations studied, the majority (68 percent was the lowest figure) of the subordinates reported that they did not know clearly how management evaluated them. Some typical comments were:

1. No, I really don't know how he feels about me. Oh, I get indirect signs once in a while.
2. The only way I know how he feels about me is that I seem to be getting raises.
3. No, I don't know how he feels about me. How do you find out about these things, can you go up to a fellow and ask him?
4. I know how he says he feels. He's extremely open about this day by day.

The difficulties were compounded by the fact that most subordinates questioned the executive committee's understanding of their world. For example, in Organization B, 80 percent of the research managers evaluated the executive committee as one that feared taking risks. Ninety-two percent of the research managers evaluated the members of the executive committee as high in conformity.

1. After being in this company for a long time, I would say that the function of the executive committee is to make sure that no real risks are taken.
2. I think they are all conformists.

At the next lower levels nearly 50 percent of the research managers evaluated the executive committee as high in conformity (and the majority of the remainder said they did not know the committee well enough to evaluate it). Also, 60 percent believed that the executive committee would prefer not to take risks. Finally, 72 percent of the same research managers reported that their views were not well understood and correctly represented to the executive committee. About 60 percent of the next lower level administrators and senior researchers reported the same views.

As these processes continue, the distance between top management and the researchers increases, the trust decreases. It is not long before two cultures may arise. In one are the researchers; in the other the management.

The researchers begin to have different work experiences from those of their managers. For example, in Laboratory B, 86 percent of the research managers reported that the most important problems they faced daily were (1) getting people to work together, to communicate, to be flexible and accept administrative rulings, and (2) for themselves to keep up with budgets and other financial problems. Researchers, on the other hand, described their major problems as dealing with technical issues (83 percent). Another illustration was that 79 percent of the research managers gave effective. The researchers reported three sets of factors as being examples of administrative factors that inhibited them from being critical in inhibiting their work. First was their own technical limits; second, the frequent changes in projects and personnel; and third, the conservatism of the company in long-range research.

As one might expect, the majority of supervisors in Laboratories A and B described their most satisfying experiences as those where (1) they were able to complete a job on time and with payoff to the company or (2) they were able to sell a project to the top. The researchers, on the other hand, reported their most satisfying experiences came from finding out from research that their technical ideas were sound. Again it was not surprising to learn that over 86 percent of the research managers aspired for administrative promotions, whereas less than 10 percent of the researchers reported similar aspirations. Most of them (nearly 75 percent) reported that they wanted to remain in research and go up the technical ladder. (The remainder reported no aspirations but to remain where they were.)[7]

Under these conditions the directors of the actual research be-

[7] By the way, I should like to repeat my hypothesis that this bifurcation of aspirations is at least equally caused by the system of the laboratory and by some childhood interests developed by the researchers. In a laboratory where administration and research were not separated, many of the first-class researchers reported a willingness eventually to go into administration.

come men in the middle. They find themselves harrassed by the lower-level researchers and by the upper levels of management. They may spend increasing time in filling out reports, fighting fire, making and changing budgets, and keeping the upper levels informed and off the researchers' backs. As one man put it, "I have become an assistant to the director rather than an assistant director." Another said, "The brain power is frittered away on trivia." Still another described the research administrator's plight as follows:

> Here's a case where one can seldom plan a quarter of a day's work, and actually execute it within the time space that the office is open. I find that for me to accomplish what I want to accomplish for a day's work, I've got to do most of it off hours. Now the reason for it is that I'm like a guy with one bat and 16 ping-pong balls. And I've got to keep hitting these things to keep the game going. So even when I have a crisis situation, I can't shut off the phone.

One research executive related an example of how next year's budget was rewritten three different times to please the next higher level. He said it was truly discouraging to return to the researchers and ask for new information because someone "on top" got a new idea on how budgets should be presented. The degree of harassment is eloquently described by a group of research managers at a meeting held by their own top management to explore how the organization could be made more effective. For example:

> A: I have a whole page full of things to say, do you want to hear them? I wish they were more constructive—I think what I have done here is put down a bunch of problems—not necessarily any solutions to stress. A certain amount of stress I guess is good. It is productive. Lately, however, we have been going through a lot of nonproductive stress, a lot of things which don't pertain at all to the research work we are doing. I really feel that our technical output is suffering from lack of management attention. The reason for this is because the management is diverted.
>
> B: You're talking about it at the division level?
>
> A: I'm talking about the division level and I'm not sure it doesn't go higher. They are diverted by things which are certainly stress production but not necessarily producing any product, any technical output.
>
> B: Do you have any examples of what you mean by that?
>
> A: Well, I can cite some examples in my own shop. These things probably haven't showed up yet on the outside; they are

going to. These are mistakes that probably I should have done something about, if I could spend the time doing it. Now, either we have to have more management so some of them can go to meetings and some of them can stay home and apply their abilities to the main function of the division or we're going to have to cut out something.

C: You say that there are just too damn many meetings going on.

A: Meetings, paper work, so forth, trying to learn to live with a new organization, a new accounting system, all of these things at once, plus change in top management, and each time that changes, there are a whole bunch of things that have to happen, re-education, new things that people want to know, and I really think that our technical effort is suffering. You're going to start to see our customers complaining about mistakes here and mistakes there and things we should have done, why didn't we do them.

B: Do you think that all this would tend to disappear if we just sat around and didn't make any more changes for a while?

A: Well, you're going to have to live with the mistakes that we made.

B: I'm talking about the diversion of the top management, mostly the meetings.

A: I think we ought to decide a timetable of the things we are going to do. Maybe not try and do them all at once. Take the most important thing we have to do and then spend a certain amount of time on that and put the next ones on the next year's program or the year after that. Maybe an associate director would help, but I don't really know if it would be worth the extra money that would have to be put into that. I just feel that I have myself and my assistant directors and frequently the section heads all doing so many things that we just can't concentrate on our main product.

C: Can I reinforce that? This thing means a lot to me. You mention an associate director or the equivalent of it. I support it. We had to get one by the back door. We used to have one, but we were told we couldn't have an associate director. I finally had to compromise with the boss to have an assistant director whom I'll call an administrative director (*laughter*).

A: Don't misunderstand me, I'm not making a pitch for an associate director because I don't really know that I need one. I'm making a pitch for less of this, what I consider less productive work and stress-producing work and let's stress the technical.

C: There was a fabulous change in the productivity and the technical quality of our output in engineering when we put an associate director in to help with these management problems like he is talking about.

B: Just like the department stores that have a guy in the fire now and then when someone complains. To get back to these meetings a little bit, let's say there are a hell of a lot of them; do you consider them unnecessary or necessary, temporary or what?

A: Well, they have a purpose obviously, but I think that you have to weigh the importance of them versus the other things that you have to do. And I think we have gotten out of balance. We've always had some of this going on, and I think we have a double or triple dose of it right now. We haven't really made any adjustments in our personnel to handle it. Nor do we even think that maybe we do need to have extra people around just to do this sort of thing.

E: I detect more in what you're saying then just attendance at meetings.

A: Oh—any time you go to a meeting you come back with a job, and every time you put a new special staff man on, he thinks up things for you to do.

C: For instance, this joke about breaking in a new president or a new vice president or whatever he happens to be is no joke. It takes up a lot of time if for nothing else than the uncertainty in knowing how to deal with problems that you got to submit for decisions. We run into a real dilly that has chewed up a week for the three top people in our organization on this damn space problem.

B: It's enough, too, that every time there is a new guy in the organization, everybody has to find out how he likes to work.

F: I feel myself that the organization has been building a much more complex bureaucracy.

B: You mean the staffs?

F: Well, yes, and I'm not sure just what causes it. I think one of these problems is a much greater degree of conformity between the various divisions—you have staff groups trying to set up rules on how to be uniform, and then you have to get the divisions in and the committees to figure out how to do it; get everybody to agree on something, and the staff people and this includes the service groups, suddenly set up something and do it. Then you get all sorts of repercussions, and then the division management gets all involved in trying to straighten it out again. And it's just a lot of little things. I'll give you a ridiculous thing that has taken an amazing amount of time in the division. Someone decided to take the water coolers out of our building because they cost $1,000 a year or something like that. I don't know just what it was, and so one day they just trotted in and took them out.

D: And do you think the staff groups support those things?

A: Yes, they are all staff groups—service groups—and so the first thing you know there were meetings in the hallways and people making economy studies on how much money was lost with people running back and forth to the drinking fountain, and then the next week the darn drinking fountains all broke down in the building. I swear top management spent several days on that darn thing. And we didn't even know it was going to happen. Well, I really spend a lot of my time with the services. I had one this morning where all of a sudden I find out that the accounting system that we thought we had, had been changed. I probably spent an hour on the phone with —— on why he can't make the changes just now. He's got his troubles obviously, but this is the kind of thing that takes your time. Yesterday it was my analytical budget, and so forth. I think we are spending an inordinate amount of time on the cost-cutting type of efficiency improvement. We are missing the real efficiency improvement. We have some analyses, one of them that was just made was that our real efficiency of research is 30 percent. Somebody else came up with making a study of projects, that is, only one third of the projects we do get are used, the others fold somewhere along the way. This is a very rough number. But what that means is if management spent a little bit more time looking at this other two thirds and then deciding not to do it, we would be a hell of a way ahead of trying to save $25,000 on cafeteria costs or something like that.

C: I certainly agree with that.

A: I don't say that we shouldn't be doing these things, it's just a question of emphasis.

C: You think the way to get it done is to provide more time for your division to do it?

A: You mean to make somebody available—I guess I'm not sure I understand the question.

C: Well, I gather from what you say that if we were to spend more time analyzing these projects, well then, maybe eliminating the ones that weren't going to be any good anyway—we'd be a hell of a lot better off.

A: I don't mean an analysis in retrospect—I mean me devoting my time looking to project selection and looking at what other people are proposing and using what judgment I have on helping to develop programs and follow them along. Take the support people. They're making decisions which vitally effect my business and what I am able to do and I don't have any say in it; they will come tell me about it, but they won't change what they are trying to do. So I say, all right, I can give you a certain amount of money to do analytical work, that's all I can afford. I'll cut back personnel in my division because I want to have this much money for analytical work. This is an example, this just happened. And they will say fine, for this much money you can buy so many people here and so many people there, and somehow or other they have decided how many will be professional and how many will not be professional by talking to other divisions and then making up their own mind on it.

Then we just decided we are going to change our accounting system. We are going to change the rates from professional to nonprofessional. Now, because the decision was made that they are only going to give me three professionals and all the rest non-professionals, I've lost so many thousands of dollars out of my analytical budget.

B: For the same service?

A: For the same service. Now I could keep that money for something else. I had to take out of my budget, professional people, in order to give them so much money.

D: I think something similar to this happened down in my division. To cut back more professional people and to get more analytical service which is badly needed. So in effect we gave the money to the analytical people, which is fine. Then what happens? Due to an arbitrary decision in the budget, they cut the whole analytical division, and we get cut proportionally. If I had known this I would have done the analytical work in my own division.

A: Well, did you actually lose in analytical service?

D: Sure I lost in analytical service.

Another way to indicate the impact of the organization is to quote from a study conducted in one of our leading industrial research organizations. The top department research managers were asked to describe what they felt were their major responsibilities. These reports were given to an expert on organization for his comments. He wrote, "The writer is stuck by the degree of downward and inward looking exhibited by the managers. The department is seen as a thing unto itself, and one of the manager's prime roles (from his view) is to preserve it." The writer continued:

> Before reading the reports, I jotted down what seemed to me to be the most critical problems for R and D today. My understanding of these included: (1) increasing the unit value of the technology to the company, (2) increasing the unit output of technology, (3) lowering the unit cost of technology.
>
> In going over the letters I find that these factors are almost totally absent in the testing of the managers' *personal* responsibilities. What comes through to me . . . is an emphasis on the maintenance of the existing institution.

Of the 142 managerial responsibilities listed by these men, less than 18 were directly relevant to the above critical problems. Apparently, most of their time was spent in "keeping within budget," "looking for people," "representing the department," "altering programs," "keeping informed by subordinates and informing them."

In another research organization I found the following notes made by a frustrated research manager:

Company relies on me for technical supervision of work and getting it out on time and for allotted money. I spend about 30 percent of my time on this. I handle about 45 jobs/month in section —means perhaps one hour per job, on average, to delegate, guide, review, and pass judgment.

In contrast, I spend nearly twice this time on administrative duties and meetings with outsiders.

If some way could be found to handle the administrative load more efficiently, more effective work direction should result in better quality and quantity of output.

Examples of administrative jobs.

Work scheduling.
Keeping staff informed.
Manpower balances.
Cost control.
Month-end progress reports.
Newsletters.
Status bulletins.
Explain overruns and poor service.
Preparation of absorbed budget.
Monthly check on percent complete for absorbed job.
Personnel matters.
Straightening out political conflicts.
Organizing meetings with clients and other divisions.

Company pays a price for the above situation

Time and money restrictions prevent evaluating alternatives— exploring creative ideas. Thus, initiative is discouraged.
Men complain they don't get enough guidance from section head.
Short-term demands may get precedence over best long-term development of engineers.
Work particularly of new men, tends to be more slipshod.

Research manager is frustrated by situation where he has responsibility without corresponding authority.

Has authority to make technical decisions, but not enough time to get that involved.
Doesn't have authority to make decisions on administrative matters—the rules are spelled out in great detail and so are the deadlines.

RESULT: Manager does a lot of bookkeeping, to the exclusion of creative research.

QUESTION: Is this present balance recognized, and is it to be long-range benefit to the company?

As is the case of the meeting above, most of the research managers report that little is gained by being open and frank. In most cases nothing seemed to result. In a few cases the more outspoken ones have had the impression that they hurt their reputation with the research executives.

According to our analysis, nothing will tend to be done. But, it is not because the upper levels do not wish to act or that they are inconsiderate. It is because the negative activities have developed so fast, enmeshed so deeply in the research organization that they have become complex systems in their own right. It now becomes difficult to change the situation even if people suddenly became more open and risk taking. One can imagine how improbable it is that a defensive organization can overcome these complicated, multiconnected activities.

It is now easier to see why the characteristic voted most important in a "good" leader was to leave people alone. In a culture such as this (and with the probable low interpersonal competence of the leader), the best possible situation was to be left alone. The other factor mentioned slightly more frequently is that a "good" leader is technically competent. The importance of this factor may now be even more clearly appreciated. Not only would it be important to have a technically competent supervisor because the work is technically complex. In a world full of spinning of wheels, the technically competent supervisor should be able to understand more easily and more quickly the reasons why the subordinates are having technical difficulties and why they cannot meet the schedules.

But the probability of the supervisor remaining technically competent in a world where he is forced to spend so much time on administrative problems is quite low. It is interesting to note that the majority of the supervisors and researchers in Laboratory A (the young one) felt that they were not technically obsolescent, although the supervisors admitted they could become so if they were not careful. In the older and larger research laboratory, over 85 percent of the supervisors felt that technical obsolescence was a crucial problem.

By the way, the majority of the senior researchers reported opposite views. They felt that every good researcher could keep himself up to date. If there was a problem of obsolescence, it was either because the man was not keeping himself up to date or that the organization did not give the researcher adequate time to keep abreast of the field. For example:

> 1. I'm sure there must be some technical obsolescence, but I don't think it exists the way the administration thinks it does. They started training courses during the day, but I am against that. It takes people away from their work, and I consider the best way to keep up to date is to read the technical journals rather than take courses, and I still think there are many people who could work on their own job and continue their education.
>
> 2. This is a sore point with me and my blood boils when I read in the journals about obsolescence. If you run into obsolescence in a company like this, I feel quite sure that the company has an awful big hand in it. If you spend your time doing routine jobs in a company, then I think you have a great probability of becoming obsolete. If I am obsolete, this is the reason why. I've had to spend hours and days and weeks of time doing routine things.

The administrators and the less competent researchers on the other hand, felt that there was a definite problem of obsolescence. They believed that the research organization should develop courses for individuals. One wonders if the emphasis placed by administrators upon obsolescence is partially a way to reduce their own anxiety about having become technically obsolete. I might add that the average number of years in industrial research laboratories of the supervisors (as supervisors) in Laboratories A and B was about the same. Thus, one could not attribute the views of the supervisors in laboratory B to longer membership in industrial laboratories. Indeed, the majority of the supervisors in Laboratory A came to that organization because they felt that they were no longer managing research in their previous setting and could, therefore, become obsolete.

Under these conditions researchers could begin to *see* their organization as second class. In one of the laboratories studied, for example, 79 percent of the top research administrators felt that the organization was not utilizing the potential of the researchers and was "average" or "below average" in output. Sixty-two percent of the senior researchers reported similar feelings. To make the situation worse, the researchers eventually began to see themselves more as conformists and less as risk takers. For example, in the same organization, nearly 50 percent of the top-level researchers admitted (reluctantly) that they conformed more than they liked to acknowledge. As one put it, "When it really comes down to it, I conform. It's the system." The same researchers perceived their superiors as being low in risk taking (50 percent).[8] Only 13 percent felt that their supervisors were low in conformity. Of those who rated their superiors low in risk taking and high in conformity, over 85 percent spontaneously added that, in their opinion, the major causal factor was the system. "I watch Dr. —— in a meeting and I can tell he hates to conform to decisions that he believes are wrong. But, as he asked, what the hell can anyone do. I see his point of view." Another research manager put it this way, "As individuals I think our people are risk takers. But in groups, in this place, they have been clobbered so much that they take few risks."

Another consequence is that if views such as these are held long enough, they may become so internalized that the researchers may eventually *expect* second-class research from the organization.

1. Well, I think this company is about average and if they are not careful they are going to go down. I ran into some problems; for example, I developed something that was new in the company and I had to deal with people above me who knew nothing, absolutely nothing, technically speaking. And who I just didn't feel would give my side of the argument a fair chance.

2. I think the efficiency as I see it, although I might be wrong, has succeeded reasonably well in maintaining a good image on the outside through the quality of products. And we have put out some good ones. But I think this has been done really at a great cost. It takes an awful lot of money to be quite inefficient. I think many of our problems have been caused by company attitude rather than by contributions of the people. I think the company attitude has been quite poor. Some people give me the feeling they don't know where they want to go, and sometimes they give me the feeling they don't want to take any risks.

3. I guess the company is doing its best, but I don't think it is utilizing its people as effectively as it could be. I think one thing that could happen is to try to avoid having political matters dominate the scene and to have a little better appreciation for demonstrated abilities for accomplishing things.

---

[8] $n = 50$ in Organization B.

Another thing is that we have grown to be quite large and matters are much more impersonal, and I feel the breach between effective management and the worker is just so great that this leads to undesirable effects. It would be very nice if the man who is making assignments and putting effort behind things knew the workers really well. If he knew their interests, their skills, and their weak points, he could then take these into account when making assignments.

4. I don't think our effectiveness is as high as it could be. I think we have so many people being moved around just like chessmen.

Conclusions and Recommendations

First, may I again remind the reader that this theory of the deterioration of research and development organizations is a theory. Although some evidence exists for parts of the framework, it has yet to be tested.

If subsequent research confirms these hunches then we may conclude:

1. Assuming that the researchers are technically competent, their interpersonal competence will tend to be much lower. Indeed, the possibility may be raised that one reason why individuals go into research is that it may provide a legitimate way by which not to face up to their capacity to generate difficulties in interpersonal situations. One wonders if the researchers' tremendous emphasis upon autonomy and freedom may be partially motivated by an unconscious desire not to find out how interpersonally incompetent they are. However, when they are placed in situations where they must work cooperatively with others, then they have to face up to their relatively low interpersonal competence. This is what seems to happen to many researchers who find themselves on team projects. Many of them told us that their biggest frustrations were those with people.

Another reason why researchers may emphasize being left alone is that they have learned that contacts with superiors (who are also researchers) tend to be dissatisfying. To tell this to the superior would get them into an emotionally laden situation which both parties (and the culture) tend to abhor.

Finally, it is tempting to speculate that the researchers' mistrust and disregard for organizational authority and control may be partially their way of preventing themselves from seeing their own similar needs, which, for some reason they do not tend to accept. As long as they condemn organizational authority, who can suggest that their values are identical (in many respects) to those of the organization? This is not to deny the legitimacy of the complaint against organizations lodged by many researchers.

The point is that if our data are valid, then researchers who become administrators (and many do) tend to behave in the very way that they condemn. Moreover, as I analyzed their complaints, most of them were not against authority per se, but the way it was used. For example, many of them complained about the unilateral way in which projects were defined, supported, altered, dropped, and evaluated. Many complained at the increasing sense of mistrust shown by management through the increasing use of budgets and other control mechanisms. Others complained about the constant sly remarks made spontaneously by some administrators which implied that research represented unnecessary overhead; that researchers knowingly conducted research much beyond the time that the project was obviously a failure; that researchers did not have any concern for the organization, etc. These facts are not inherent in the nature of authority and control. The way in which authority is used is related to the leadership styles of the research administrators. It is the way authority is used that leads to these complaints.

2. The relatively low interpersonal competence at all levels leads to lack of awareness and misperceptions at all levels. This, in turn, leads to each group reacting to the other in such a way as to make the situation worse. The result is an organization increasingly tied up with defensive activity that no one seems to appreciate or to be able to alter. Indeed, if it goes on long enough, it may become accepted as "part of life." This results in an organization that manifests activities that, once triggered off, seem to be uncontrollable, compulsive, and repetitive. An organization that is controlled by internal activities that no one desires may well be on its way to becoming neurotic.

Roberts[9] has developed a flow chart of the factors that may affect technological accomplishment on the project as well as re-

_____

[9] E. B. Roberts, "Engineer Dynamics and Productivity in Research and Development Projects," Working Paper: Organizational Research Program, A. P. Sloan School of Industrial Management, 1963.

search productivity. If this analysis is valid, then the organization as a system would tend to develop these factors in such a way that they inhibit researcher productivity. For example, in Table 7–1 the variables listed by Roberts are shown on the left-hand side and their probable effect on the impact observed in Organizations B and C (and less so in A) are noted in the two columns on the right-hand side.

If this model is correct, it suggests that lavish working conditions and high wages cannot overcome the frustration of being required

TABLE 7–1

Factor	Predicted Impact of B and C Social Systems upon the Factors	
	Increase	Decrease
1. General capability of management.....................		X
2. Delays in effects...................................X		
3. Effect of project experience.......................		X
4. Delay in acquiring new knowledge...................X		
5. Delay in absorbing new knowledge...................X		
6. Project schedule pressure..........................X		
7. Other influences...................................		
Unilateral changes of projects*.....................X		
Unilateral changes of men..........................X		
8. Relative productivity of researchers.,.................	X	
9. Motivational forces for productivity..................	X	
10. Average absence and off-job time....................X		

* Added by the writer.

to do relatively routine, customer-defined and controlled, unpredictably altered, second-rate research. Nor will autonomy lead to increased research effectiveness. Actually, autonomy may be necessary because—to put it rather strongly—if two or more researchers are required to work cooperatively under supervision, their interpersonal competence will tend to be low enough that they will tend to create difficulties for one another. These difficulties, in turn, could create emotional problems which could affect the research. Granting autonomy, under these conditions, would be rewarding interpersonal incompetence.

In addition to the usual reasons cited for the importance of autonomy, I believe that it is valued by researchers (as would be the case of anybody who is in the same predicament) as a *defense* for low interpersonal competence and not because they know how to utilize it. For example, I was quite surprised when over two thirds of the senior researchers ($n = 50$) in one organization told me that if researchers did not produce they would recommend *rigid* and *close* control of their work. Further supportive data came in some preliminary observations of teacher-student relationships at a large university. The conformity scores were as high and the risk-taking scores as low, as in any business meeting observed to date.

The model may also provide an explanation for the findings that research teams seem to lose their effectiveness as they age. In the culture outlined above, one would predict that the longer people exist in the system, the less the innovation. How can productivity be a guideline if the researcher decreasingly defines the project, controls its level of technical challenge, and is permitted to finish it to a point where it may produce some worthwhile contribution? Indeed, a research organization could reach the point where completed projects might indicate the skill of the researcher to pick or become part of relatively safe, easy, projects that have little challenge and make even less of a contribution to knowledge. Moreover, the more programmed, service-oriented the research, the less the probability that a researcher would want to publish it.

To put this another way, both management and researchers tend to behave in such a way that they tend to inhibit, dissatisfy, and frustrate one another. They do not do this because they want to frustrate and dissatisfy. They do it, I would suggest, because they are not interpersonally competent to do otherwise and because neither has a theory of administration that would lead them to behave in a more instructive, innovative, and facilitating manner. The model also sheds light on why size seems to be crucial in research organizations. The larger the defensive system, the more difficult it must be to administer and, as we saw, the more hopeless the participants seem to feel about successful change for the better.

And while we are speculating, we may ask what is the meaning of criteria used for assessing creativity that depend upon superiors' ratings, papers published, and projects finished? For example, supervisor ratings will probably be more valid in the early stages of the life of a research organization. In the latter stages, the supervisor may be so harried, technically tired and obsolete, as well as ignorant of the literature, that his ratings of subordinates' innovativeness would be questionable. Nor, if our data are valid, do peer ratings help. As we have seen, few researchers reported that they knew the work of their peers; even fewer reported that they believed that their work was well understood and valued by their peers. Many reported a sense of rivalry and competitiveness, and peers across project or division lines tended to underrate one another.

The research also raises some questions about the frequently used distinction of "cosmopolitans" (usually technical people) and "locals" (usually the administrators).[10] The concept of cosmopolitan has meant an individual who is not centrally identified with the organization in which he belongs. He has identified with a reference group that exists beyond the boundaries of the organization. The local, on the other hand, is organization-centered. He is less interested in outside reference groups and more centrally involved in the effectiveness of the organization.

In this research, I found that these distinctions had to be broken down even further. First, I found, as others have noted, organization-centered individuals who were less concerned about the relevant professional scientific and engineering reference groups. I also observed individuals who were mostly identified with the technical, scientific, and engineering societies and seemed little involved in the organization. Many of these, I believe (but do not have systematic evidence), became cosmopolitan out of frustration with organizations and interpersonal relations. I believe that if they did experience more meaningful satisfactions in these areas, they could become locals and cosmopolitans.

The professionals who reported the highest degree of self-actualization, challenge, and success at their technical work were also the most closely identified with the organization. This group was composed primarily of the best researchers (as evaluated by the organization), who were still highly productive.

Interestingly these extremely highly actualizing individuals answered many questions significantly differently from those researchers who were also actualizing but not at what seemed to be at

---

[10] Alvin W. Gouldner, "Cosmopolitans and Locals: Toward an Analysis of Latent Social Roles—I," *Administrative Science Quarterly*, Vol. 2, No. 3 (December, 1957), pp. 281–306.

such a high degree. The overall trend was that they were highly identified with the organization and their professional societies. They saw their organizational life and their work interests as a "perfect marriage."

They rated the organization as "an excellent place to work," innovative, a workplace "without parallel." They expressed little anxiety about promotion. "This organization has been so good to me, all I want to do is make sure at the end of each day that I have truly earned my pay." They could recall no dissatisfying situations except those caused by their own limitations and could repeat endless numbers of satisfying experiences, all of which were related to technical accomplishments.

They either did not agree with the majority or they played down the importance of unilateral changes in research, shuffling of people, budgets, administrative pressures. However, they admitted that they were usually left alone to do their work as they wished. None could think of anything about their organizational life that they would change except "to expand the day to 48 hours instead of 24 hours."

They did not believe their managers were conformists. Rather, they described them as having a "cooperative attitude" or being "good soldiers." The few who felt the technical ladder was not a resounding success quickly gave reasons why this was not the company's fault. "After all, this was an unusual experiment and it will take time to iron out the kinks."

In short, their reports contradicted the trend. Indeed, if the model above is valid, they may be described as more company-oriented and "blind" to the laboratory's problems than the most involved and upwardly mobile administrators.

Only a very few individuals in the two research organizations (less then five) were interviewed who could be included in the final category of being withdrawn from the organization and the technical work. The number was higher (about 25 percent) in the consulting firm.

The point is that, as reported by others, researchers do tend to fall into the categories of cosmopolitans and locals. However, unlike the implication usually drawn, the first-class basic researchers who also were productive were both cosmopolitan and local and not simply extremely cosmopolitan.

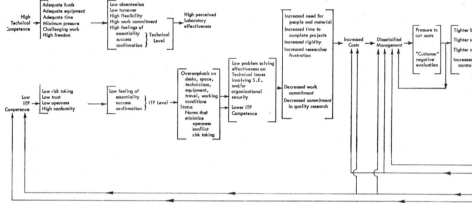

FIGURE 7-1.   A Model of R&D Deterioration.

Summary

In the Figure 7-1, I try to bring together the major points developed so far in the form of a self-maintaining system.

The input is relatively low interpersonal competence. This leads to the participants experiencing low feelings of essentiality, psychological success, and confirmation on the interpersonal level. The participants react by an overemphasis on desks, space, technicians, travel, and status as well as by developing norms to minimize openness, conflict, and risk taking. This should result in low problem-solving effectiveness on *technical* issues that involve the participants' self-esteem and/or their organizational security (which tend to include many of the crucial technical problems).

As problem-solving effectiveness decreases, the need for people, materials, and time increase as do the researchers' frustration and rigidity toward change. At the same time, I believe, the researchers' commitment to work and aspiration toward high-quality research decrease. These factors should tend to increase costs, which dissatisfies top management, leading it to react by increasing pressure to cut research costs and by seeking customer evaluation of the payoff of the research activities. Since the latter tends to be negative, there is a feedback to make top management more satisfied. This, in turn, may lead management to tighten budgets, research schedules, and capital expenditures, and to give the customer increased influence over the research.

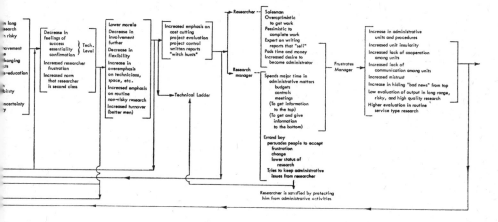

The researchers react by decreasing the long-range risky research. The organization feels increasingly the need to shift researchers to projects according to the customer demands. The researchers become more frustrated and experience a decrease in their feelings of success, essentiality, and confirmation of technical competence. This feeds back to increase costs, as well as to lower researcher morale, involvement, and turnover (of the better researchers), and overemphasis on technicians and space, and flexibility. There is a feedback to increased management dissatisfaction which, in turn, increases management's emphasis on cost cutting, project evaluation, project control, "witch-hunts," and leads to the creation of the technical ladder. All these factors also feed back to increase research costs, which dissatisfies management, and the cycle becomes circular.

The researcher is increasingly impelled to become a salesman, overoptimistic in order to get work, pessimistic about when the job can be completed. He also pads budgets of time and money and learns to write reports that "sell" his point of view.

The research managers spend increasing amounts of time on administrative activities designed to pressure and control researchers. They also feel that they become "errand boys" as well as "protectors" of the first-line researcher from the top.

The end result is that laboratory units may begin to fight one another and to protect their sovereignty by developing boundaries; cooperation and communication decrease and mistrust increases.

The practice of hiding "bad news" from the top increases and so do new projects designed to evaluate researcher effectiveness. The increasing mistrust and lack of communication leads to a feedback activity that supports and reinforces a relatively low interpersonal competence. This closes the loop, and we have a self-maintaining system becoming slowly less effective and innovative.

What Can Be Done?

If two recent articles are accurate, the answer provided to this question seems to be increasing pressure upon research organizations to become more efficient.[11] Increasing intervention by the line departments, tighter research budgets, more systematic evaluating research, more rigorous (hopefully) quantitative indices for evaluating research payoff, more use of charts to control the flow of research, closer link with the marketplace and a weaker tie with basic research, and finally an increase in the use of top-level committees to oversee research, can be expected.

I question if these activities will solve the problems of research organizations. First, they imply that research is being inefficient because researchers want it to be that way. According to this theory, a researcher pads budgets, becomes overoptimistic, sells research, and decreases the quality of his work because he sees no other way to keep the organization intact. Once an organization becomes sick, the choice offered to a researcher is between two alternatives that lead to illness; he does not have a choice between alternatives that lead to illness or health. As one researcher put it, "It is a choice of whether the organization will destroy itself today or tomorrow." It seems to me that the strategies of tighter controls may increase the control that management has over already (and increasingly) inefficient activities. The unintended consequences however, will be (1) an increasing feeling on the part of the researchers that they are not trusted, respected, or understood, which will lead (2) to further defensive behavior on their part, which in turn (3) will probably be responded to by management with even greater controls, and so (4) these will develop and

---

[11] David M. Kiefer, "Winds of Change in Industrial Chemical Research," *Chemical and Engineering News*, March 23, 1964, pp. 88–109; James B. Quinn and James A. Mueller, "Transferring Research Results into Operation," *Harvard Business Review*, Vol. 41, No. 1 (January–February, 1963), pp. 49–66.

strengthen the undesirable and uncontrollable defensive activities that can make the organization even less flexible, changeable, open, and innovative. It is not too farfetched to predict that if these processes continue long enough, they could help to make research organizations sick organizations.

I am *not* implying that controls, clear-cut objectives, and valid evaluation procedures are not useful. They are necessary, and the less defensive an organization is, the more it can generate and accept its own controls. I am implying that few committees will operate effectively, few evaluation procedures will tend to be accurate, few research schedules will tend to be realistic, and even fewer researcher-customer relationships will be made effective by these corrective measures. These measures do not get at the heart of the problem. At the core of the problem is the basic tendency for researchers to be uncomfortable with feelings, openness, and risk taking in interpersonal relationships. This leads to a research culture that will tend to reward conformity, mistrust, antagonism, and fear of risk taking. As fear, mistrust, and frustration with others increases, the individuals begin to question the motives of others. "Why is he doing that to me?" "Is he trying to get even—if so for what?" These questions and fears eventually act to make *technical* problem solving less effective.

An organization that has tied itself up in knots with organizational defenses must first untie itself. No one can order this to occur. Indeed, as I have suggested, the researchers can't make it occur even if they are intellectually aware of the problems.

What is needed is that the researchers, especially the research administrators, be helped to increase their interpersonal competence and decrease the incongruence between their values and their behavior. I believe that organizations that tie themselves up with "neurotic" interpersonal knots can extract themselves by focusing on the causes of these compulsive and repetitive defensive activities that tend to inhibit effective problem solving.

To my knowledge, there is no single plan available that can be used by organizations to become less compulsive and more effective in their problem solving. Each organization must examine itself. It must be able to look within, at precisely those factors that it has been unable, to date, to discuss openly. An organization can go from one that is problem creating to problem *solving*, if its members are able to own up to how they really feel, become more open and receptive, take more risks and support the norms of individuality, concern, and trust. In short, again I return to the requirement that (assuming high intellectual and technical competence) the first step toward increasing organizational health is for the top to increase its interpersonal competence.

Samples of Categories

Level 1. Individual Behavior

Owning (i or f)

Taking responsibility for, admitting ownership of, having possession of an idea, a feeling, anything that is one's own.

To "own up"

"I believe . . . the following"
"In my opinion we should talk about. . . ."
"I do not agree with so and so."
"I feel. . . ."

Not owning (i or f)

Not taking responsibility for, not admitting ownership of ideas, feelings, anything that emanates from "within."

Some examples are:

"I am not upset" (although flustered and red-faced).
"I do not mind being misunderstood and not appreciated. I am used to that." [When he previously complained of the same problems.]
"Who, me? No, I'm not bothered by it" (when it is clear he is flustered).

Openness (i or f)

Being accessible to new ideas and feelings from self and others. By "new" we mean "new" to the individuals. Ready to receive, to be affected by ideas and feelings. Asking questions with the objective of learning.

Not closed, ready to consider new facts and feelings.

Strives to hear people the way they wish to be heard (implies nothing about accepting ideas or feelings: to accept is to own).

> "Please tell me more. . . ."
> "I am not sure I understand you. . . ."
> "What do you mean. . . ?"
> "I am now just beginning to realize that I have feelings. . . ."
> "I wonder why I have never been able to see that before. . . ."

Not open (i or f)

Not being accessible to new ideas and feelings from self and others. Not ready to receive new ideas and feelings. To close, to shut, to confine, to limit, to wall off.

Does not strive to hear people the way they wish to be heard.

> "I don't want to hear what you have to say."
> "I'm sure that I'm right. There's no need for more information."

Experimenting (i or f)

Examining ideas and feelings for the *purpose of disclosing* New aspects. To be willing to subject ideas and feelings to a test, to permit difficulties, ideas, or feelings to undergo the test of actual experience.

> "Let's give it a try and see what happens."
> "I'm willing to try this out, although I've never done it before. . . ."
> "I've never said this to anyone including myself, but now I realize. . . ."

Rejecting experiment (i or f)

Not examining ideas or feelings for the purpose of disclosing new aspects. Not willing to subject ideas or feelings to a test, to difficulties.

> "I refuse to participate in an exercise—in an experiment."
> "This is nonsense—I don't want any part of it."
> "There's no sense to continuing this because you're wrong."

Level I: Interpersonal Behavior

Helping others to own (i or f)

The behavior is similar to owning except it is to help others to own.

> "If I understand you correctly, you are suggesting. . . ."
> "May I try to be of help. . . ?"
> "Bill has a point that we ought to help him get across to us. . . ."

Not helping Others to Own (*i* or *f*)
The behavior is similar to not owning except it is influencing others not to own.

> (*Cuts person off and states*): "Let me tell them what you are saying. You're bungling it up."
> (*To a person who is upset and who has just said he is not*): "O.K., if you can say you're not upset, that's enough for me."
> (*Cuts person off*): "I know what a better example of the same point is. . . ."

Helping others to be open (*i* or *f*)
The behavior is similar to openness except it is focused on helping others to be open.

> "May I help you explore that further . . . ?"
> "Would it help to consider the following ideas . . . ?"
> "Since you have asked for clarification of the point that is confusing to you, let me try. . . ."

Not helping others to be open (*i* or *f*)
The behavior is similar to not being open except it is aimed at preventing others from being open.

> "In my opinion, you'd be a fool if you listened to him."
> "Why do you spend time raising these issues?"
> "Enough of that, let's get back to the facts that we all have."

Helping others to experiment (*i* or *f*)
The behavior is similar to experimenting except that it is aimed at helping others to do so.

> "I sense that this is a very difficult topic for you, please go on."
> "I should like to do everything that I can to help you understand this difficult problem."
> "If Bill wishes to discuss this, I should like to help him even if the subject is a difficult one for him to discuss."

Not helping others to experiment (*i* or *f*)
The behavior is similar to not experimenting, except it is aimed at preventing others from doing so.

> "This is crazy. You'd be a fool if you continued talking about it."
> "For your sake, let's get off this subject. If you don't, it may upset you."
> "Don't try it since you don't know where it will lead you."

Level II: Norms

Individuality (*i* or *f*)

Emphasizes the appropriateness of the expression of individual ideas or feelings. It is good for a person to say what he believes. Emphasizes that individual is an entity; personal independence. To behave (think and/or feel) in a way that is congruent with one's own internal feelings and ideas. Autonomous—internal commitment.

Conformity (*i* or *f*)

Behavior that leads to no choice, cuts down alternatives as speaker demands, requires dependence, behaves definitively. Behaving in accordance with what one believes to be congruent with someone else's desires or commands. (Mimicking others—being dependent on external commitment.)

Concern (*i* or *f*)

The norm emphasizes, in addition to the expression of individuality (*i* or *f*), the appropriateness of manifesting interest in, involvement with, ideas and feelings of self and others as well as with subjects. Expressing *a need to explore further, curiosity, sympathy, attention, forethought*. To care, be responsible,—a watchful regard or attention for self and others. Unconditional regard, nonevaluative feedback, and confirmation.

Antagonism (*i* or *f*)

Not mindful of, concerned about, self and others. Hostility toward self and others. Little regard—conditional regard. Evaluative feedback.

Trust (*i* or *f*)

To think in ways—or express feelings—that mean the individuals take risks. To risk one's sense of self-esteem in a relationship. This implies nothing about risking the relationship, because if there is a fear of "breaking the relationship" then there is no trust.

Mistrust (*i* or *f*)

Fear of risking one's self in a relationship. Fear of risking the relationship.

The observer makes an inference of what is a risk. In doing so, he infers (*a*) the culture of the group and (*b*) the "strength" or "level of learning" already achieved by the individual. For example, the observer would infer:

No risk: When the individual experiences little anxiety talking about X, and some others also experience little anxiety.

Risk: When the individual experiences little anxiety talking about X, but most of the members experience much anxiety.

Risk: When the individual experiences high anxiety when talking about X, but most of the members experience little anxiety.

Risk: When the individual experiences high anxiety when talking about X, and the same is true for most of the members.

Illustration of Various Combinations of Categories

Own i–individuality i

"I believe the following. . . ."
"In my opinion, I would. . . ."

Own f–individuality f

"I feel strongly about this. . . ."
"My feelings in this matter are. . . ."

Open i–concern i

"Are you saying that . . . ?"
"I am very much interested in learning what you believe."
"Please tell me more about what you think of my ideas."

Open f–concern f

"I should very much like to know if you feel we are taking your feelings into account."
"Please tell me how you feel about me. It would help me to understand our relationship."

Experiment i–trust i

"I'd like to throw out an idea which may really be crazy, but let me try it."
"Let me explore that because if you are correct, my entire view would be incorrect."

Experiment f–trust f

"I should like to share some feelings with you which are most difficult for me to express."

H.o. own i–individuality i

"I believe that it is our job to make sure everyone's ideas get a hearing."

H.o. open ı–concern i

"Won't you please consider this idea [or feeling for *f*]?"

H.o. experiment i–trust i

"I should be glad to help you explore this idea and I realize how upsetting it could be to you if . . . [or feeling for *f*].

Not own i–antagonism i

"No, I refuse to consider that foolish idea [feeling for *f*]."

Not experiment i–mistrust i

"Oh no, I'm not going to get in your logical trap. I don't trust you [feeling for *f*]."

Not helping others own i–conformity i

"Don't speak."

Not helping others open i–antagonism i

"You let him talk you into listening to his crazy ideas and you'll become crazy, you fool."

Not helping others to experiment i–mistrust i

"Be careful, don't try that out with him. You can't trust that guy's logic."

Samples of Imbalance Behavior
Helping others own i–conform i

"As I sense it, you've done quite a bit of thinking on this problem. Give us your views."
"I think Bill has a good point. *Go ahead*, Bill, now!"
"I like your point; it is a good one. But what is really needed here is something else."

Owning i–conformity i

"If you'd just do this, everything would be all set. There would be no problem."
"You don't need a new organization. That's for sure."
"I think that problem x is a problem, *but* the *main problem really* is. . . ."
"I should like to suggest that we do the following (*without asking begins to do so*)."
"That was unjust of him to do that. You should have done [the following]."

"I thought we'd start by my presenting my ideas first and let's see, perhaps we might be able to add to them."

"Their biggest problem is that they have stamped out ideas, created conformity."

Openness i–conformity i

"I wonder if I am out of order. Is this O.K. (*continues without checking*)?

Asking questions in a legal manner in order to get a man to see what you believe is wrong thinking on his part.

"May I say something about this [does not want a response]? "The *real* problem here is. . . ."

Own f–conform i

"My distinct feeling is that you guys better stop talking or you'll get yourselves into further trouble."

Open i–antagonism i

"It happens in life; why can't it happen here?"

Own i–antagonism i

"It shattered your self-images!"

Group: *g.n.h. own i–antagonism i*

Question (serious to asker) followed by laughter.

Own i–mistrust i

"You walked out of class because you read a book when this was done and you have been wanting to do it all year."

Own i–antagonism f

"Whenever we talk to Dr., Mr., or X, he says he's uncomfortable, uneasy . . . but never says why. . . ."

Imbalance among Units[1]

"All right, I'll tell you what we're going to do [full of feelings of being fed up]. I'll move Susie Q and five others out of there *providing we are not held responsible.*"

Own i–individuality i
Not exp. (no risks)–*mistrust f*

---

[1] This category is not used in the researches that are included in this report. Much research is needed before its usefulness can be ascertained.

Closed–dislike, antagonism (The feeling score)

It is the observer's inference that A is feeling strongly, but A does not say he is feeling strongly, thus the closed and antagonism.

A to B: "If you wanted to ask a good question, you'd ask how long it would take to fire three people."

Own i–conform i
Not open f–antagonism f

(A is *owning up i, conform i* toward B and is not being open with his feelings of antagonism.)

A to B: "Look here, I am assuming that you are a responsible person and you wouldn't do it that way [irritated]."

Own i–individuality i (A's assumption about B)
Not open f–antagonistic f (irritation)

Interobserver Reliability Studies

Interobserver Reliability Study I

THE WRITER and graduate student A observed a laboratory training program for the first study. Most of the nine sessions scored were T group sessions. Several T group sessions, however, turned into discussion sessions where the participants explored various kinds of interpersonal theory.

The procedure followed was that both observed the T group meetings. However, they were not scored during the meeting. They were scored later on by listening to the tapes of the sessions. While observing the group, each observer took whatever notes he felt were relevant to describe the "output" categories of the group. These categories were not well developed during this study, and therefore we took the opportunity to obtain as many insights as we could about them. Later on, as we shall show, interobserver reliability studies were conducted on these categories.

Immediately after each session, the two observers went to another room where the tape was played and scored. The procedure followed was for each unit to be scored at a time. One observer usually "called" the units for a period of time, and then the other observer did so. Out of 4,958 units, there were disagreements as to what constituted a unit in 11 cases. (The disagreement regarding the categorization of the unit was, as we shall see, higher.) Once each observer had scored the unit, then a comparison was made. If there was agreement, this was noted and the scoring continued. If there was a difference in how each scored the behavior, it was discussed until resolved. If, after adequate discussion, no agreement could be reached, then this was noted. Also noted was who did the influencing in getting the other to change. This was important especially since, in this case, someone might hypothesize that a graduate student might constantly "give in" to the senior researcher. As the data show, this hardly ever occurred.

It is realized that many small-group researchers have attempted to develop scored categories that are scored so easily that each observer could score an entire tape separately and then compare their results with each other. We did not believe this was possible, nor necessary, nor desirable. It was not thought to be possible because of the molar nature of the categories and the relatively small experience that either observer had with the categories. As was indicated previously, it is our hypothesis that too often categories have become the slave to methodology. If they could not be used easily and by relatively unsophisticated observers, then they have not tended to be used.

Interestingly, this is not the practice in such fields as medicine. There, wherever possible, the categories used are derived from research and models about the nature of the human body. Moreover, in most cases, highly intricate and accurate machines are used. Finally, again in most cases, their "observers" are either highly trained technicians or even more highly trained nurses and medical doctors. The point that we are emphasizing is that medicine seems to take an opposite strategy from the one that is common in the behavioral sciences. Instead of simplifying the categories, they tend to develop more complex ones. To use these effectively, they develop complex machines and better-educated observers. This is not to imply that they do not wish to develop simple indices. This is the goal of any science. It is to suggest that they will not sacrifice focusing on the meaningful because the present crop of observers cannot observe with a respectable degree of reliability. For example, the author observed a team of radiologists spend hours discussing their views about the meaning of a dot on an X ray before finally deciding on its meaning.

Another advantage of the constant discussion among observers was that the scoring sessions provided an excellent training arena for the observers. Also, there were times when each observer began to feel tired, if not "fed up" with the many hours involved in scoring tapes. In most cases, the fatigue or boredom set in at different times for each observer. Consequently, one observer was always able to influence the other so that the quality of the scoring did not depreciate appreciably.[1]

Why should we not permit this kind of flexibility in our observations? It simply means that reliability and predictive validity (if high) cannot be obtained without some effort. And why should human behavior be more easily scorable than a dot on an X ray?

The interobserver reliability scores for the first study were as shown in Table B–1.

TABLE B–1

FIRST INTEROBSERVER RELIABILITY STUDY—OBSERVERS A AND B

Sessions n = 100	Total Time of Meeting (Minutes)	Total Time Scored (Minutes)	Total Units Scored	Total Agreement	% Agreement	Total Disagreement	% Disagreement	A Influences B	B Influences A	Agreement after Discussion (Percent)
1......	85	55	180	161	89	19	10	9	10	100
2......	95	65	180	156	87	11	10	5	6	100
3......	95	60	180	156	87	24	24	13	14	100
4......	75	55	180	160	88	20	12	12	8	100
5......	85	45	100	91	91	9	9	2	7	100
6......	100	55	180	155	86	25	14	15	10	100
7......	75	55	180	168	93	12	7	6	6	100
8......	90	55	180	168	93	12	7	12	10	99
9......	90	55	180	159	88	21	12	8	13	99

Two comments about the scores: First, A (the author) influenced the graduate student in about the same number of cases as B influenced A. Second, these scores are truly not indicative of the actual interobserver reliability. Actually a *disagreement* was scored as occurring when there was not agreement as to the categories as well as when there was lack of agreement as to whether the behavior should have been scored as (*i*) or (*f*). Thus, every time

---

[1] This advantage was not enjoyed in the later studies where, for most of the time, each observer observed different groups. Under these conditions, one has to depend upon the feelings of responsibility of the observer as well as the sample size. The final check, of course, lies in the kinds of predictions one is able to make and confirm.

behavior was scored, there were four comparisons made. They were comparisons on (1) levels I and II, (2) i or f on that level, (3) level III, and (4) i or f on that level. However, the percentage figures for agreement did not give credit for the agreements for the i's or f's but did give a debit for any disagreements about i or f.

The first results were encouraging, and, therefore, we turned to a second study.

Interobserver Reliability Study II

The same results were obtained in the next interobserver reliability study. This study was conducted by the author and the second graduate student. These studies were all conducted in the same

TABLE B–2

Sessions	Num- ber of Units	Total Agree- ment	% Agree- ment	Total Dis- agree- ment	% Dis- agree- ment	A In- fluences B	B In- fluences A	Total Final Agree- ment	% Final Agree- ment
I. T Groups									
1..............100		86	86	14	14	7	7	99	99
2..............100		84	84	16	16	10	6	100	100
3..............100		85	85	15	15	8	7	100	100
Total $n = 300$									
II. Case Discus- sions									
1..............100		88	88	12	12	4	8	99	99
2..............100		86	86	14	14	8	6	100	100
III. Board of Directors									
1..............100		86	86	14	14	8	6	100	100

manner except that no observations were made of actual groups. The raw data used were tapes of actual sessions.

The studies consisted of scoring (a) three T group sessions, (b) two case discussion sessions, and (c) one decision meeting of a board of directors.

Interobserver Reliability Study III[2]

The third interobserver reliability study was between the two graduate students. These studies were conducted in an identical manner to those described above.

---

[2] Further interobserver reliability studies are presented in Chapter 6.

A closing comment. Although the interobserver reliability scores seem satisfactory, it should be pointed out that not all categories were used with equal frequency. For example, as we shall see in the case discussion studies, the majority of the scores clustered around owning, openness, concern, and conformity.

There are two points to be made in this limitation. First, as our studies included more and different kinds of groups, more and more of the categories were placed into use. Thus, as we shall see, in one study of a T group that truly "orbited" we found a wealth of the

TABLE B–3

INTEROBSERVER RELIABILITY STUDY

Sessions	Total Units Scored	Total Agree- ment	% Agree- ment	Total Dis- agree- ment	% Dis- agree- ment	A In- flu- ences B	B In- flu- ences A	Agree- ment after Discus- sion	% Agree- ment	% Dis- agree- ment
I. Board of Directors Meeting										
1........200	174	87	26	13	11	9	197	98	2
II. Case Discus- sions										
1........200	174	87	26	13	9	8	197	98	2
III. T Group										
1........200	177	88	23	12	8	11	200	100	

hard-to-find categories such as *experiment f*. Also, in a study of an executive group we found a great number of instances of such categories as *not owning, not open,* and *not helping others.* Since interobserver reliability studies were conducted in each case, we were able to ascertain the degree of agreement possible in using these categories.

The second point to be emphasized is that our theory predicts certain categories will not tend to be observed with great frequency in organizational settings in our culture. Thus, for a great number of research projects that will concern us, we will probably not observe those categories about which we have inadequate reliability data. Should they arise, however, with increased frequency, it would be quite simple to conduct such studies during that project. Indeed, as we conduct new research projects, we will add to the reliability studies.

We close with an item analysis of the interobserver reliability studies. The reader may be concerned about the uneven frequency with which the categories have been observed as well as the absence of several of the negative categories. This concerns us, and we are conducting further research. At the moment, it looks as if this spread is inherent in the kind of universe that we are studying.

TABLE B–4

ITEM ANALYSIS OF INTEROBSERVER RELIABILITY STUDIES*

Level I	Frequency	Level II	Frequency
own i	1177	concern i	942
open i	473	conform i	428
own f	372	individuality i	312
help others own i	135	concern f	307
not help others own i	83	individuality f	153
open f	59	antagonism i	151
help others own f	58	antagonism f	103
experiment i	35	conform f	37
group not help others own i	26	trust i	30
not help others to be open i	20	trust f	16
experiment f	16	Total	2479
help others to open i	9		
help others to experiment f	6		
help others to experiment i	4		
not own i	3		
not own f	2		
respect experimenting i	1		
Total	2479		

* This includes studies made in decision-making groups, case study groups, and T groups.

Explorations in Interpersonal Competence[1]

Describing and Predicting Individual Interpersonal Competence

THE HIGHER the plus scores the greater the individual interpersonal competence (on the individual or group level). In order to explore this hypothesis several studies were conducted with T groups which have as an objective the increase of individuals' interpersonal competence.

The members of two T groups in one executive laboratory and two T groups in two other executive laboratories were used as subjects ($n = 51$). Their behavior was scored and for each individual total plus and minus scores were developed. By subtracting the minuses from the pluses, an overall competence score was developed for each member. Each individual was ranked relative to all other individuals in his T group. These scores and rankings were not divulged to the faculties or to the executives.

The rankings were divided into thirds. The top third represented the "high" interpersonally competent members. The next third were "moderate" and the next third were the "low" interpersonally competent members.

The two staff members and the observer (where possible) in each T group were asked, at the end of the program, to rank each individual in their group in terms of the three categories. They were asked to do this independently of each other. Naturally, they

---

[1] The appendix is part of an article that appeared in *Applied Behavioral Science*.

TABLE C–1
Rankings of Individual Competence

Group I

Person	Quantitative Score	Rank Based on Quan. Score	Rank— High = H, Low = L, Medium = M	Rank by Staff A	Rank by Staff B	Rank by Observer
A	204	1	H	H	H	H
B	138	2	H	H	H	H
C	133	3	H	H	H	H
D	119	4	H	M	H	M
E	113	5	H	H	H	M
F	111	6	M	M	H	M
G	100	7	M	M	M	M
H	96	8	M	L	M	H
I	92	9	M	M	M	L
J	90	10	M	M	M	M
K	85	11	L	L	L	L
L	33	12	L	L	M	L
M	30	13	L	L	L	M
N	3	14	L	L	L	L
O	0	15	L	L	L	L

Total agreement of qualitative scores....11
Total disagreement....4
Statistical significance....00182

Group II

Person	Quantitative Score	Rank Based on Quan. Score	Rank— High = H, Low = L, Medium = M	Rank by Staff A	Rank by Staff B	Rank by Observer
A	150	1	H	H	H	H
B	137	2	H	H	H	H
C	103	3	H	H	H	H
D	101	4	H	M	M	M
E	96	5	H	H	M	M
F	92	6	M	M	H	M
G	90	7	M	M	M	M
H	87	8	M	H	M	H
I	69	9	M	M	M	M
J	61	10	L	M	M	L
K	56	11	L	L	L	L
L	55	12	L	M	M	M
M	50	13	L	L	L	L
N	44	14	L	L	L	L
O	33	15	L	L	L	L

Total agreement of qualitative scores....11
Total disagreement....4
Statistical significance....00182

were not told about the rankings that had been developed from the quantitative scores. In all cases except one, the faculty were not familiar with the categorical scheme. In the case of the writer, who was fully acquainted with the schemes, his judgments did not seem to be any more accurate than the others.

The following three tables compare the ranking given each individual on the basis of the quantitative scores with those given him by the two staff members as well as the observer. Groups I and II

TABLE C-2

RANKINGS OF INDIVIDUAL COMPETENCE

		GROUP III				
Person	Quantitative Score	Rank Based on Quan. Score	Rank— High-H, Low-L, Medium- M	Rank by Staff A	Rank by Staff B	Rank by observer
A................323		1	H	H	H	H
B................286		2	H	H	H	H
C................270		3	H	M	M	M
D................262		4	H	H	H	H
E................250		5	H	H	H	H
F................240		6	M	M	M	M
G................234		7	M	M	M	M
H................210		8	M	M	M	M
I................184		9	M	M	M	M
J................173		10	L	H	H	H
K................143		11	L	L	L	L
L................133		12	L	L	L	L
M................116		13	L	L	L	L
Total agreement of qualitative scores............11				11	11	
Total disagreement........................... 2				2	2	
Statistical significance........................				.000632		

are grouped together in one table since they were studied at the same laboratory. Groups III and IV were studied at a different time. The degree of agreement in all cases is statistically significant and encouraging.

Interesting data were also obtained a day after the program was completed when the executives in Groups I and II were asked to evaluate their experience. They could, if they wished, sign their comments. Of the executives who turned in some comments, 10 in Group I and 11 in Group II were signed. The comments were read by a professional social scientist but one who was not associated with the program nor with the research. He was asked to rank the comments into three categories, namely, very pleased, moderately pleased, and displeased with the educational experience. These evaluations were correlated with our quantitative scores. The data suggests that the men's perceived degree of learning and satisfaction with the laboratory experience correlated highly with the quantitative scores. See Table C-4.

TABLE C-3

RANKINGS OF INDIVIDUAL COMPETENCE

| Person | Group IV | | | |
	Quantitative Score	Rank	Rank by Staff A	Rank by Staff B
A	312	H	H	H
B	281	H	H	H
C	234	M	M	M
D	210	M	L	L
E	207	M	M	M
F	170	M	M	M
G	154	L	M	M
H	140	L	L	L
Total agreement	6			6
Total disagreement	2			2
Statistical significance	P		$<$	.05

These results, although encouraging, are by no means conclusive. It could be, for example, that the judges are somehow distorted in their judgments and that the distortion is in the same direction as the one that may exist in the scheme of categories. Research is also necessary to ascertain how well an observer could rate the individuals without having the benefit of the categories. It may well be that, for prediction purposes, our categories are not much more effective than an educated guess.

Describing Individual Growth

The next step was to attempt to develop, on the basis of the competence scores for each session, the individual's "growth curve" during the total number sessions.

These curves must be interpreted with caution. First, there are no norms available from which to define, in precise terms, the meaning of "high," "moderate," and "low" competence. Up to this time all we have done is arbitrarily divided any given group of subjects into three subgroups. However, since no norms exist, an individual who may be "high" in one group could be "moderate" or "low" in another group.

This points up another characteristic of these categories that must be kept in mind. All the evaluations of individual competence are related to the particular group in which the individual was a

TABLE C–4

COMPARING SCORES WITH INDIVIDUALS' REPORTED SATISFACTION WITH COURSE

Person	GROUP I		GROUP II	
	Rank by Score	*Rank by Individual*	*Rank by Score*	*Rank by Individual*
A......................	H	NIP*	H	H
B......................	H	M	H	NIP
C......................	H	NIP	H	H
D......................	H	NIP	H	H
E......................	H	NIP	H	NIP
F......................	M	L	M	H
G......................	M	M	M	NIP
H......................	M	M	M	M
I......................	M	M	M	M
J......................	M	M	M	M
K......................	L	L	L	M
L......................	L	L	L	NIP
M......................	L	NIP	L	L
N......................	L	L	L	L
O......................	L	L	L	L

Total sample.................... 10   Total sample....... 11
Total agreement.................. 8   Total agreement.... 9
Total disagreement............... 2   Total disagreement.. 2

* No identifiable paper.

member. An individual's competence is highly influenced by the growth of this group. If his group learns much, then the probability that he can earn higher scores increases. The opposite is the case when an individual is in a group that has not learned very much.

Conversely, the group's growth is partially influenced by the growth of the individuals. But, the influence the individuals have upon the group is not simply the summation of their learning. There is a process of interaction which makes the group learning more than a sum of the individual learning curves. For us to hold such a position may seem odd, since our group curves are constructed by summing all the individual contributions. This apparent contradiction can be explained if we recall the two aspects of our scoring procedure. The "norm" categories are designed to "capture" the interaction effect of the interpersonal relationships. The pattern of norms that each group develops is unique to that group. The second factor is the interdependence of the individual and interpersonal categories. If many members are owning ideas (but not feelings) a norm of *individuality i* may become established which then (we hypothesize) sets to influence the individual's behavior toward more *owning i* and less *owning f*, or *openness i* or *f*, or *experimenting i* or *f*. Although we have group scores that are summations of individual contributions, these individual contributions are highly influenced by the individual contributions of others (as well as by the norms).

All our curves (so far) are limited to groups that have met for only a week or, at the most, two weeks. Time, therefore, is another crucial factor that must be taken into account.

Finally, none of our groups are preselected according to personality patterns of members. Shutz has shown, for example, that if individuals of a particular personality predominate in a group, they can significantly influence the dynamics within the group.

Let us now turn briefly to Graph C–1. The objective is to suggest that the scores might be capable of describing individual differences in learning in T groups.

The first curve represents the best individual curve that has been obtained to date (which also came from the best group that ever has been measured). The second and third are moderate and low competence members from the *same* group. Individual curves exist from other groups whose "highest" learner is close to the bottom end of the "moderate" learners in this group.

The first aspect of interest is that all three curves are not smooth, constantly increasing curves. All the individuals have periods of learning followed by periods of little or low learning. The moderate and low learners, however, had significantly higher negative scores than the high learner. Thus, although they seemed to be able to increase somewhat (and cyclically) their plus behavior, they were unable to correct their defensive behavior. The low learner had much more difficulty in this than did the moderate learner.

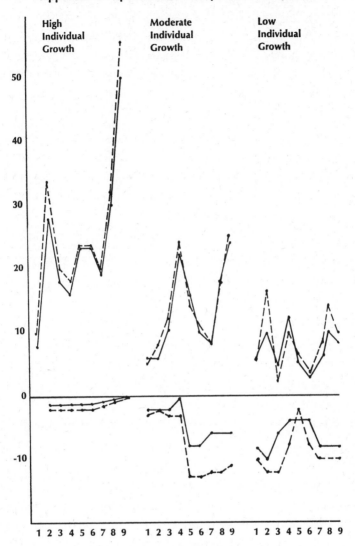

High
Individual
Growth

Moderate
Individual
Growth

Low
Individual
Growth

NO. OF SESSIONS

———— Level I (individual-interpersonal)
- - - - - - - - Level II (norms)

GRAPH C–1
Individual Growth Curves

Although the moderate learner seemed to have corrected his defensive (minus) behavior somewhat, he did not reduce it as much as he increased his plus behavior. If this trend were to continue (i.e., the plus scores go higher but the minus remain constant or increase), he may turn out to be an example of an individual who is either "in transition" or a person who "got religion." If he is in transition, it would mean that he has learned how to increase the plus aspects of his behavior and would eventually learn to decrease the minus aspects.

An examination of the categories shows that high learners tended to have more idea scores in terms of *openness, helping others to own, to be open*, and *experimenting* as well as more feeling scores in each of these categories than moderate or low learners had. The minus scores of the high learners were very small. If they decreased in competence it tended to be in terms of decreases in their plus scores rather than increases in their minus scores. Perhaps they had control over their defenses so that when they began to operate ineffectively they tended to withdraw or asked for help rather than becoming more defensive.

The moderate learners tended to differ from the high learners in that they had lower *openness* scores, and only a few of them were related to feelings. Moreover, they had significantly lower *helping others* scores. It is as if they were spending most of their time worrying about their own difficulties in interpersonal competence. The moderate learners tended to have almost none or, at the most, one *experiment* score.

Not all moderate learners had as low minus scores as the one depicted. But where the minus scores were low, the plus scores were also low. This suggests that if a moderate learner's defenses are low, his capacity to contribute to his own and others' growth may also be low. Although no systematic data are available, we would like to suggest another difference between high and moderate (and also low) learners. The high learners seem to have the capacity to *make* the T group experience a learning experience. They seem to *give to*, to *invest the group with* learning potential.[2] The moderate learner, on the other hand, is capable of learning, if

---

[2] I believe this finding jibes with Abraham Maslow's findings of the self-actualizors. In his terms, the high learners are able to develop "peak experiences" in a T group.

the group culture is capable of helping him to learn. He will "take" from the environment to learn, but he does not seem to be capable of "giving" to the environment. The low learner seems unable to "take" or to "give" to the environment.

Describing and Predicting Group Interpersonal Competence

The next step was to test the validity of the hypothesis that the higher the plus scores, the greater the group competence. Again the studies were made in two T groups.

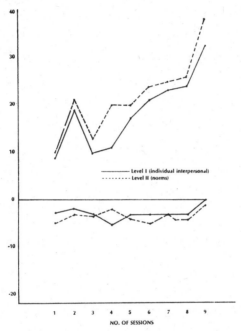

GRAPH C–2.   October, 1962—Group I.

In Group I (Graph C–2) we have a graph of the best group that we have studied to date. The curves represent the group's scores without the trainer.

The group began well, ran into difficulty,[3] and was then able to overcome the difficulty so that it seemed to continue to increase its competence over time. The individual and group "plus" curves

---

[3] The phenomenon "things must get worse before they get better" may be derived from the theory as being necessary for all groups that begin with relatively low competence.

continued to go up and in about the same relationship to each other. The norm scores tended to be slightly higher, partially because it might be easier (especially at the outset) to contribute to group growth than to one's own or to that of another specific individual.

The negative scores were much less frequent in the group. They, too, became worse but then became better. Toward the end the total individual negative scores reached zero, whereas the norm negative scores were almost zero.

How valid are curves like these? One method available to us to determine the validity was as follows. Since the theory suggests that the higher the plus scores and the lower the minus scores, the greater the competence of the system, then Group I should be perceived, by its members or outsiders, as becoming increasingly competent.

From our and others' empirical experience, we developed ten indices or criteria of group competence. They were:

1. Contributions made within the group are additive.
2. The group moves forward as a unit; there is a sense of team spirit; high involvement.
3. Decisions are made by consensus.
4. Commitment to decisions by most members is strong.
5. The group continually evaluates itself.
6. The group is clear about its goals.
7. Conflict is brought out into the open and dealt with.
8. Alternative ways of thinking about solutions are generated.
9. Leadership tends to go to the individual best qualified.
10. Feelings are dealt with openly.

Each of these criteria was included in a questionnaire as a dimension on a continuum of 1 through 5. The "1" represented the low end of the continuum and the "5" the highest possible score. An alternative of "don't know yet" was included for each dimension.

At the end of each session, all the participants, staff, and the observer filled out these questionnaires in terms of their evaluation of the group as a whole. These data were kept by the observer and were not seen by anyone. They were tabulated *after* the laboratory was completed.

In addition each individual indicated (on a continuum of 1 through 5) how much he liked the group. This was taken as an overall indication of his feelings about the group. Also he was asked to predict how well he felt others liked the group.

Several analyses were made. First the scores for all the questions per session were combined, and averages were computed to indicate each individual's feelings about the group in terms of the ten in-

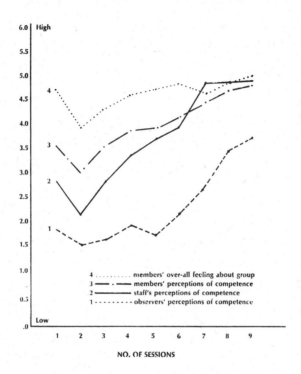

4 ·········· members' over-all feeling about group
3 ——·—— members' perceptions of competence
2 ———————— staff's perceptions of competence
1 ········· observers' perceptions of competence

NO. OF SESSIONS

group contributions add up	group is clear about its goals
moving forward as a unit	conflict is dealt with
decision by consensus	alternatives are explored
Members' commitment to	leadership is appropriate to
decisions	skills
constant self-check	feelings are dealt with openly

GRAPH C–3.   October, 1962—Ardon House Outputs.

dices. All these were summed so scores were developed of the total group's competence as perceived by (a) the observer, (b) the staff, and (c) the participants in terms of the ten indices.

These scores were plotted in a graph (see Graph C–3). It is interesting to note that there is a large measure of agreement among the four curves. The four curves are, with one exception, highly congruent with the group curve presented in the graph.

In order to obtain a quantitative indication of this congruency among the curves, a correlation was computed between each of these curves and a curve computed from the scores obtained on the basis of the observations (Graph C–2). The results were as follows:

Correlation between Group Curve and	r. i. j.	Statistical Significance
Observer's evaluation	.86	.0150
Educators' evaluations	.83	.0188
Members' evaluations	.93	.0086
Members' overall feelings about the group	.54	.2112

We were also able to correlate the curve describing each of the ten indices with the group's curve based upon the observations. The results were as follows:

Indices	Correlation with Group Growth Curve
1. Group contributions add up	.60
2. Moving forward as a unit	.79
3. Decision by consensus	.76
4. Strong member commitment to decision	.73
5. Constant internal check of group effectiveness	.78
6. Clarity about goals	.84
7. Conflict is dealt with openly	.62
8. Alternative solutions explored	.76
9. Leadership varies and is functional	.85
10. Feelings are dealt with; not suppressed	.81

All of these correlations are statistically significant at least at the 5 percent level, with exception of number 7. (It is close.)

Some readers might wonder, since the correlations are so high, if we may be measuring the same phenomenon or there are one or two factors that underlie them all. We doubt this possibility for all the indices except 7 and 10, which we believe are overlapping.

The behavior implicit within each of the remaining factors seems significantly different. Clarity of goals, contributions "adding up," "decision by consensus," "exploring alternative solutions," functional leadership," "strong internal commitments" seem to the writer to be criteria on different levels of analysis. This assertion may be best defended by asking the reader to visualize what would be necessary to help a group learn how to perform each of these activities effectively.

The results for the two questions regarding "liking the group" were analyzed separately. First, there was no statistically significant correlation between the individual's perception of the effectiveness of the group or the "actual" effectiveness and his liking for the group (.54). The correlation is even lower when we asked the individuals to predict how they feel others will feel about the group at the end of each session (.36).

In a second study encouraging results were also obtained. Again we found a significant relationship between the members' and staff's evaluations of the group and the competence scores developed by the observers. They were:

Correlation between Group Curve (Not Shown) and	r. i. j.	Statistical Significance
Educators' evaluations	.77	.01
Members' evaluations	.83	.01

However, opposite results were obtained in the "liking" questions. In this study, the members' liking of the group for each session "grew" closely with the competence scores (.85). Also they predicted more accurately than the previous group members how well others liked the group (.79).

Discussion

During the studies of T groups we learned that it was possible to score an individual's behavior and to plot his aspects of his learning during the T group sessions. We utilized the same procedure to evolve a quantitative score of the individual's competence.

Needless to say, further studies are needed to validate these findings. Aside from the obvious problem of a small number of cases (especially in terms of faculty ratings) there is the problem of ascertaining if the relatively high predictive validity of the scores remains high when the individuals who are being rated have been through a relatively poor or extremely effective T group. It may be that we were able to obtain the encouraging results because the individual competence showed an adequate spread which made it easier for the raters to rate and increased the probability that the predictions would be accurate. What would happen if we had to predict in groups where all the individuals learned much or little? Another possibility is that the faculty variance is much greater than the amount represented within the present study. It is conceivable that another group or faculty might have greater difficulty in scoring the individuals or might not, but in either case it might develop significantly different ratings.

Also, studies are needed to validate the individual growth or learning curves that were presented. If such validation is obtained then it may be possible to begin to understand the dynamics of human personality and its relationship to learning.

Studies are also needed where the categories are used to represent the more extreme of the cognitive learnings (logic, concept formation) as well as more interpersonal and clinical learnings (therapy groups). Such studies might help to produce observations in the infrequently observed categories of our scheme. At the moment, one of the major weaknesses of our scheme as a total scheme is that many of its categories have hardly been used in the situations studied to date.

As these studies are developed it should also be possible to begin to conduct research that focuses on learning that is simultaneously cognitive and interpersonal. This should help us to begin to understand the interrelationships between the two levels.

Turning to the small group level, it was shown that the growth of one group's competence (which is quantitatively different from the growth of any individual in it) could also be ascertained with encouraging validity.

In the case of group learning or growth we were able to conduct a study to explore the relationship between the curve of group learning (developed from the scoring procedure) and the members' perception of their group's development. The results were encouraging, but again the number of cases was small.

One of the interesting avenues for further research is the area between individual and group growth. For example, the same individual could be studied in groups where there is relatively great learning and in groups where there is relatively little. The writer's competence scores in two T groups were 300 and 150 respectively. Is it possible that the dynamics produced in the second T group helped the writer to be less competent? If so, why?

Studies could also be conducted where the participants were selected according to (1) the degree to which they held the pyramidal values, or (2) their need for power, inclusion and affection (Schutz), (3) dependence and counterdependence (Bennis and Shepard), (4) complexity *vs.* simplification or abstract *vs.* concrete (Harvey, Hunt, and Schroder), to mention but a few. Experiments could also be conducted where groups were permitted to develop up to a certain point, and then the members were "transplanted" systematically.

Laboratory Education and T Groups

The research may help those practitioners interested in making laboratory education more effective. If these preliminary findings are replicated, the set of categories can provide a meaningful measurement of individual learning and group growth. It would then be possible to conduct research which would help the staff identify individual behavior styles and group conditions under which learning can be increased.

Moreover, faculty members can be studied under varying conditions. The resulting knowledge might help us become more efficient in understanding how a given staff member's behavior facilitates and inhibits growth. Such knowledge should be helpful to the staff members as it attempts to increase their own competence. It should also be useful in pairing staff members to develop "optimal" learning conditions for the group. Also, it may be possible to switch faculty members as the groups develop so that they obtain that kind of help that they need the most at any given phase of their development.

The same kinds of alternatives can be considered for the participants. Groups could be composed and recomposed as a function of the individual pattern of scores. Participants can be matched more effectively with those staff members with whom they would probably learn the most.

Another interesting possibility is for the individual and group curves to be used to provide feedback to the members as to how their performance compares with (1) other members in their group, (2) their group as a whole, and (3) other members in other groups with or without the same pattern or same position, status, etc. The same kind of study could be made on the group level.

The best way to use the data in order to increase learning is still not clear. One would have to be careful to try not to let the data become perceived as evaluative (i.e., whether the people are good or bad). Rather, the hope would be that the scores provide them with information which they can use to help them become more competent. Thus if a man sees that his learning curve is not rising, he might look at it more analytically to see why this is so. He might find out, for example, that he is manifesting much behavior that is *owning i* and *conform i* or *owning i* and *concern i*. Examining his "scores" he may see that he could be helped if he *owned up* to his feelings more; or he could strive to become more *open* (*i* and *f* levels); or even attempt an *experiment i* or *f*. In short, the data could be used to help the individual just as the shooter uses the feedback he gets from someone who "scores" his target to show him where he is hitting. Such information can help the shooter decide what he must do to come "on target."

In comparing individual and group data one will also have to be alert to note if the feedback of the data tends to generate individual competition and/or group rivalry. Again, it is the writer's belief that too little is known about the positive and negative aspects of each on learning. According to Deutsch,[4] for example, competitive experience can decrease cooperation and a decrease in cooperation in a T group could decrease the probabilities of individuals helping each other and thus limiting their own and others' growth possibilities.

Blake and Mouton[5] have shown that intergroup rivalries of the win-lose variety can also be harmful to learning. However, he has also suggested that if such rivalries occur, the staff may use them as rich data for the group members to examine and from which to begin to derive important learning experiences.

Summary

Exploratory research has suggested that the categories can be used (1) with an encouraging degree of reliability, (2) an encouraging degree of predictive validity, and (3) as the basis to describe increases or decreases in individual and group competence.

---

[4] Morton Deutsch, "An Experimental Study of the Effects of Co-operation and Competition upon Group Process," *Human Relations*, Vol. 2, July, 1949, pp. 199–231.

[5] Robert R. Blake and Jane S. Mouton, "The Intergroup Dynamics of Win-Lose Conflict and Problem-Solving Collaboration in Union-Management Relations," in M. Sherif (ed.), *Intergroup Relations and Leadership* (New York: John Wiley & Sons, 1962).

Index of Names

Index of Subjects

This book has been set on the Linotype in 11 point Janson, leaded 2 points, and 10 point Janson, leaded 1 point. Chapter numbers are in 14 point Deepdene; chapter titles are in 24 point Deepdene. The size of the type page is 26 by 44 picas.